Rougher Justice

Rougher Justice

Anti-social behaviour and young people

Peter Squires and Dawn E. Stephen

WILLAN
PUBLISHING

Published by

Willan Publishing
Culmcott House
Mill Street, Uffculme
Cullompton, Devon
EX15 3AT, UK
Tel: +44(0)1884 840337
Fax: +44(0)1884 840251
e-mail: info@willanpublishing.co.uk
website: www.willanpublishing.co.uk

Published simultaneously in the USA and Canada by

Willan Publishing
c/o ISBS, 920 NE 58th Ave, Suite 300,
Portland, Oregon 97213-3786, USA
Tel: +001(0)503 287 3093
Fax: +001(0)503 280 8832
e-mail: info@isbs.com
website: www.isbs.com

ISBN 1-84392-111-1 paperback

British Library Cataloguing-in-Publication Data

A catalogue record for this book is available from the British Library

Project managed by Deer Park Productions, Tavistock, Devon
Typeset by GCS, Leighton Buzzard, Beds.
Printed and bound by T.J. International Ltd, Trecerus Industrial Estate, Padstow, Cornwall

Contents

List of abbreviations

ABA	Acceptable Behaviour Agreement
ABC	Acceptable Behaviour Contract
ACORN	A Classification of Residential Neighbourhoods
ALG	Association of London Government
AS	anti-social
ASB	anti-social behaviour
ASBO	Anti-Social Behaviour Order
ADHD	Attention Deficit Hyperactivity Disorder
ASPD	anti-social personality disorder
BCS	British Crime Survey
CDRP	Crime and Disorder Reduction Partnership
CJ	criminal justice
CJS	criminal justice system
CPTED	crime prevention through environmental design
CS	community safety
CSJ	Commission on Social Justice
CSO	Child Safety Order
DTO	Detention and Training Order
FPSC	Family Policy Studies Centre
HMIP	Her Majesty's Inspectorate of Prisons
IPPR	Institute for Public Policy Research
ISSP	Intensive Supervision and Surveillance Programme
LR	left realism

MMPI	Minnesota Multiphasic Personality Inventory
NAO	National Audit Office
NDC	New Deal for Communities
ODPM	Office of the Deputy Prime Minister
PAT	Policy Action Team
PYO	persistent young offender
RJ	restorative justice
RO	Referral Order
RSD	Research and Statistics Directorate, Home Office
SEU	Social Exclusion Unit
SCP	situational crime prevention
SSP	situational social policy
YIP	Youth Inclusion Project
YJ	youth justice
YJB	Youth Justice Board
YOI	Youth Offender Institution
YOT	Youth Offending Team

Preface and acknowledgements

This book emerged both from a number of separate research projects and a series of our academic interventions into debates about youth crime and disorder and community safety policy-making. While we were undertaking these various projects, the concept of anti-social behaviour was rapidly developing and taking shape around us. By 2004 it had become, apparently, the central crime and disorder question.

The main projects drawn upon in pulling this book together were, first, a project examining young people's motivations for vehicle taking and 'joyriding' which was sponsored by Sussex police. We are grateful to Inspector Dave Stringer for his help and support with this work. Secondly, the book is based upon a project evaluating the use of 'Acceptable Behaviour Contracts' in the East Brighton 'New Deal for Communities Area' (EB4U): here we are grateful for the help and support of John Mitchell and his community safety team colleagues. Thirdly, the book draws upon a number of Youth Justice Board project evaluation exercises conducted by Peter Squires and Lynda Measor in the South East and London. Here we are grateful for the assistance of a wide range of Youth Offending Team managers and their staff. Above all, in each of the aforementioned projects, we are grateful to the young people (and their families) for agreeing to be interviewed and to the many youth workers who 'sponsored' our approaches to the young people.

Finally the project draws upon a 'Perceptions of Anti-Social Behaviour' project undertaken for the London Borough of Sutton. Here we are grateful to Clare Demuth and Duncan Grant for their support with this work and to Liz Cunningham, Marylynn Fyvie-Gauld and Carlie Goldsmith who undertook important aspects of the fieldwork.

Parts of Chapter 4 were presented in a Social and Legal Studies Association conference at the University of Edinburgh in 2001 while parts of Chapter 6, and the themes of Chapters 2 and 3 were presented at British Society for Criminology Conferences in 2002 and 2004 respectively. This text also draws upon and develops ideas first published in two journal articles: Stephen, D.E. and Squires, P. (2003) ' "Adults don't realise how sheltered they are". A contribution to the debate on youth transitions from some voices on the margins', *Journal of Youth Studies*, 6 (2): 145–64, and Stephen, D.E. and Squires, P. (2004) ' "They're still children and entitled to be children". Problematising the institutionalised mistrust of marginalised youth in Britain', *Journal of Youth Studies*, 7 (3): 351–69.

Peter would like to thank Kathy and Matthew for enduring his anti-social behaviour with varying degrees of tolerance. Dawn would like to dedicate the book to her late grandmother Mary for her strength of spirit, wisdom and humility.

Peter Squires
Dawn E. Stephen
Brighton

Chapter 1

The new politics of behaviour: anti-social behaviour as a contested terrain

If I am acquainted with my neighbours and have some sort of network close to me, I have an easy time if some youngsters misbehave in my hallway. I can call for someone who might know some of them, or I can turn to the athletic neighbour one floor up – or perhaps better still – I can ask for help from the little lady I know as particularly good at handling local conflicts. But without a network, and with all the information on the increase in crime in mind, I would have locked the door and called the police. I would thereby have created conditions for encouraging unwanted behaviour, and for giving that unwanted behaviour the meaning of crime. (Christie 2004: 69–70)

While undertaking some of the fieldwork discussed in this book we encountered a claim, often promulgated by anti-social behaviour (ASB) enforcers (the new class of social control agents dedicated to the task of policing ASB in some of its contemporary manifestations). The claim was that our recent preoccupation with ASB should be taken as a positive sign. The implication read into this development was that a community's major crime problems had already been tackled and no longer posed the threat or generated the fears they once did, thereby allowing community members to move on to a lower tier of concerns affecting them. In the words of the proverb that many of us will undoubtedly recall from our childhoods, the pounds (the bigger and worrying crimes) having been taken care of we now need only look after the pence.

Perhaps it goes without saying, but we were never given much convincing evidence to support this wishful claim. Subsequently when interviewing residents of an area (an area of urban social housing) often associated with crime and ASB we found them to be concerned about a very familiar series of criminal and disorderly behaviours (Girling *et al.* 2000). Crime levels in the ASB target areas often remain high and have seldom fallen to such a living memory all-time low that communities can now breathe a collective sigh of relief and move on to other issues.

While we were deliberating upon these questions, the first Annual Report of the Home Office campaign, *Together: Tackling Anti-Social Behaviour* was published (Home Office 2004), its launch accompanied by the familiar Blair and Blunkett double act keen to celebrate the government's latest successes. The opening lines of the document boldly reiterated the upbeat governmental theme: 'As crime has fallen, anti-social behaviour has become a major cause of concern in communities across the country.'

Our interest lies not primarily in relation to the claim about falling crime. The most recently available crime data suggest significant reductions in British Crime Survey (BCS) recorded crime in the risk of becoming a victim and levels of worry about major types of crime – and ASB (Dodd *et al.* 2004). Furthermore, year on year quarterly comparisons suggest an annual 5 per cent reduction in police recorded crime, but an overall total still hovering around the five million offences per year mark (Finney *et al.* 2004), although precise trends are difficult to discern because of the counting rule changes after 1997. Significantly, violent and sexual offences recorded by the police show increases in the range 13–18 per cent and, while the Home Office rightly claim that a large part of such increases will be attributable to improved recording practices, it is nevertheless important to register the particular significance of violence in shaping public fears and perceptions (Zimring and Hawkins 1997).

Rather than dispute the evidence about an apparently falling crime trend, our main concern here is with what this means, how it is interpreted and whether we are permitted to make the leap from falling crime to, therefore, this new priority of Anti-Social Behaviour. To a large extent we share Tonry's (2004) observation that New Labour have made a specific priority of ASB, not so much *inventing* the idea as reappropriating it to serve a particular politics of enforcement. The kinds of problems that ASB has come to represent are not by any means new issues (juvenile nuisance, the moral standards of 'the poor') but in tapping into these concerns, creating what Frank Field has called 'a new politics of behaviour', New Labour have certainly connected with and orchestrated a wide range of late modernity's 'respectable fears' (Pearson 1983). Tonry has suggested that this may prove to be a high-risk strategy, although there is already plenty of evidence to suggest that the government are aware of this and are taking steps to stop a risk becoming a liability for, as we argue later, managing public perceptions is an important aspect of 'tackling ASB'.

Given that the naming and problematisation of ASB has been, in a number of important respects, government led, we are not convinced that its emergence as an issue has anything much to do with 'falling crime'. As we indicated earlier, crime and disorder levels in the kinds of areas targeted for ASB enforcement often remain high. They have not fallen so obviously and significantly that residents of the most deprived communities can now relax and seek out other issues to worry about. For a start, even a quick glance at the Home Office's typology of anti-social behaviours (see Chapter 2) reveals that a majority of the acts now classified as ASB are already crimes anyway. This points us to a different problem. The Home Office referred, in particular, to what it has termed 'the justice gap' (Home Office 2002a), the fact that a majority of offenders are not brought to court (to justice) and that an overwhelming majority of harmful, offensive or anti-social behaviours appears to achieve no redress. In this light, the politicisation of anti-social behaviour, thereby bringing corporate responsibility to bear upon a collective problem, appears as an attempt to close the 'justice gap' through more effectively targeted and streamlined enforcement.

Here, we are in agreement with the important insights of Hansen *et al.* (2003) that the problem of ASB is perhaps best understood in relation to a perceived 'enforcement deficit'. This is so in a number of senses. For Hansen and his colleagues, this 'enforcement deficit' concerns the fact that traditional criminal justice interventions tend to individualise their response around particular incidents and offenders and have no mechanism for addressing the collective and accumulating impact of harm and distress across a community. For these authors the precise contribution of a community safety perspective lies in the way it facilitates a shift in the ways in which we think about the cumulative impact of crime and disorder incidents (which, taken by themselves, might seem isolated and relatively trivial) upon communities and victims. The concept of ASB provides this perspective with both a rationale for taking this behaviour seriously and a mechanism for intervening. Thus ASB is anti-social in the way it undermines community cohesion, fragments shared values and erodes social capital. Disparate acts of an 'anti-social' nature are not victimless offences but, rather like the 'incivilities' described by Wilson and Kelling (1982), have a cumulative impact creating both climate and context in which ever more serious transgressions become normative and have to be endured.

Unfortunately, in the process of grounding this conception of the 'justice gap' within community safety discourse and policy, a subtle shift has occurred in the meaning of the concept. It first arose in a publication of the 1992 Commission on Social Justice (CSJ 1993) where it referred to the growing evidence of inequality and social exclusion in a society founded upon principles of equal citizenship. For community safety it became the dilemma of ensuring criminal justice in the absence of social justice, as evidence began to mount of the devastating impact of crime and disorder and concentrations of victimisation in the most deprived areas. Yet as Crawford has commented, a higher priority is accorded 'to crime prevention – as opposed to poverty prevention' (Crawford 1998: 121). Finally, for the Home Office, the 'justice gap' has become a question of criminal justice system performance – justice through enforcement.

A second aspect of the perceived enforcement deficit relates directly to questions of youth offending. During the 1990s and, especially after the defining moment of 1993, the abduction and murder of James Bulger, had passed, we began to see an increasing level of complaint regarding the alleged impunity with which young 'delinquents' could act, apparently confident that neither the police nor the rest of the youth justice system could touch them. This emerging complaint was not especially new but it was effectively orchestrated by a policing lobby (Faulkner 2001) and came to focus specifically upon a number of perceived weaknesses of the youth justice system. In due course, these criticisms were articulated in the avowedly ideological title of the white paper *No More Excuses* published by New Labour 1997 (Home Office 1997a). A number of issues surfaced – the policy of diversion, repeat cautioning, delays, inadequate enforcement and 'bail bandits'. Taken together, these suggested a system in need of substantial reform – riddled, as it were, with 'justice gaps'. Given that young people were seen to be responsible for a substantial proportion of the ASB endured by communities (Campbell 2002a) and that ASB itself was seen as a seedbed of future, more persistent, delinquency (Audit Commission 1996; Farrington 1996), here were two compelling reasons to tackle this 'enforcement deficit'. This is also why, in this book, we consider it essential to address ASB and youth justice in tandem. As we argue later, each policy area informs and complements the other.

A final aspect of this perceived 'enforcement deficit' relating to ASB involves a number of areas of concern relating to social policy agencies and their engagement with the family. Lately these issues have acquired a new coherence under the guise of a 'responsibilisation strategy' (O'Malley 1992; Garland 2001: 124). Through this strategy, in a more explicit application of contractual and communitarian principles (although plainly authoritarian versions of these ideas), an increasing number of policy functions have been delegated to families and communities. In essence, these processes are similar to the 'governing through the family' described by Donzelot (1979) or the establishment of governmental relationships (Foucault 1990; Garland 1996) between the family and other state agencies which we have earlier referred to as a kind of 'disciplining' or criminalising of social policy (Squires 1990). This 'policing of the family' manifests itself most obviously in the attempt to discipline parents (Parenting Orders) and hold them ever more criminally responsible for the offending behaviour of their children. Obviously this is by no means a new dimension of British social policy (Stedman-Jones 1971; Wohl 1977; Utting *et al.* 1993; Morris 1994) and, drawing upon this history, Jones and Novak were clearly correct in their observation that the burden of the new laws proposed to discipline parents would not fall upon the affluent families of middle England (1999: 150) but upon the inhabitants of Britain's poorest and most deprived neighbourhoods, social housing estates and communities.

Accordingly, as the New Labour 'social exclusion' agenda unfolded (Social Exclusion Unit 1998; Howarth *et al.* 1999, 2002) and a series of 'joined-up' situational social policy initiatives were installed in these 'most deprived' areas, there seemed no little irony in the fact that, where New Deal initiatives were established, the relations of scrutiny and discipline could be ever more acute. Crime and disorder issues had always been a key component of New Labour's understanding of the problems of the poorest areas. In this respect at least, the government's inheritance from left realist criminology remained intact. For example, the Social Exclusion Unit presented the issue in the following terms, foregrounding the residents' perceptions of and concerns about crime and ASB:

> Poor neighbourhoods are not just a housing problem ... there is no single definition of a poor neighbourhood ... they have poverty, unemployment and poor health in common and crime usually comes high on a list of residents' concerns. (SEU 1998: 13)

A subsequent report by Policy Action Team 8, set up by the SEU to help develop responses to ASB, further elaborated the problem:

> ASB is a widespread problem. It is a problem that is more prevalent in deprived neighbourhoods. Its effects are often most damaging in communities that are already fragile and where services are overstretched. Serious hard-core perpetrators are small in number but their behaviour has a disproportionate impact on large numbers of ordinary people ... Anti-social behaviour is perceived to be twice as high in deprived areas than nationally ... is considered to be a medium to large problem by three-quarters of social landlords ... and appears to be increasing. (SEU 2000: 7)

However, in practice, when attempting to address such issues politically, some of the language employed betrayed levels of contempt and intolerance reminiscent of Victorian society's treatment of the supposed 'underclass' (McLaughlin 2002). According to the Prime Minister, the scourge of so many deprived communities were 'young people with nothing to do [but] make life hell for other citizens' (Blair 1997). And from such pronouncements it is then but a short step to the demonisation of 'louts', 'yobs' and 'neighbours from hell'.

In New Deal for Communities areas, the newly established community safety teams began to use the additional leverage afforded by their housing management responsibilities to address problems of crime, disorder and anti-social behaviour. In this they were able to draw upon the developing experience of local authorities using housing management powers and tenancy agreement provisions to address neighbour disputes and the unacceptable behaviour of tenants (Burney 1999). While the Labour Party, still in opposition, had outlined its plans for taking tougher action against nuisance neighbours, drawing a clear connection between the effective management of ASB and community safety (Labour Party 1995), the Conservatives' 1996 Housing Act had conferred new enforcement powers upon social housing landlords (Flint 2002). In this way, social policy institutions became useful vehicles for exercising a certain leverage over parents. Although the focus of much of this new enforcement action concerned housing management, a survey of social landlords in 2001 found that 77 per cent of the latter identified 12–17 year olds as the most relevant group for their ASB enforcement action (Hunter and Nixon 2001). With the coming of Anti-Social Behaviour Orders (ASBOs) and Acceptable Behaviour Contracts (ABCs) the emphasis on youth control which had been at the heart of this enforcement activity became all the more explicit. No less obvious was the emergence of a pattern of 'postcode enforcement' practice. By virtue of their status as social housing tenants, residents of certain communities could be subjected to a more intensive scrutiny of their lifestyles, behaviour and relationships and rendered more vulnerable to enforcement action. The power to evict problematic tenants was the leverage available to social landlords and, in due course, as we describe in a later chapter, it was this threat of eviction which was employed to give teeth to the ABCs. The threat of eviction was used to give parents an additional 'incentive' to manage their children 'more responsibly' and curb their offending and disorderly behaviour. The threat of eviction was said to 'get their attention and concentrate their minds wonderfully'. In a similar vein, later proposals extended an idea of reducing or withholding social security benefits paid to offenders, perpetrators of ASB or offenders failing to comply with the terms of their community punishment or reparation orders.

The proposal emerged from the same 'contractual' model of citizenship that New Labour had espoused long before it took office (Commission on Social Justice 1993); rights were to be linked to duties, responsibility was to earn respect. Only the fact that withholding benefits to some of the poorest and most inadequate offenders might just be the most criminogenic and counter-productive option conceivable persuaded some, not least the probation officers who would be managing the pilot projects, to voice their opposition. In any event, proposals of this sort, imposing tougher discipline and social controls upon the poorest through social welfare interventions, are scarcely a new feature of social policy (Piven and Cloward 1972). The difference now may simply be the degree to which social policy has become crime and disorder focused (or 'criminalised'). Paradoxically, this may be occurring just as the problem of crime itself is becoming rather less clear cut, absorbed and obscured by a growing and diverse range of perceived risks, insecurities, fears, harms, immoralities, dangers and 'anti-social' threats, behaviours – and persons – for which and for whom our society is having to evolve new responses. It is, in this broadest sense, that we relate the problem posed by ASB with a series of perceived 'enforcement deficits' with which late-modern nation-states are now struggling to cope (Crawford 2002).

It is for these reasons that, in this book, we approach the question of responding to youth offending and 'tackling' anti-social behaviour through the perspective of a perceived enforcement deficit. Our argument is almost entirely contrary to that ventured earlier by, among others, politicians, local authority enforcement officials (the new class of ASB coordinators) and summarised in the *Together* campaign's first Annual Report, namely that 'as crime has fallen, anti-social behaviour has become a major cause of concern'. By contrast, we are witnessing crime and disorder being reproblematised as 'anti-social' activity, thereby lending a spurious new integrity to the politics of exclusion, to intolerance and to inequality. A whole new raft of enforcement opportunities are being developed to address the perpetrators of these offending behaviours. Unlike earlier discourses we no longer prioritise 'treatment', 'cure' or 'education', and still less do we attempt to improve the disadvantaged social, domestic or environmental contexts in which an overwhelming majority of today's anti-social (and offending) young people fail to develop into successful and responsible adults. We overlook the criminogenic social contexts bearing down upon the 'delinquent' and concentrate largely upon their choices and behaviour. This leaves us with relatively few options in either understanding or dealing with their behaviour. We interpret the behaviour as typical of 'that kind of person', as Christie (2004: 49) has noted, offensive and anti-social people 'are their own explanation' thereby ensuring our overreliance upon discipline, punishment and containment.

For us this problematisation of ASB marks the arrival of an increasingly insecure, divided and intolerant culture. Likewise, the policing of ASB suggests an increasingly disciplinary society and, contrary to contemporary political rhetoric regarding social inclusion, a markedly more exclusive one, selectively targeting a particular range of stigmatised behaviours and individuals for reasons that are often beyond the perpetrators' control and, at best, for which they are seldom solely responsible.

In the first chapter which follows, we attempt to trace the emergence of this new discourse on ASB, linking current concerns about youth and ASB to wider preoccupations with the 'condition of Britain' by which New Labour in general and Tony Blair in particular have been concerned. What was needed was a firmer sense of social responsibilities, 'tougher love' and stricter discipline in our key social institutions. Many of New Labour's reforms to youth justice and youth policy were designed to bring this about.

In Chapter 3, while tracking the evolution of a discourse on ASB, we link the emergence of an explicit public and political concern with ASB to the problematisation of 'juvenile delinquency' during the Second World War and the immediate period of postwar reconstruction. Then it was recognised, in the emerging social democratic criminology of the time, that children whose families were disrupted by wartime, who may have been evacuated and may not have seen their parents for months or even years, who may have been abused, bereaved or bombed and who were, in any event, deprived of a normal childhood, may develop certain anti-social characteristics. For us, that presumption still applies. Children and young people growing up in communities undergoing rapid social change, in urban environments that barely accommodate them and amid a tantalising consumer culture they cannot afford, maybe deprived, maybe neglected, maybe abused and forced to grow up too fast, are also likely to exhibit a variety of behavioural adjustments. Their 'delinquent solutions' (Downes 1966) may be to shoplift, to steal cars, to bully others over whom they have a little leverage or perhaps just to play football, in so doing churning up a patch of grass on the estate that older residents had once considered sacrosanct.

We encountered an intriguing illustration of this particular intergenerational dilemma in the course of some of our fieldwork looking at perceptions of ASB in an urban residential area. Both the perception of the issue and responses to it have changed markedly over time. Children playing street football and apparently 'spoiling' an area of grass on a residential estate saw the erection of 'No Ball Games' signs on their favourite pitches. Others repeatedly kicking their ball against the 'goal' of a neighbour's ground floor flat were supplied with lightweight foam footballs which did not thump so heavily on the wall and which were less likely to damage parked vehicles. Compare these with an article written in 1950 in the first issue of the newly launched *British Journal of Delinquency*. In the article Spencer considered how wartime conditions had impacted on young people's lives and opportunities. Five years after the ending of the war, however, he had noted, with some obvious satisfaction, the return of normal, healthy pro-social activities – street football – to the streets of the neighbourhood he was researching (Spencer 1950). Unfortunately, perhaps, as we have already seen, this conception of positive social activity has not lasted so well and it now generates a range of complaints.

In the course of the fifty-plus years since Spencer's original article, the street football pitches have become on-street car parks where a stray shot might result in some expensive damage. What has not changed is the behaviour. Around it everything has changed – the perspective of the viewer/complainant, the sense of context, the physical occupancy of space, the interpretation of the behaviour and now, perhaps finally, the law itself. Street football has become anti-social behaviour. Yet many writers and researchers have commented upon the importance of the street in childhood and youth cultures. The street was once the principal setting for children's play and recreation. Yet today there is no doubt that the car, in particular, has had an unprecedented impact upon how children and young people use streets or feel able to wander safely in and around the neighbourhood in which they live. An IPPR study, *Streets Ahead*, has recently argued that:

> The age of the motor car has undoubtedly had a profound effect on children's freedom of movement. The visibility and freedom of children is surely one of the marks of a civilised society. If the freedom of children is constrained in the motor age, then public policy should seek to rebalance the rights and responsibilities of road users towards children's rights and motorists' responsibilities.
>
> (Grayling *et al.* 2002)

By contrast, Moss and Petrie (2002) cite a community safety consultation initiative in Stirling where local residents objected to the use of a playground for skateboarding while demanding that the local authority fix 'No Ball Games' signs adjacent to almost every green space on their estate.

Whether foam footballs, the outlawing of street football or ASBOs really appease an older generation for whom the mere presence of groups of young people has increasingly become perceived as threatening remains an open question. The older people alluded to earlier, who objected to children playing football adjacent to their homes, were not just concerned about the state of the grass. Their concerns were typically more deeply rooted within their perceptions of a variety of changes in their immediate environment and wider society, for instance changes bound up with a range of factors including the allocation policies of social housing agencies, and housing officers cautiously administering their increasingly scarce resource and, in the older generation's eyes, permitting the 'intrusion' of problematic families with young children into hitherto quiet areas. Accordingly there are relatively few surprises in some recent Home Office analyses of BCS data on public perceptions of crime, disorder and ASB. Fears and concerns about local ASB problems appear to be triggered, above all, by an abiding sense that levels of disorder were running out of control locally and that the police, criminal justice system (CJS) and local authority were not performing well. These perceptions were at their most acute in social housing areas. In other words, with perceived levels of disorder rising, the protection and support that people felt they had a right to expect (in part, perhaps, an outcome of an increasingly consumerist orientation towards policing services: Squires 1997) no longer seemed to exist. Large numbers of young people 'hanging about' were the most common focus for these concerns (Finney 2004; Thorpe and Wood 2004).

Capturing this picture of perceptions of change and decline in local communities and an associated retrenchment in public services, Young has described the sense of 'ontological insecurity' which results (Young 1999). The picture incorporates several echoes of the 'broken windows' criminology of Wilson and Kelling (1982) and corresponds with the inter-generational conflicts described by Girling et al. (2000). Crime, disorder and anti-social behaviour are latched onto by those feeling insecure as a tangible sign of the risks they (and we) run. They legitimate our defensiveness, authenticate our fears and even underpin our secular modern fatalism, but at the same time they vindicate our own sense of ourselves as moral and worthy: respectable as opposed to disreputable. We do not seek to be fearful and we do not enjoy it, rather fear and insecurity are the travelling companions of our desire to differentiate and reaffirm ourselves, our values and beliefs.

And to do this we need the 'Other', the enemy, all that we are not (Taylor 1999). In recent years especially, youth, so often a metaphor for change and the 'condition of society' (Cohen 1973; Pearson 1983), have come to assume this role, the visible, even tangible presence on your street, outside your shops and in your parks. And according to Lea and Young (1984) it is not just the question of what young people are or the behaviour they exhibit but rather what they represent, for crime and anti-social behaviour are only the end point of a continuum of disorder. [They are] not separate from other forms of aggravation and breakdown. It is the run down council estate where music blares out of windows early in the morning; it is the graffiti on the walls; it is aggression in the shops; it is bins that are never emptied; oil stains across the streets; it is kids who show no respect; it is large trucks racing through your roads; it is streets you dare not walk down at night; it is always being careful; it is a symbol of a world falling apart. (Lea and Young 1984: 55)

In due course, such a litany of concerns became the seedbed of left realism, envisaging a new 'victimised community' and a new project, 'community safety', against whom the 'anti-social' would come to be defined. But on a wider scale, it is worth reflecting, in this 'symbol of a world falling apart', just whose world was this? Postwar criminologists spoke of 'delinquent generations' (Wilkins 1960) whose experiences, options, life chances and attitudes were laid down during the chaos of wartime and who, partly in consequence, adopted different lifestyles and significantly (or so it appeared) more 'delinquent' pathways than their prewar peers. In a similar fashion we might speak of similar 'post-welfare' generation(s). People entering adulthood during the 'progressive' and optimistic years of postwar reconstruction and enjoying expanding opportunities, full employment, rising general affluence and standards of living and 'cradle to grave' welfare until, that is, this cycle of rising expectations was brought to an abrupt stop. There may be no inevitable association between ageing and increasing concerns about victimisation, even though this is often how the issue is represented – crime perceived as a virtual age war (James 2001; Mawby 1988). Yet for this generation and their immediate successors who, perhaps, may never have had it quite so good after all, confronted now by worries about the adequacy of their pensions and the availability or affordability of housing, health and social care (anticipated in social policy circles from the mid-1980s), and witnessing the dereliction resulting from local authority spending restrictions, then maybe the rowdy congregation of local youths on the street corner could feel like a final straw. In such circumstances the behaviour, dress, mannerisms and language of 'youth' (about which no one, least of all their parents, seemed willing to do anything) could well acquire a profoundly 'anti-social' quality.

Yet whereas fear of crime is often taken as a seemingly unwavering fact of contemporary life, delinquency and anti-social behaviour usually demands some explanation. Our own view, by contrast, is that we can only arrive at an adequate understanding of contemporary preoccupations with ASB by an informed appreciation of both. As the observation by Christie with which we commenced this chapter makes plain, we are currently creating the very conditions most likely to encourage unwanted and anti-social behaviour, and in which we view that behaviour as threatening and malicious to be viewed primarily through the prism of crime (Christie 2004).

Picking up from these themes and issues, Chapter 4 develops our core argument that that ASB management, prevention and enforcement activities have now become central and indispensable features of contemporary youth justice. We relate this interpretation of ASB to the more general changes occurring within the youth justice field and within the context of the series of relatively new and emerging commentaries attempting to describe, explain and evaluate recent changes in youth justice. These include the emergence of a new 'actuarial' penology and the governmentality perspective emphasising the strategy of 'responsibilisation' and new modes of exercising power. In the latter half of the chapter we develop these themes in relation to key dimensions of Cohen's (1985) 'dispersal of discipline' argument.

The following two chapters describe the findings arising from two distinct research projects exploring aspects of youth justice and ASB management. Both pieces of research are informed by our developing critique of existing youth justice practice and our commitment to informed qualitative research methodologies designed to give a voice to the young people at the centre of questions of Youth Justice (YJ) policy and ASB enforcement. The first (Chapter 5) involves a project developing an in-depth analysis of the establishment and enforcement of ABCs by a community safety team in a New Deal area. We explore the views and commentaries of members of the community safety team (and those of related agency and professional interests) and compare these to the views of the families and the young people themselves with regard to the effectiveness, implications and, in some cases, unintended consequences of the contracts. The critique we develop of the ABC enforcement process both broadens and develops our critique of ASB management and the New Youth Justice.

Chapter 6, also based upon a qualitative empirical study takes issue with one of the central objectives of the reformed YJ system, the supposed severing of the link between ASB and more serious and persistent patterns of offending. The project was directly concerned about the motivations of young people and their involvement in vehicle taking. We explored the reasons they gave for their initial involvement (the choices they took, as it were, in the context given by the opportunities they perceived) and looked at the factors which proved influential in their persistence. The research was intended to offer a critical reflection upon the dominant paradigms of 'criminal career onset' research by trying to place the perspective of the young person at the centre of the analysis.

Finally, in Chapter 7, we attempt to draw these several themes together through a consideration of the processes of marginalisation and criminalisation endured by the youth of the lower social classes. The critical perspectives we bring to bear upon these issues derive from the interactionist studies of the 1960s and 1970s, especially the work of Edwin Schur, whose Radical Non-Intervention (1973) perspective poses perhaps the most direct challenge to today's punitive early interventionism. Yet our attempted revival of Schur's insights must now be situated within the context of late modernity's particular fears and insecurities.

In particular, this entails a new politics of perceptions and reassurances in which, in the criminal justice field, the policing of anti-social behaviour features as the foremost example of a new discourse of governing through 'precautionary injustice'. Unfortunately, vague definitions of ASB and enforcement mechanisms concentrated in relatively deprived areas where problematic behaviours of all kinds might be more readily discovered (not least because we seek them there with greater vigilance) seem likely to exacerbate the government's political and systemic difficulties with marginalised youth. Pitts, for one (2004: 149), fears that New Labour may well have painted itself into a corner on this very issue: it has to play the 'tough card', but being tough does not work and only creates greater injustice. In this difficult climate our argument in the final chapter is presented as a contribution towards a more humane, fair and civilised system of youth justice. More specifically, we have in mind a system of youth justice which does rather more than create and circulate a species of 'politically and economically useful' delinquency (Foucault 1977: 277) wherein the most marginalised of young people are misspent in the pursuit of electoral advantage and a given conception of social order.

Chapter 2

The irresistible rise of anti-social behaviour

Anti-social behaviour, however defined, causes much unhappiness; and sizeable proportions of both public and private resources are consumed in an effort to deal with it ... No-one can embark on a discussion of anti-social behaviour without making assumptions as to the criteria by which any specific actions are defined as such; and those assumptions are bound to reflect, not only the norms of a particular culture, but in some degree also, the subjective preferences of the person who makes them. What is understood to be unacceptable behaviour varies from place to place and from time to time; and even where standards are much the same, actual manifestations will vary. (Wooton 1959: 13)

Feedback from the doorstep canvassing during the 2004 local and European elections confirmed what the New Labour leadership had long suspected: 'anti-social behaviour' had become, apparently, the number one concern of the British people. But how had this issue risen so quickly and to such prominence? A few weeks later, polling results from two by-elections in the Midlands confirmed the picture. Labour's successful election coordinator told journalists:

'If we had not been seen to be on the people's side over anti-social behaviour we would have lost the election. Without a shadow of a doubt, it is the number one issue on the doorsteps in urban areas and has been since I have been an MP. It is teen gangs, graffiti, fireworks, the quality of life issues that cumulatively make life a misery for too many people'. (Wintour, *The Guardian Analysis*, 20 July 2004).

The remark poses a number of important questions, not least the idea of government 'being seen to be on the public's side'.

However, one searches, largely in vain, for any extensive mainstream criminological treatment of the issue and only fleeting references to it in some of the critically defining texts of recent years. For example, there was no entry on ASB in the first *Dictionary of Criminology*, published in 2000 (Muncie and McLaughlin 2000). It is as if, being not quite crime, ASB had slipped the criminological leash or, alternatively, that it fell somewhere beyond the discipline's theoretical radar and there left to another tier of 'community safety' evaluators, practitioners and commentators to go where critical criminologists feared to tread – or, perhaps, from where they had been excluded. In a Home Office press release of October 1999, Jack Straw firmly rebuffed criticism of the ASBO from 'certain academics and civil libertarians' who thought the ASB provisions 'too sweeping' or 'incompatible with the European Convention on Human Rights'; 'the Government does not accept that' he concluded (Grier and Thomas 2003). More generally, perhaps criminology had simply been outpaced by a government deeply committed to, indeed hugely dependent upon, leading on 'law and order' (Garland 2001; Tonry 2004).

Law and social order had been the making of New Labour and, seemingly, a central crusade of its leader, Tony Blair. In office, however, the competing strains of politics, policy and perception worked their own difficulties. New Labour wanted to be seen to be delivering on its law and order promises but, although reported and recorded crime were generally falling and have continued to fall into the government's second term of office, larger and larger percentages appear to believe crime is increasing. And this occurred, even as the BCS evidence suggested that people were now worrying less about about significant crime types (burglary, car crime and violence). Nevertheless, according to Finney, (2004), 'seventy-two percent of adults thought the crime rate had increased in the country as a whole over the previous two years and 54% thought [it] had increased in their local area … Almost a half (47%) of people thought both national and local crime levels had increased' (p. 25). In particular, much research tended to suggest that people's concerns about ASB – especially the ASB of young people – was connected to wider preoccupations about deteriorating standards of living or their perceptions of declining neighbourhoods (Hancock 2001). More recent analysis of British Crime Survey data has tended to reinforce such a context- or environment-driven perception of anti-social behaviour problems. People living in social

housing estates or poorer areas tended to report more anti-social behaviour problems (Thorpe and Wood 2004).

Although New Labour's law and order agenda was to be 'evidence
based', the careful development of 'what works', many commentators
(Muncie 2000a; Faulkner 2001; Pitts 2003; Tonry 2004) ventured the view
that New Labour's crime policies often relied upon a fairly selective
reading of the evidence and were invariably far more preoccupied with
politics and with winning (or chasing) public opinion than the 'evidence-
based policy-making' extolled by ministers. It may well have been this
'dissonance' which discouraged, or excluded, a more mainstream criminological scrutiny, but a consequence was that few major challenges were
made to the sweeping discourse of anti-social behaviour until such time as
the new legislation (Anti-Social Behaviour Act 2003) was in place and
Crime and Disorder Reduction Partnerships (CDRPs) had appointed their
ASB coordinators and were well into the process of formulating their local
ASB strategies.

Risks and representations

For the government, then, the invention – though perhaps 'reinvention'
would be a better word, and (as we shall see) 'rediscovery' better still – of
anti-social behaviour was an attempt to close the awkward circle of
politics, policy and perceptions referred to earlier. Criminology has long
been aware of important disconnections between the risk of crime and the
fear of crime (Hollway and Jefferson 2000) but this posed the government
with a serious problem when its crime reduction achievements were not
perceived and widely applauded by the public. Despite the extensive
reworking of the criminal justice system in the wake of the 1998 Crime and
Disorder Act, especially the reorganisation of youth justice, the public
have continued to complain about a wide range of phenomena – either
'conditions of late modernity' or 'unacceptable behaviours' depending
upon the perspective adopted – impacting upon their quality of life. In
'official' crime prevention circles, these conditions and/or behaviours
were increasingly expressed in the 'broken windows' discourse inherited
from Wilson and Kelling (1982) which emphasised the moral
responsibility of individuals towards their communities, sanctioned the
intolerance of 'incivilities' (the forerunner of today's ASB) and helped
inaugurate a campaign for the 'zero-tolerance' policing of troubled
neighbourhoods. Even so, Young is undoubtedly correct to note that the
traditional uniformed police may only be a necessary, though far from
sufficient, component of this new urban governance (Young 1999). The
'broken windows' perspective is important for, undoubtedly, the ways in

which one perceives such social phenomena become a crucial factor in determining how one reacts to them and, more importantly, how communities and social agencies (the police, the government, the law) seek to respond. And under New Labour, social policy, urban policy and community regeneration were to become increasingly driven by crime and disorder management priorities.

As Crawford has noted (2002), the raft of policy measures which cohered around the notion of 'community safety' entailed new ways of looking at the multiplicity of issues framing 'the crime problem'. These included a concern with prevention and with wider social problems, with fear and a broader more holistic sense of the 'quality of life' relating back to notions of 'ontological security'. It is at this level that the cumulative 'societal' or 'communal' identity to which ASB is construed as a threat can be understood. However, both the local and global problems and insecurities to which community safety strategies are meant to be a response also expose many of the limits and contradictions of the contemporary state's sphere of action and its objectives. As Zedner (2000) has noted, the pursuit of security (against what, or against whom?), like the promise of community safety itself, can be an ultimately unachievable goal because it depends upon the construction of symbolic risks or threats ('the anti-social') against which the society or the community need to be defended. The strategy of social inclusion, in other words, depends upon the construction of an excluded (and in this case anti-social) 'other'. In this respect, for Crawford, the significance of community safety work and anti-social behaviour prevention of enforcement strategies lies precisely in their representational value. In a globalised, scary and dangerous world, they represent a sphere of policy action in which governments can achieve something. 'The current governmental preoccupation with petty crime, disorder and ASB reflects a sense of "anxiety" about which something can be done in an otherwise uncertain world' (Crawford 2002: 31–2). Drawing upon Bauman's insightful analysis of the scope of state action in a world of rapid globalised finance, we get an intriguing glimpse of a new 'nightwatchman' state once associated with laissez-faire liberal capitalism (or anticipated in Nozick's [1974] libertarian utopia). 'State governments are allotted the role of little else than oversized police precincts, [with] the quantity and quality of the policemen on the beat, sweeping the streets clean of beggars, pesterers and pilferers' (Bauman 1998: 20) emerging as the key governmental priorities.

Crime control and disorder management represent the sine qua non of Blair's 'New Labour' strategy, while any ambiguity implicit in Blair's famous slogan 'Tough on crime, tough on the causes of crime' has tended to be resolved in favour of tougher social discipline and the reinforcement of 'responsibilities' rather than more broadly preventive social policies. As

Pitts has noted, in this interpretation of crime, in this case youth crime, 'the idea of youth crime as a product of poverty, social inequality or psychological disadvantage is supplanted by an emphasis on individual and family responsibility' (Pitts 2003: 47–8).

New Labour did embark upon a range of broader social and community initiatives to address the processes of social exclusion, for example: New Deal for Communities, Sure Start, On Track, Education Action Zones and the Youth Inclusion Programme. And collectively these policies did, as Barton and Gilling (1997) have argued, carve out a new home for social policy within the emerging community safety field, but this was increasingly social policy for crime prevention or, as it was also expressed, the criminalisation of social policy. While New Labour could undoubtedly make a case that it was serious about being 'tough on the causes of crime' an infinitely stronger case could be made for the fact that it was actually becoming much 'tougher on criminals', with young offenders in particular appearing to bear the brunt of the emerging populist intolerance. And, as Smith has noted, 'the rhetoric of social inclusion is consistently undermined by the intensified focus on individuals ... the Youth Justice system ... demonstrating less and less interest in the causes of crime as far as [the] individual is concerned' (Smith, R. 2003: 72).

In view of all this: first, New Labour's commitment to crime reduction being apparently undermined by a growing public perception that crime was rising, not falling; second, growing evidence that in certain 'more deprived' and especially poorer urban areas concerns about anti-social behaviour seemed to be instrumental in driving up the fear of crime and thereby eclipsing any crime reduction gains; and, finally, the awareness of a model of police-led, 'incivility targeting' and community regeneration which seemed to be successful in the USA – the government was led to shift its emphasis. Thus, if public perceptions seemed to be hindering an appropriate acknowledgement of the effectiveness of New Labour crime control policies, it became important to address these perceptions directly. This is not so in the more populist and familiar sense in which the government has often been accused of being far too preoccupied with the 'spin-doctoring' of public information, but rather that public perceptions of anti-social behaviour had to be engaged with directly.

Writing in the *Observer* (4 July 2004) Asthana and Bright discussed the government's latest measures to deal with the intolerable and anti-social behaviour of 'neighbours from hell', but they note that this is a 'high-risk strategy'. The government, they claim, 'invented the expression "anti-social behaviour" to describe a range of activities from vandalism to assault [but] now has to demonstrate that it can do something about it.' The suggestion is that this is a central feature of the contemporary discourse of anti-social behaviour, that it is, in part at least, an attempt by government to engage directly in a politics of representation about law, order and public safety, an attempt to influence public perceptions directly. It would certainly not be the first time that government has invoked such a representational strategy to put itself 'on-side' with respect to public sentiments or to shape public attitudes. For example, the often referred to 'war' against crime, beginning with a Home Office White Paper with this name in 1964 (Home Office 1964) clearly invokes a particular kind of (in Faulkner's eyes, inappropriate) symbolism with regard to anti-crime strategies (Faulkner 2001: 144). More recently the infamous 1992 Car Crime Prevention Year campaign which employed the image of packs of marauding hyenas to represent the, seemingly almost feral, insolent and amoral, groups of young vehicle takers and thieves, arguably took this form of law and order politics to a new level (Campbell 1993). Indeed, it is possible to argue that this particular imagery of young offenders has had a lasting impact upon (and done lasting damage to) images of young people in a way which has fed directly into today's anti-social behaviour debates (Brown 1998). The frequency with which congregations of young people are described as 'almost feral' by police or other spokespersons (Jeffs and Smith 1996), in the course of an argument being made for either greater control, dispersal or greater discipline, would suggest that this is not just a coincidence, but a direct result of a former government's crime prevention propaganda.

Yet if demonising youth in the manner alluded to above has chiefly contrived to increase the public's fear of groups of them occupying public space – and thereby increase the fear of crime and so frustrate the Government's purpose of winning the war of perceptions over crime reduction – then the government's recent upping of the stakes in respect of anti-social behaviour carries even further risks. As Tonry has recently observed, recent analyses of the British Crime Survey, provide 'striking evidence of the perverse effects of overemphasis on crime and crime prevention concerning anti-social behaviour' (Tonry 2004: 57). Looking at the proportions of BCS respondents who thought the particular types of 'incivility' and disorder that we now group together under the collective label of ASB were 'big problems', an intriguing pattern emerges. The BCS was conducted every two years between 1992 and 1998 and then annually since 2000, and for most of the problematic behaviours the trends were flat or falling until 1998 'when the Government began trumpeting its campaign against anti-social behaviour ... and have risen markedly and steadily ever since' (ibid.). And, he concludes, 'by making anti-social behaviour into a major social policy problem, and giving it sustained high visibility attention, Labour has made a small problem larger, thereby making people more aware of it and less satisfied with their lives and their government' (ibid.).

However, the representational aspect is not the whole of an explanation for the irresistible rise of anti-social policy behaviour. Convenient as this notion was in opening up a new field of action for a government committed to a disciplined model of citizenship and to reading social conditions in terms of their resulting behaviours – for which individuals are held responsible, it is nonetheless possible to read New Labour's rediscovery of anti-social behaviour as a culmination of a number of developing policy strands during the 1980s and 1990s.

In a speech prefacing the announcement of the government's five-year strategic crime reduction plan in mid-July 2004 (Home Office 2004d), the Prime Minister spoke of creating a 'new consensus' on law and order (Blair 2004). In the speech Mr Blair referred to his first political campaigning experiences and of encountering deprived and run-down, high-crime areas, where 'people were too scared to open the door and where the letterboxes had burn marks around them through which lighted rags had been shoved.' Reflecting on these experiences in an article for *The Times* he recollected using, for the first time, the phrase 'anti-social behaviour'. This was in 1988. However, despite the strong sense of continuity of purpose implied within Blair's 'recollection', anti-social behaviour did not arise, perfectly formed, in the mind of a politician in 1988. Rather, it re-emerged as a result of a complex combination of influences. Chief among these were:

- First, the overall shifts in perspective within criminology and criminal justice policy associated with the 'broken windows' perspective in crime prevention and the contrasting criminological 'realisms' emerging during the 1980s.

- Second, a concern with social exclusion and victimisation, especially within deprived and excluded communities. In such neighbourhoods, chronic rates of crime, disorder, violence and victimisation compounded the intolerable experiences and disrupted life chances of residents.

- Third, there has been a process of 'residualisation of social housing' after 1980 to which social housing agencies responded with more stringent enforcement of tenancy conditions (Burney 1999). Proposals for 'probationary' or introductory tenancies culminated in the new enforcement powers in the 1996 Housing Act (Hunter 2000; Flint 2002) while the 1995 Labour policy document, *A Quiet Life: Tough Action on Criminal Neighbours*, expanded the notion of ASB while placing it firmly at the centre of the Party's approach to community-oriented crime and disorder management (Labour Party 1995).

- Finally, there was a rediscovery of the sense in which unchecked youthful or adolescent anti-social behaviour was perceived as the seedbed of a persistent criminal career. Liberal youth justice policies were held to be mistaken in holding to a developmental optimism that young people would 'grow up out of crime'. Rather, in the deprived and excluded communities referred to already, the chances were that they would not do so. In such cases, high rates of 'nuisance', 'delinquent', 'disorderly' and 'anti-social' behaviours amongst the young people were both a symptom of the underlying problems and a sign of the worse criminality to come.

Left and right realism and broken windows

From Conservative realism in particular came an emphasis on punishment, deterrence and, above all, an unmitigated individual responsibility (Roshier 1989) which was to be the foundation upon which an increasingly punitive targeting of the criminal and anti-social was to be constructed. From 'left realism', (LR) along with the generic injunction to take crime 'seriously' came a focus upon the victim, and especially the hidden victims, who had not hitherto found their way into the crime reports. For a variety of reasons, significant sections of the population seemed disinclined or reluctant to report all the offences they experienced. This could be the result of their known relationship with offenders (in the case of domestic violence, bullying or acquaintance violence), intimidation or the threat of repercussions, or their membership of a group unaccustomed to having the police follow up their complaints diligently. Evidence suggested that this under-reporting could be particularly significant in some communities and in deprived and high-crime areas (Maynard 1994) where reported crime marked only the visible tip of an entire iceberg of victimisation. This insight from LR, In particular, that an entire field of harm and victimisation existed, working its corrosive influence largely beyond the sphere of the criminal justice system, is a key step towards the contemporary rediscovery and re-problematisation of ASB.

Another important theme, contributing to the construction of a discourse on ASB and emerging from left realism, concerns social cohesion and 'community capacity'. To some extent this theme, which we discuss in more detail later on, connected with the broad thrust of Wilson and Kelling's (1982) 'broken windows' analysis mentioned already. It is this to which Tony Blair was alluding in his July 2004 speech. Crime and victimisation were dynamic aspects of social exclusion (Hope 2001); they compounded the deprivation and vulnerability of the already poor, the excluded or those enduring discrimination. In turn, crime corroded the ability of communities to cope with existing problems: businesses closed, community facilities become vandalised and unusable, areas gained a 'reputation', those who were able to leave did so (Skogan 1990; Bottoms and Wiles 1997). In such an analysis, left realism displayed something of its intellectual debts to the Chicago School 'social ecology' of crime in which environmental and situational factors determined crime levels. In due course, this largely environmental reading of the causation of crime patterns subdivided to produce two strands, both of which came to impinge upon the anti-social behaviour debate. One key strand here concerns the important shift by which environmentalism combined with a resurgent and neoclassical conservative criminological realism to sponsor the design-driven deterrent variants of crime prevention: 'defensible space', crime prevention through environment design (CPTED) and situational crime prevention, also known as 'target hardening' (Gilling 1997; Hughes 1998).

Neoclassical conservative criminological realism was crucial to this hugely important paradigm shift in crime prevention and criminology and essential to the formulation of contemporary notions of ASB. Conservative realism did not seek to understand crime at all, simply to prevent as much as possible of it (or apprehend as many as possible of those responsible for it). It is this which has prompted the debate about whether classicism and or neoclassicism were genuinely *criminological* theories at all (Radzinowicz 1999). After all, Classicism tended to accept that humans were, by nature, individualistic, self-interested, interest-maximising and both opportunistically and calculatedly dishonest. That is, it tended to assume, as given, more or less everything that criminology had sought to turn into a science. Conservative realism stressed authority, deference to law and tradition and, above all, personal and individual responsibility, and then punishment, for wrong-doing. We might catch an echo of this changing emphasis in a former Prime Minister's comment, in 1993, that society should 'condemn a little more and understand a little less', while discussing the perceived crisis in youth crime patterns following the abduction and murder that year of two-year-old James Bulger. John Major's statement was said to have signalled the newer more punitive approach to youth justice developing in the 1990s (Wilson and Ashton 2001: 18).

From this conjunction of conservative realism and environmental criminology were derived both the explicitly utilitarian 'rational choice' theory and the instrumental 'routine activity' theory (Felson 1994). Neither appeared very much interested in understanding criminality or criminal motives; their concern was with preventing (or, at best, managing or lowering) crime as a form of aggregated behaviour. The fact that such theories have largely avoided any attempt to explain or understand criminal behaviour has led some commentators to question what we can really learn from them. The beguiling and supposedly 'common sense' of 'rational choice' or 'routine activity' theory becomes a weakness. This is an issue for researchers when seeking to evaluate criminal justice and crime prevention initiatives and, arguably, especially so for a government committed to a 'what works' criminal justice agenda. For, as Tilley has argued (Tilley 2000), an evaluation might tell us what 'worked', where and when, but without the 'why' and the 'how' we lack any reliable basis upon which to replicate an apparently successful project at another time and in another place. So however plausible these theories were, the explanation of criminal or disorderly behaviour was always beyond their grasp. Crime and disorder were not just *misunderstood* behaviours but, rather, behaviours which were incapable of being understood and the motivations behind them remained quite opaque.

There is no little irony in the fact that when commentators, horrified by a latest criminal atrocity, are apt to refer to the seemingly 'mindless violence', what they are really saying is that they don't understand, can't understand, even don't want to understand the motivation(s) for it. Of course this is not a new phenomenon – the seeming 'mindlessness' of criminality is a staple characteristic of crime commentary and reporting. It is as if any knowledge of the motivations of the perpetrator, any capacity to understand them, is itself an acknowledgement of inherent corruption. The point is, however, and it has been for some time, that we have now placed ourselves in precisely the same position with regard to understanding anti-social behaviour, especially youthful anti-social behaviour. It is a behaviour exhibited by 'them', part of their very 'anti-social' otherness, nothing more nor less than we would expect from those types: the 'neighbours from hell', the almost 'feral' and undisciplined kids, and the 'drunken louts' and, more recently, 'the loutettes'. The labels stick, they serve as shortcuts to an entire worldview of crime and punishment: 'Evil people are their own explanation. The discussion comes to a stop, the phenomenon is understood, there is no further need for intellectual efforts,' and we know what we must do (Christie 2004: 49). There now seems a huge and growing social distance between 'us' and a variety of 'them', now compounded by class and culture, generation and ethnicity. While it has typically been a characteristic of postwar adulthood's misunderstanding of youth and youth's 'rebellion' – for instance, the dress sense, the music, the culture and language often adopted to shock and confront, and especially the 'hangin' about', the 'doin' nuthin'' and the affected pose of bored disengagement (Corrigan 1979) – this incapacity to understand has now become institutionalised within the youth justice system itself. This is an issue we discuss further in a later chapter.

There are more than a few echoes of these aforementioned themes in

Tony Blair's July 2004 speech embracing a 'new consensus on law and order' and repudiating the culture of permissiveness he believes characterised the 1960s. Describing the 'cultural revolution' of the 1960s which culminated in a new approach to social and criminal justice he refers in particular to a 'law and order policy still ... understanding the social causes of criminality'. But 'here, now, today,' he continues, 'people have had enough of this part of the 1960s consensus.' Later he talks of working 'through instinct' and embracing a new common sense about society and crime. Central to this is a reaffirmation of social order and a tough and intolerant attitude to the 'anti-social'. Almost by definition, the anti-social stands opposed to some conception of society or social order: the question here concerns precisely *which* forms of society and social order. Mr Blair's, it seems, comprises only the 'responsible, respectable ... decent law abiding majority ... those that play by the rules do well and those that don't get punished.' Contrary to Mrs Thatcher's infamous claim, for Blair, 'there is such a thing as society' but New Labour's commitment to social inclusion was always more qualified and conditional, subject to acceptance of a social contract imposing discipline and duties (Levitas 1996) and now, apparently, requiring the expulsion of the 'anti-social'. The lines of inclusion/exclusion appear to be being redrawn. In the light of Mr Blair's reflections on the 1960s, one is tempted to recall a cartoon of that era and how it might also now be redrafted. The picture showed an ageing hippy with a pen, altering a piece of 1960s graffiti sketched on a wall – 'Never trust anyone over 25' asserted the original slogan. Over time, as the graffiti artist has aged, the age in the slogan has been crossed out and replaced, 'Never trust anyone over 30' and then 'over 40' have been scribbled in. Now, by contrast, the same generation of slogan writers appear to be reversing the process, 'Never trust anyone under 25'. Young people appear to be shouldering a substantial portion of the blame for social disorganisation, crime and disorder and, especially, anti-social behaviour.

Communities and exclusion

This community and environmental dimension to the discourse of anti-social behaviour is also influenced by the 'broken windows' model of crime prevention. Similarly, as we shall show, perceptions of the behaviour and activities of young people are typically quite central to the way both residents and responsible agencies define the problems.

There is a good deal of evidence emerging to suggest that people's concerns about ASB – especially the ASB of young people – is connected to wider preoccupations about deteriorating standards of living or their perceptions of declining neighbourhoods (Hancock 2001; Budd and Sims 2001; Thorpe and Wood 2004; Finney 2004). This can involve the physical appearance of their immediate residential areas, a sense that services and amenities are poor or, at least, not what they should be. This might be combined with relative isolation and a growing sense that local authorities (specifically local councils, the police and criminal justice institutions more generally) are failing to halt this sense of decline or deal effectively with the perpetrators. More generally, as Girling et al. (2000) remark:

> It has in recent years become commonplace to assert that petty crime and disorder are in the main activities of the young and that public anxiety about crime attaches itself in large measure – among adults at any rate – to these 'incivilities'. The gathering of male and female teenagers, unsupervised, in public spaces – on front walls, street corners, in town centres, by the local shops – is said to prompt anxiety and unease among local residents and other (potential) users alike. Such a preoccupation with the activities of the young (and associated calls for somebody to take tough action) certainly comprises the staple diet of much party political and media discourse on 'law and order'. (Girling et al. 2000: 71)

It is important to address such concerns as well as the now more specific perceptions about anti-social behaviour surfacing. As we will argue, even if young people could not be said to be responsible for these underlying urban problems, they are often seen to be closely associated with them and their behaviour is often held by many to make many such contexts even more worrying (Smith, R. 2003). Hancock's analysis of community safety initiatives in relatively disadvantaged neighbourhoods helps to capture this general sense of youth 'out of control' in communities 'in decline' (Hancock 2001). As R. Smith notes (2003: 171), contemporary anxieties may often be as much a question of perceptions as of genuine material changes or serious risks of crime and disorder. However, as we have already argued, much of the Government's action on anti-social behaviour has been driven precisely by a concern to address such perceptions about young people slipping 'out of control'.

Like the unsupervised youth referred to by Girling et al., Hancock's interviewees drew attention to the common denominator of large numbers of young people hanging about, occupying public space, discarding litter, perhaps becoming drunk and rowdy, breaking windows, causing criminal damage and graffiti and generally disconcerting or intimidating older residents (Hancock 2001). Acknowledgement of these issues has led Hansen et al. (2003) to a particular interpretation of the role and purpose of ASB enforcement action which relates closely to what we refer to as the 'enforcement deficit' argument. Their argument is that there are a number of systemic pressures within criminal justice procedures which essentially individualise both offences and responses to them and have no means for addressing the cumulative impact of, perhaps individually relatively trivial, acts of nuisance or harm. There is, they argue, a mismatch between the 'accumulating distress for victims and [the] non-accumulating impact for offenders' (Hansen *et al.* 2003: 81–2). The issue here is the cumulative 'society-effect' of 'anti-social' activities. The ASBO, they suggest, is the one provision that comes closest to recognising and helping address the cumulative impact of disorderly and offending behaviour. 'Refocussing attention from crime to antisocial behaviour occurs because of a failure of criminal justice to punish persistence in crime in ways commensurate with community impact' (ibid.: 87).

Expressing the need for ASB enforcement action in this fashion shifts the frame of reference back towards discourses centred upon quality of life and the governance of community safety. At the same time it still emphasises an enforcement-driven perspective. In other commentaries the notion of an 'enforcement deficit' has been made rather more explicit. A telling illustration of this can be found in Campbell's 2002 review of ASBOs for the Home Office Research Department. The supposed 'enforcement deficit' (to which the ASBO was construed as a solution) was said to contribute to a sense of relative impunity for juvenile offenders. Campbell recycles precisely this (populist) idea about juvenile impunity (and the supposed licence it gave to youthful troublemakers) and notes that juveniles 'were able to commit their anti-social behaviour in the full knowledge that there were few criminal sanctions that could touch them.' Completing the picture, she continued, 'this situaton can often cause local frustrations, as juveniles are often perceived as the cause of many anti-social behaviour problems, and anti-social behaviour is often used as a synonym for problems with young people' (Campbell 2002a: 2).

The association between young people, anti-social behaviour and disorder and neighbourhood decline appears to be fairly widespread (NACRO 2003). The London Anti-Social Behaviour Strategy Consultation Document (ALG 2004) and the Scottish Executive Report on Anti-Social Behaviour Consultation Responses (Flint *et al.* 2004) both drew a close connection between youth and anti-social behaviour. Typically, the concerns here are both strategic and developmental. Anti-social behaviour is a priority to be addressed for two reasons other than its direct and immediate impact. The first reason involves the perpetrators. ASB is seen as an entry route into more serious and persistent criminality and this has to be addressed (a question of youth). The second reason involves its cumulative and 'chronic' impact upon communities (a question of contexts, environments and communities).

Questions concerning the cumulative 'quality of life' and levels of satisfaction people derive from their area of residence involve a number of social, psychological and emotional factors. We have already noted, in the BCS findings reported by Thorpe and Wood, that there was a strong relationship between perceptions of problems with anti-social behaviour and enjoyment of living in an area (Thorpe and Wood 2004). However, as the authors acknowledge, this relationship might tell us different things.

On the one hand, levels of anti-social behaviour may be largely responsible for the levels of dissatisfaction people feel about the area in which they live. On the other hand, anti-social behaviour may be the 'last straw', the immediate and tangible issue upon which people focus when already unhappy with their neighbourhood for a variety of reasons. In this sense, concern about anti-social behaviour may be symptomatic of broader concerns in much the same way as the 'fear of crime' is said to crystallise a number of more diffuse anxieties about (late) 'modern life' (Crawford 1997). Thus unruly teenagers were a major preoccupation of council estate residents and this group (second only to 'affluent urban' residents) were the most likely to report 'insulting, pestering or intimidating behaviour' to BCS interviewers. Equally, higher levels of concern about anti-social behaviour was clearly associated with higher levels of fear of violent crime, burglary and vehicle crime, offences known to feature prominently in the profiles of high-crime estates. None of this proves any kind of causal or developmental connection between anti-social behaviour and more developed criminal careers, which is one of the government's central justifications for targeting juvenile anti-social behaviour. Rather, both anti-social behaviour and more serious crime can be the result of similar sets of circumstances and conditions, chiefly social deprivation and what is termed the lack of 'community efficacy' or 'social capital' – the capacity of a community to deal with social problems it encounters (Harcourt 2001).

Yet, in this sense, a lack of 'social capital', understood as personal networks, family, friends, 'good neighbours' – people one could turn to at times of difficulty or from whom one could gain reassurance and support – might itself be a reason for people feeling unhappy with an area of residence. Equally, facing fear, harassment, intimidation and anti-social behaviour all alone could certainly accentuate one's sense of vulnerability. Even in relatively high-crime areas people are apt to cite family, friends and good neighbours as reasons for why they are content with where they live (Squires 2004). Where such social capital is lacking, crime and disorder problems could loom much larger. This is an area specifically addressed in the London Anti-Social Behaviour Strategy, where problems are described as especially difficult around areas of public housing (ALG 2004). As Thorpe and Wood note, 'only 12% of those who said that people in their local area looked out for each other also perceived high levels of anti-social behaviour, whereas 40% of those who said people in their area did not look out for each other perceived high levels of anti-social behaviour' (Thorpe and Wood 2004: 65).

Significant differences in the reported prevalence of anti-social behaviour may also have something to do with the repeated identification of relatively high levels of crime (and now anti-social behaviour too) with a group we might call the 'same old culprits' living in the 'same old areas'. The identification of chronically crime-prone areas has a long history although the present focus on these issues more directly dates back to the Chicago School environmental criminology of the 1920s and 1930s (Bottoms and Wiles 1997). In the UK since the first British Crime Survey in 1982 and the construction of the A Classification of Residential Neighbour-hoods (ACORN) classification of areas by socio-economic status it became possible to more directly pinpoint relatively high crime areas (Osborn and Shaftoe 1996). From the early 1980s onwards it is possible to identify a growing preoccupation with the increased crime, disorder and anti-social behaviour problems in social housing areas – council estates (Hope and Shaw 1988; NACRO 1988; Coleman 1998; Osborn and Bright 1989; Safe Neighbourhoods Unit 1993).

It seems beyond any reasonable doubt that the process of 'residualisation' (or 'americanisation' – Hough and Mayhew 1982) of council housing after 1980 (Hope and Foster 1992; Page 1993; Flint 2002; Pitts 2003) exacerbated the underlying problems facing such areas. This happened as the social composition of social housing estates was altered and the housing management options of social housing landlords became more restricted with the poorer, 'more difficult' and 'problem families' becoming concentrated in a diminishing supply of social housing. Likewise, Hope's work, analysing British Crime Survey returns over a number of years, has clearly documented the major redistribution of victimisation occurring during the 1980s and 1990s (Hope 1994, 2000, 2001). Estates that had already gained reputations as sources of trouble were seen to deteriorate while left realist criminology's renewed attention to communities and to victims refocused political attention on these high and rising crime areas. Such areas ceased to be seen exclusively as the *source* of the wider community's crime problems and instead the exposure of hitherto hidden and under-reported rates of victimisation revealed the far greater crime and disorder problems of these neighbourhoods. In other words, for the 'same old culprits', things were even worse. In turn, the targeting of such areas for special interventions tended to reinforce the perception that the crime and disorder problems themselves derived from the nature of the areas or (especially) the types of people resident within them. At the same time they increased the likelihood that a range of 'target' behaviours and activities would be identified, reported and recorded. As the 2004 BCS analysis itself shows, people do now appear to be significantly more sensitised to crime, disorder and anti-social behaviour issues. When residents of low-crime areas encounter ASB they may attribute it to 'other' kids from estates with the bad reputations (Girling *et al*. 2000; Measor and Squires 2000). By contrast, when residents of these same estates report ASB it is because they are threatened by it and weary of it – but at last someone is listening.

Teenagers and youths continue to appear at the top of people's lists of perceived anti-social behaviour perpetrators. As we have noted, this relates *both* to the more familiar question of adult perceptions of juvenile deviance to the more recent, enforcement-informed, prescription that today's 'anti-socials' become tomorrow's criminals and it is necessary to nip criminal careers 'in the bud' (Muncie 2002). Even where recent research exists casting doubt upon the apparently inevitable transition of the young 'anti-social' into the young adult offender (Australian Institute of Family Studies 2004; Bright 2004) it appears to make relatively little impact upon prevailing assumptions. As Skelton and Valentine (1998) have noted, such Anglo-American conceptions of childhood appear to derive more from a cultural tradition in which children are seen as, in potential at least, 'little devils' only kept upon the straight and narrow by punishment and strict discipline. This is a tradition closely associated with the classical and deterrent criminological tradition. This being the case, it would seem to follow that anti-social behaviour plays an important role in broadening and operationalising Classicism or, in other words, justifying its crossing of its traditional self-imposed boundary between the strictly criminal and a much wider sphere of anti-social acts.

Growing out of crime, or not

It should already be fairly clear that, to a large extent, complaints about anti-social behaviour are very often complaints about youth. As we have noted, there has been a marked and recurring tendency (an argument we will develop more fully later) for the authorities to demonise certain categories of young people (Pearson 1983). This is especially so in respect of the working class youth and of ethnic minorities and, again as noted already, especially since 1993, this demonising of youth became a central feature of both British crime prevention policies and related propaganda. An intriguing outcome of this official preoccupation with the criminal and disorderly behaviour of youth is captured in the British Crime Survey finding that members of the public tend to significantly overestimate the extent of juvenile involvement in crime (Mattinson and Mirrlees-Black

2000). In fact, it is known that virtually 90 per cent of 'known offenders' are aged over 18. There may be, as R. Smith (2003) acknowledges, some ambiguities here regarding the definition of 'youth'. Criminal and disorderly young people, perhaps well into their twenties, caught in what Pitts (2003) has called a period of 'protracted adolescence' and who, by virtue of their lifestyles, dress or habits may well have been contributing to a perception of youth as increasingly troublesome. Equally, although the peak age of offending may well lie within the teenage years, this is quite a different issue from the claim that teenagers commit a majority of offences. In fact, the evidence would point us in quite a different direction, for serious or persistent offending by teenagers is relatively rare (Hagell and Newburn 1994).

As Muncie has acknowledged, official data on juvenile offending does present 'a somewhat controversial and contradictory picture' (1999: 15) because the generally declining official figures of youth crime implied that youth offending was becoming a less significant problem, whereas many people's experiences (especially people living in deprived or 'high-crime' areas) might suggest quite the opposite. Commentators have sought to explain this disparity in a variety of ways (Bright 1997). Faulkner, on the other hand, refers explicitly to a largely effective police-led campaign during the early 1990s to convince people that 'large parts of the country were being overrun by serious and persistent juvenile offenders – children who were out of the control of their parents and who the police and the courts were powerless to prevent' (2001: 209).

Developing his point, Faulkner explains:

> The police claim, and the public and political perception that juvenile crime was rising, and that juvenile offenders were becoming both more persistent and nastier, was difficult to reconcile with the statistics or to substantiate with more than anecdotal or impressionistic evidence. With hindsight, the fact is that the police themselves were probably ignoring quite a lot of juvenile crime, perhaps in the belief that 'nothing would happen' if they made an arrest or began a prosecution. (Faulkner 2001: 123; see also Anderson *et al.* 1994; Measor and Squires 2000: 207 215).

In due course, the managerialist eye of the Audit Commission, bemoaning the ability of the youth justice system to cost so much to achieve so little while satisfying so few, appeared to confirm that youth offending was unlikely to have fallen. On the other hand, it presented no evidence to the effect that youth crime was spiralling out of control. In this, the evidence reviewed corresponded closely with data produced in a recent report by Communities that Care (Beinart *et al.* 2002). This self-report study, titled *Youth at Risk?*, found that while as many as 48 per cent of 14–15 year olds admitted to some offending activity (excluding substance misuse) the overwhelming majority did not offend on a regular basis and did not continue into persistent offending careers. All things considered, the increasing public and political profile attaching to youth crime during the mid-1990s and the abrupt turnaround in official policy appears to have stemmed primarily from factors other than major changes in the underlying rates of youth involvement in crime.

Yet, for all that, the abrupt U-turn in approaches to youth crime during the period 1988 to 1996 was certainly dramatic. Four key government documents demonstrate the extent of this rapid about turn in the underlying philosophy of youth justice. These documents comprise a Home Office Green Paper from 1988 *Punishment, Custody and the Community* (Home Office 1988), the 1991 Morgan Report, then the Audit Commission Report, *Misspent Youth*, of 1996 and finally New Labour's White Paper *No More Excuses* (Home Office 1997) which laid the foundations for the new Youth Justice strategy contained in the 1998 Crime and Disorder Act.

In 1988, a Conservative Green Paper argued, in words even the most liberal of labelling theorists could hardly fault:

> Most young offenders grow out of crime as they become more mature and responsible. They need encouragement and help to become law-abiding. Even a short period in custody is quite likely to confirm them as criminals, particularly as they acquire new criminal skills from more sophisticated offenders. They find themselves labelled as offenders and behave accordingly. (Home Office 1988: 6, para. 2.15)

Three years later, the influential Morgan Report summed up its analysis of the troubling behaviour of young people: 'the vast majority of criminal activity by this age group involves less serious offences and a considerable amount constitutes behaviour which is rowdy or anti-social rather than strictly criminal.' Furthermore, the Report concluded, 'most young people grow out of delinquency as they move through adolescence.' (Morgan 1991: 24). In the latter comment it is also instructive to note that anti-social activities were clearly distinguished from criminal acts.

By contrast, only five years later, in 1996, the Audit Commission firmly squashed these dangerously complacent liberal ideas. Things were now very different: young people, apparently, no longer grew out of crime. Thus 'young males are not growing out of offending as they used to.' (Audit Commission 1996: 12). And a year later the new Home Secretary introduced his youth justice White Paper *No More Excuses* in the following terms:

For too long we have assumed that young offenders will grow out of their offending if left to themselves. The research evidence shows that this does not happen. Today's young offenders can easily become tomorrow's hardened criminals. As a society we do ourselves no favours by failing to break the link between juvenile crime and disorder and the serial burglar of the future. (Home Office 1997a)

Later, the White Paper, drawing heavily upon the Audit Commission's preceding report, went on to provide further details about how these links between 'anti-social behaviour' and crime and disorder were to be broken. Crime had to be 'nipped in the bud', children 'at risk' had to be prevented from being drawn into 'persistent or serious offending' or protected from being drawn into 'criminal and anti-social behaviour'. Rather than separate entities, it is notable that in the White Paper, 'anti-social behaviour' and 'crime and disorder' had now become aspects of a single range of behaviours.

As Pitts has argued (2003: 8–9), the earlier view of juvenile offending, reflected in the 1988 Green Paper and the Morgan Report, was sustained by a series of interrelated assumptions about youth and delinquency. Expressed briefly these were: first, that the criminality of working-class children and young people was not generally serious or persistent; second, that the patterns or forms of victimisation were not usually serious; third, that rehabilitation or treatment was ineffective and often did more harm than good; fourth, that young people had rights and that they (and their families) deserved protection from the well meaning but also often counterproductive interventions of 'welfare professionals'; fifth, that interventions, as well as being ineffective, could be costly; and, finally, that, all things considered, most young people could be safely left to grow out of crime as 'more indigenous mechanisms of social control' (family, community, maturity, employment, relationships) came to exercise their influence.

Conversely, by the mid-1990s these assumptions no longer appeared to hold sway. Some of the offending by young people could be very serious and damaging. As we have noted already patterns and forms of victimisation were now seen in a quite different light, especially in socially deprived and excluded areas and especially for certain groups of the population. Rehabilitation had been, to some extent, supplanted by more punitive responses, and by a robust, albeit ideologically motivated, defence that 'prison works' while successive governments committed themselves to a more rigorous investigation of what works and cost-effectiveness in youth justice, and to prediction, targeting and risk-assessment. Here, of course, the contributions of the Audit Commission were quite central. Finally, the increasing concentration and overlapping of criminalisation and victimisation in socially deprived areas (Hope 2000, 2001) meant that 'protective factors', 'indigenous social controls' or 'social capital' offering opportunities or routes out of criminality were few and far between (Pitts 2003). In some areas, therefore, 'growing out of crime' was unlikely or not even an option. Such wider evidence, pointed to different kinds of problems, issues that the Audit Commission was less interested in and with which it was less equipped to deal. Its main concern had been to assert a more effective grasp over the disparate elements comprising the youth justice 'system' and engineer a change of perspective in youth offending and youth justice (Anderson 1999; Jones 2001a; Smith, R. 2003). We consider these issues more directly in a later chapter.

Returning to the anti-social behaviour connection, as Pitts shows, during the mid-1990s a renewed concern about a growing company of so-called 'persistent young offenders' – or 'pre-pubescent super predators' – came to exercise a tight grip on debates about youth justice, greatly influencing New Labour's youth justice strategy and significantly shaping the 1998 Crime and Disorder legislation, 'turning it into a means whereby the criminal law would penetrate the previously sacrosanct realm of childhood' (Pitts 2003: 48–9).

And of course it is here that the newly rediscovered notion of anti-social behaviour was to prove so useful. Anti-social behaviour was the seedbed of 'future persistent delinquency'. As Home Secretary Jack Straw put it in the foreword to the government's *No More Excuses* White Paper on Youth Justice (Home Office, 1997), echoing the words of the 1996 Audit Commission Report, the central objective was to break the links between juvenile anti-social behaviour and crime. But of course, expressing the problem in this way involved an assertion that there already was some kind of developmental connection between youthful anti-social behaviour and persistent criminality. Rather than breaking links, New Labour was making them. Initially, the particular concerns addressed by the emerging discourse of anti-social behaviour involved those actions or behaviours which either fell short of outright criminality or which, for other reasons, did not attract the intervention of the criminal justice system, most specifically of the police. At least, in its first official manifestations, ASB seemed to fall below the radar of the criminal law. It was nuisance or 'pre-criminal' behaviour, or behaviour indulged in by those beyond the reach of the criminal law (until 1998, for example, those aged under 14).

Few genuinely new research findings justified the remarkable turn-around in approaches to youth justice or, indeed, prompted the rediscovery of anti-social behaviour. Quite the contrary, for as we have seen the complaint from many criminologists (Faulkner 2001) had been precisely how little impact their work had had on the shaping of new policies. The prevailing reaction of academic criminologists (Muncie 2000a; Pitts, 2000) was that the government was rather more interested in politics than with policy and with reassuring the *Daily Mail* and its middle-England readership that it could be trusted to deliver on 'law and order'. So, although there were few genuinely new research findings to justify the new policies a powerful constellation of factors began to take shape. Taken together, the focus upon identifying the anti-social precursors of future delinquency, the concern with prevention and early intervention (because young offenders will not mature out of crime on their own) combined with left realism's preoccupation with the community and New Labour's committed politics of the family (Utting *et al.* 1993) helped resuscitate an older criminological tradition and the body of research findings associated with the work of Farrington and West. This work, which we will discuss in greater depth in the following chapter, had itself originally prioritised various conceptions of ASB far more than had been the case in the early 1990s. The time was ripe for the return of the approach to 'youth delinquency' embodied in Farrington *et al.*'s work. It drew together the elements that New Labour sought to address and offered an academic and 'evidence-based' justification for the way it wanted to go.

Together with the 1996 Audit Commission Report, the Social Exclusion Unit's Policy Action Team (PAT) Report 12 on *Young People* framed the new direction (Social Exclusion Unit 2000). In many respects, although the PAT report confirmed the broadly social and environmental reading of the causes of youth offending and related anti-social behaviour (Bright 1997; Graham 1998) in conjunction with the new youth justice strategy, primary attention was given to the development of managerial and organisational solutions (Jones 2001a).

The Audit Commission's, by now familiar, analysis of the causes of youth crime and of the interventions required to address it drew significantly upon the extensive work by Farrington (1996), the studies by Graham and Bowling (1995), Utting *et al.* (1993) and research sampled by Utting (1996). Thus 'anti-social behaviour', now officially recognised as the precursor to a youthful criminal career, emerged from the cluster of personal, familial, communal and environmental factors reiterated by a wide range of criminological researchers. As Pitts has argued (2003: 44), these are now read less as factors in a complex aetiology but more directly as simple cumulative 'risk factors':

> poverty and poor housing, poor parenting (including neglect, abuse, harsh and inconsistent discipline, lack of supervision and marital conflict); association with delinquent peers, siblings and partners;

low measures of intelligence, poor school performance and persistent truancy; high levels of impulsiveness and hyperactivity; and
being brought up by a criminal parent or parents. (Graham 1998: 7)

Equally, research suggested, exposure to multiple risk factors increased
the likelihood that individuals might progress to serious or persistent
offending patterns as did the earlier onset of involvement in criminal, anti-
social or disorderly behaviour (Graham and Bowling 1995; Farrington
1996). In turn, the Audit Commission promised the 'joined-up' measures,
addressing the personal and familial failings and the dearth of local
opportunities in order to break into this 'cycle of anti-social behaviour'
(Audit Commission 1996: 90). The document itself had rather less to say
about the more community-oriented interventions. In this respect, it
suffered from a common affliction of community crime prevention
planning, namely the tendency to confuse 'community' with a given range
of local social interventions in a given geographical area (Lacey 1995;
Measor and Squires 2000). Ultimately, individuals and their behaviour
have been foregrounded while communities and their needs have been
less directly addressed.

Definitions

Although this rediscovery of anti-social behaviour firmly situated the
problem in a context given by deprived communities, poor housing
management practices and delinquent and predelinquent juvenile crime
and disorder – familiar locations and the usual suspects, as it were – there
remained a degree of ambiguity about the range of actual behaviours
covered by the concept.

By its very nature the definition of anti-social behaviour is subject to
interpretation (Bland and Read 2000; Moore and Lawrence 2000). As the
ASB research team in the Home Office Research and Statistics Directorate
(RSD) acknowledged, 'the subjective nature of the concept makes it
difficult to identify a single definition of anti-social behaviour' (Home
Office, RSD Briefing Note 2004). Accordingly, a 'range of approaches' to
the definition of anti-social behaviour are adopted and the Briefing Paper
goes on to provide a typology of anti-social behaviours for the guidance of
practitioners working in enforcement (see Figure 2.1). In the same vein, the
London Anti-Social Behaviour Strategy consultation document also
acknowledges: 'anti-social behaviour often involves clashes of values and
standards' (ALG 2004: 7).

Anti-Social Behaviour Typology
Source: Home Office, Research Development and Statistics Directorate
Numbers in brackets refer to the incidents reported during the 2003 ASB Day Count

Misuse of public space	Disregard for community/personal well-being	Acts directed at people	Environmental damage
Drug/substance misuse	*Noise nuisance*	*Intimidation/harassment*	*Criminal damage/vandalism*
Taking/dealing drugs	Noisy neighbours/cars/motorbikes	Making threats	Graffiti
Sniffing volatile substances	Loud music	Verbal abuse	Damage to bus shelters
Discarding needles and paraphernalia	Persistent alarms	Bullying	Damage to phone kiosks
Crack houses	Pub/club noise	Following people	Damage to street furniture
Presence of dealers or users (2,920)	Noise from business (5,374)	Pestering people	Damage to buildings
		Voyeurism	Damage to trees, plants or hedges (7,855)
Street drinking	*Rowdy behaviour*	Sending offensive mail	
Begging	Shouting/swearing	Obscene/nuisance phone calls	
(together, 3,239)	Fighting	Menacing gestures (5,415)	
	Drunken behaviour		

Litter/rubbish
Dropping litter
Dumping rubbish
Fly-tipping
Fly-posting
(10,686)

All can be on grounds of:
Race
Sexual orientation
Gender
Religion
Disability
Age

Hooliganism/loutish behaviour (5,339)

Nuisance behaviour
Urinating in public
Setting fires
Misuse of fireworks
Throwing missiles
Climbing on buildings

Impeding access to communal areas
Games in restricted or inappropriate areas
Misuse of air guns
Letting down tyres
(7,660)

Hoax calls
False calls to emergency services
(1,286)

Animal related problems
Uncontrolled animals
(2,546)

Prostitution
Soliciting
Cards in phone boxes
Discarded condoms

Kerb crawling
Loitering
Pestering residents

Sexual acts
Inappropriate sexual conduct
Indecent exposure
(1,011)

Abandoned cars
(4,994)

Vehicle related nuisance
Inconvenient/illegal parking
Repairs on street/in gardens
Setting vehicles alight
Joyriding
Racing cars
Off-road motorcycling
Cycling/skateboarding in pedestrian area/footpaths
(7,782)

Figure 2.1 Home Office Research and Statistics Directorate: Typology of Anti-Social Behaviour.

Aside from its use as guidance for ASB practitioners working in CDRPs, the typology was used to assist in the production of a one-day count of ASB incidents. The count was conducted for 10 September 2003, and concluded that 66,107 incidents had been recorded by over 1,500 organisations including every CDRP that day in England and Wales (a further 5,973 incident reports arrived after the 24-hour cut off point). The limitations of the data were readily acknowledged but the figures were used to produce a rough estimate of the national annual direct cost of ASB per day of £13,500 million (or £3.375 billion per year). These are undoubtedly staggering figures but, as the typology suggests (and the list of reported behaviours confirms), something over half of the incidents recorded were already criminal acts. In this light, ASB comprises not a new range of problems to which modernity has lately become subject but rather a range of very familiar crimes and disorders defined largely by reference to a new range of enforcement processes.

The definition of ASB provided in the Crime and Disorder Act 1998 refers to 'acting in a manner that caused or was likely to cause harassment, alarm or distress to one or more persons not of the same household (as the defendant).' As the RSD Briefing Note acknowledges, 'this definition is broad and allows for a range of activities to be included within it.' This, it argues, 'is appropriate, given that people's understanding of anti-social behaviour is based on individual perception and can therefore encompass a range of behaviours.' In effect, the reaction or perception, or likely reactions or perceptions, of third parties are central to the definition. In this sense certain actions or behaviour would seem to be essential but it is the (potential) reactions to these which seems to define their offensiveness. On the other hand, the legislation's future orientation in part of the definition of ASB, for instance 'acting in a manner … likely to cause', suggests that no actual public complaint need be made to constitute the anti-social behaviour. Enforcement agents simply need to consider it *likely* that harassment, alarm or distress might result. As Brown has noted, in place of crime, ASB 'substitutes a rule so vague almost anything could break it' (Brown 2004: 205). Furthermore, as Grier and Thomas point out, the 2003 ASB legislation further extends the definition of ASB to include behaviour which 'is capable of causing nuisance or annoyance to any person' (2003: 9).

Understandably this creates a potentially large area of enforcement leeway which, in practice, tends to be resolved by returning us back to certain types of behaviour which, *a priori*, are deemed to be anti-social because they are by their nature distressful or alarming. Turning to the RSD guidance on types of ASB, a final irony emerges in that a number of the activities listed are themselves already criminal acts (Grier and Thomas 2003). A growing realisation that a singular enforcement-driven rationale lies behind the government's ASB strategy was compounded by the introduction (in s.64 of the 2002 Police Reform Act) of ASBOs on conviction. Whatever else ASB might be, despite some of the associated political rhetoric, it is not a range of worryingly new behaviours unique to late modernity which had hitherto evaded the attentions of law-makers and criminal justice system personnel alike. Rather ASB is simply a convenient term for a selected group of behaviours against which a more streamlined package of enforcement procedures are being adopted. In this sense the contemporary notion of ASB is almost entirely enforcement driven and defined through the enforcement process.

Furthermore, the potentially arbitrary character of definitions of ASB need not be confined to its initial definition; our research also suggested that the precise selection of cases to be taken forwards could also be somewhat arbitrary (Stephen and Squires 2003a).

Cheap and easy enforcement?

Such issues bring us to a final dimension of this critical introduction to ASB. Many features of the new enforcement processes relating to the ASBO conform very closely to the processes of 'blurring, widening and masking' anticipated twenty years ago by Stan Cohen (Cohen 1985). Cohen's arguments drew significantly upon the work of Foucault, describing the dispersal of social control mechanisms across societies and the intensification of disciplinary relationships throughout social and policy processes.

Brown's (2004) analysis of ASBO enforcement work in contemporary crime control draws particular attention to the ways in which the notion of ASB has blurred a number of the familiar boundaries within criminal justice while neutralising some of the important rights and 'due process' safeguards of traditional criminal law. Foremost here are boundaries between the civil and criminal law, between care and control processes and concerning policies facilitating social inclusion or exclusion.

In relation to the blurring of civil and criminal jurisdictions, the lower standards of proof applicable to civil cases (the 'balance of probabilities' rather than 'beyond reasonable doubt') may suggest one tactical advantage of the ASBO to enforcers. Likewise the admission of hearsay evidence, including uncorroborated police reports and intelligence shared among partner agencies or even unsubstantiated complaints from neighbours, provides a number of others. Echoing Foucault, Cohen spoke of a 'correctional continuum' through the increasingly punitive layers of which targeted individuals were progressively drawn as their behaviour failed to correspond to stipulated norms. The government's initial justification for the ASBO, designed to deal with 'criminal *or sub-criminal activity* which, for one reason or another, cannot be proven to the criminal standard, or where criminal proceedings are not appropriate' (Home Office 1998b), seems to pose a number of questions.

Any suggestion about an inability to prove cases to the criminal standard begs major questions – echoing, perhaps, the former police practice of giving cautions 'by consent' even where evidence may not have sustained a prosecution (Jones 2001a). Thus a large measure of ASB work now consists of reactive enforcement action against crime (not pre-criminal nuisance) with the ASBO itself simply just another item on the enforcement menu to be deployed as necessary. The Home Office guidance adds rather tellingly, 'the orders are not intended to replace existing criminal offences ... but there may be circumstances where they provide alternative means to deal with such behaviour' (Home Office 1998b). As all good Foucauldians know, in criminal justice 'alternative' methods of disciplining have a marked habit of becoming additional forms of discipline. As Cohen put it, 'alternatives, become not "alternatives" at all, but new programmes which supplement the existing system or else expand the system by attracting new populations – the net of social control is widened' (Cohen 1979). And as Burney has noted, the precise advantage of the ASBO, in the eyes of some supporters, may not lie in any real hope that it alone will change an individual's behaviour but by virtue of the tariff-leaping custodial sanction that breach of an order can bring (Burney 2002).

Emphasising, now, the blurring of care and control processes, as we document in a later chapter, ASB case files to which we were given access, often running close to an inch thick, contained a wealth of information on young people within a Youth Inclusion Project. The information had been produced in the context of the delivery of local social and public services and was compiled by a range of local agencies (housing, health, education, social services – and the police). However, as an illustration of the 'criminalisation of social policy' (Squires 1990), this information now primarily justified and sustained forms of enforcement action. In other cases community safety teams made available video cameras or other recording equipment and diary templates with which neighbours might assemble their own complaints. In other words, a considerable effort of surveillance, shared by a range of partners and members of the public, helps to sustain both definitions of ASB and the enforcement action directed towards it.

Finally, even broader policy objectives appear contradicted by the current focus on expelling the anti-social from communities. This sounds much more like selective social exclusion than inclusion, especially the pejorative language, the implied social pathology and individualisation which accompanies depictions of ASB. Undoubtedly there always was something of a tension in New Labour's promise to be 'tough on crime, tough on the causes of crime', but this has now shifted into simply being toughest on criminals. Policy in this area has always been about the combination of care and control and now, in relation to the new ASB work we are seeing developed, the dynamic has become one of support and enforcement. But as we have described, for many thus targeted, the policy is enforcement led, support often a distant second or almost entirely absent. And yet, if more support had been available, the enforcement might not have become necessary. Unfortunately, for support to be effective we require an understanding of human needs and social processes and as the Prime Minister has said we are no longer interested in 'understanding the social causes of criminality ... people have had enough of this part of the 1960s consensus' (Blair 2004).

In the next chapter we develop a number of these questions and ambiguities surrounding the contested contemporary notion of ASB in the course of an attempt to unearth some of the idea's seemingly hidden history.

Chapter 3

The secret history of anti-social behaviour?

Crime is anti-social behaviour – anti-social behaviour is directed against certain fundamental values ... and no form of human behaviour which is not anti-social should ever be treated as a crime ... The reverse, however, is far from true. There are very many forms of anti-social behaviour which are not, and many others which should not be, crimes. ... The anti-social character of many human activities, as, for instance, certain business transactions or methods of business organisation may for a long while remain hidden from the eyes of the legislator and the public ... Different social classes within the community may hold different views about the merits of this or that form of human activity ... Even where universal agreement does exist as to the anti-social character of certain forms of behaviour, they may be regarded as unsuitable objects for the criminal law ... The punishment of anti-social behaviour cannot be regarded as an absolute value and the advantages it may entail to the community have carefully to be balanced against the potential harm. (Mannheim 1946)

The secret history of youthful anti-social behaviour

For much of its history, 'anti-social behaviour' has been hidden, sometimes overshadowed, sometimes absorbed, by the more familiar concepts of delinquency and crime, especially juvenile crime. When it did put in an appearance it was often seen as little more than a broad early warning sign of delinquency to come or a generic travelling companion of delinquency. Thus young people who committed offences often displayed a range of associated anti-social behaviours which may not have been specifically criminal (Rutter and Giller 1983). Aggressive, disorderly and anti-authoritarian characteristics were typical. 'Anti-establishment' attitudes and behaviours were also sometimes mentioned, but this (apart from betraying its point of origin) tends to imply a rather more relative interpretation which today's ASB enforcers might not find so comfortable. Even so, in such relativism we have a clue to the definition of the behaviour itself, an issue to which we will need to return.

By contrast, the concept we have today, encapsulated in the 2003 Anti-Social Behaviour Act and, before that, the Anti-Social Behaviour Order (ASBO) has, in one sense, been developed to address a far more specific range of behaviours. Yet, to a large extent, the precise definition of these behaviours and the operationalisation of these definitions through enforcement action is driven more by community and victim reactions and perceptions than anything particularly unique to the behaviour. Above all, ASB has been constructed as an 'enforcement point' – or a point at which something has to be done – and its introduction has been designed to facilitate more direct, flexible and effective enforcement action by local authorities (and their agents) and the police. Even so, as we shall see, there is still some demand/pressure to define ASB in relation to a series of identified behaviours: to say what ASB is. This is understandable in a number of senses. Politicians promoting new legislation want to be able to reassure the public that the kinds of behaviours troubling them now will be addressed by the new laws. Enforcement agencies want to know where best and how best to target their resources (indeed the 2003 Act requires them to establish enforcement priorities and protocols). Finally, traditional legal 'due process' itself should generate demands that persons accused of ASB should actually be proven to have done *something*, merely existing ('being there' or 'hanging about': Corrigan 1979) should not be sufficient, as it used to be under the 1824 Vagrancy Act, to constitute an offence.

Young people and ASB

If ASB has only recently begun to be identified in this more precise (enforcement-driven) way, it is equally true to say that it has long been around. The 1824 Vagrancy legislation is a case in point. The history of juvenile nuisance is rather better known.

'Children have always got into trouble,' begins the first line of Berlins and Wansell's analysis of the 1969 CYPA, but 'it was not until the beginning of the industrial revolution and the massive movement of population into the towns that children in trouble began to become a social problem' (Berlins and Wansell 1972). Equally, according to West, 'ever since statistics began to be kept they have been held to prove the increasing lawlessness of youth' (West 1967: 34).

Before the rapid urbanisation of the last century childhood mis-behaviour, even if of a remarkably similar nature to that complained of today, was not understood as youthful 'anti-social' behaviour. This was largely because, like the notion of adolescence itself, the kind of uniform consensual perspective from which this behaviour could be identified did not exist (Gillis 1981). The problem was not the 'anti-social' behaviour of given individuals, but the immoral, aggressive, villainous and deceitful social behaviour of criminals and the degraded habits of the poorest. Even Havelock Ellis, writing in 1895, makes the distinction for, when discussing the case of a man driven to murder by emotions of passion and revenge, he commented that, 'it was the strength of his *social*, and not of his anti-social, instincts which had caused his crime' (Ellis 1895: 125). Driven by defective character, biology, psychology or circumstance, the criminal social behaviour of the lower orders constituted the chief threats. Barbara Wootton made a similar comment in 1959: certain theories 'tend to assume that there is something abnormal in stealing … But to the sociologist this postulate of abnormality, as applied to districts with a heavy incidence of delinquency, is beside the mark. It is conformity rather than deviance which explains the anti-social behaviour prevalent in these areas' (Wootton 1959: 67).

So while the underlying causes may have been up for debate, the culprits were fairly familiar. It was not the somehow 'anti-social' traits of the urbanised working classes that had defined the problem, but rather their depraved and immoral behaviour which worried contemporaries. They explained the causes of this behaviour in a variety of ways and, in their own terms, sought to address it accordingly. That is, the behaviour was addressed in terms of its perceived causes whereas today, ASB is addressed by virtue of its supposedly anti-social nature. In this sense we have lost a connection with causality which has, historically, been a key component in understanding and preventing delinquency. Summarising the changes of perspective and concern which had pushed 'youth' and 'youthful behaviour' to the forefront of public attention, Gillis notes, 'in the mid nineteenth century, crime had been considered a moral disease; by the early twentieth century this proposition had become reversed, and it was assumed that immoral or antisocial behaviour should be treated as a crime' (Gillis 1981: 173).

Complaints about youth

Many commentators (from Aristotle to Rousseau and a more recent selection of twentieth-century writers) have articulated their reflections on the 'troublesome youth' of the day (Wilkins 1960; Fyvel 1961; Aries 1962; Humphries 1981; Pearson 1983). In particular, Radzinowicz and Hood describe the concept of the young offender 'and all that it implies for penal policy' as a Victorian creation (1990). However, subtle changes in the precise interpretation of apparently troublesome youthful behaviour do not appear to have preoccupied complainants. Nevertheless, we should not be misled by the apparent similarity and universality of these perennial complaints. In the same way that too close attention to the endless hubbub of complaints by the British about the weather might fail to pick up a critical shift in what these complaints signify – for instance, the onset of global warming. So concentrating only on the generality of complaints about the young might lead us to overlook critical changes in what these complaints are taken to mean, how they are used and what is done about them. We are not arguing, as is sometimes suggested, that the behaviour of youth has become uniquely intolerable in late modernity but rather, following Christie (2004), that the circumstances of late modernity seem bound to create additional tensions around youth, tensions with which these societies appear less able (or even willing) to cope. It follows that, for us, anti-social behaviour is not some uniquely late modern behavioural phenomenon at all. On the contrary, it is primarily a legitimating rationale for new forms of enforcement action in high-crime societies deeply preoccupied with the reassertion of certain forms of culture and social order thought to be in jeopardy as a result of globalising social changes (Garland 2000).

Although commentators often referred to what, today, has come to coalesce as ASB they scarcely ever used the concept itself. If nothing else, this should alert us to a number of questions about the social and cultural contexts in which a discourse on youthful ASB has emerged. For this, the necessary prerequisites would seem to be the recognition of 'youth' as a distinct phase of life (Jenks 1996), the depiction of delinquency as the particular failing of 'youth' (Platt 1969) and the emergence of some stable form of 'social' order to which the allegedly 'anti-social' behaviour of youth constituted a threat. Only the birth of 'the social' gives us a context in which its delinquent antithesis could flourish (Donzelot 1979; Hirst 1981; Garland 1985; Rose 1985, Squires 1990). Almost by definition, this tends to locate any developed conception of ASB largely within the confines of the social welfare states of the second half of the twentieth century. Barbara Wootton gives us a sense of this in the list of 'anti-social' behaviours she outlined in 1959. It contained such things as malingering and vagrancy, deserting husbands (failure to maintain), neglect of children, truancy and alcoholism. These were said to be the characteristics of a 'little company of individuals, so persistently resistant (whether by design or by misfortune) to assimilation into our culture' (Wootton 1959: 43). Yet even these few remaining 'casualties of the welfare state' (Harvey 1960) might still be won over in time. The point was, like delinquents, they were seen as a hard-core minority. Any remaining social problems began and ended with them. They were the problem. Likewise the postwar 'delinquent' was, supposedly, 'at war with society' (Jones 1956: 48). Whether by habit or delinquency these characters were little but anachronisms in the age of the welfare state. They were more than just problems, they were seen increasingly as an affront to a modern welfare society, an enemy of it and a threat to it. The point can be illustrated by comparing the pre- and postwar discourses on 'juvenile delinquency'.

Bailey's exemplary study of juvenile delinquency and juvenile justice policy-making between 1914 and 1948 (Bailey 1987), even as it charts the rise of a welfare-oriented, individualised and therapeutic orthodoxy in matters of juvenile delinquency, makes no reference to this 'delinquency' being understood as anti-social behaviour. The often stated purpose behind the developing professionalism of the services for 'delinquent' or deprived children and young people was undoubtedly one of 'normalisation' – winning the 'unfortunates' back for citizenship. However, at a time of optimism, reconstruction and postwar progress the idea that these casualties of society and victims of wartime disruption might yet be a serious threat to the new social order had not yet fully formed.

The challenge of youth

By contrast we might refer to the seminal 1947 commentary, *Lawless Youth: A Challenge to the New Europe*, produced by a distinguished committee of criminologists and child welfare experts, including Margery Fry, Hermann Mannheim, Leon Radzinowicz and Max Grünhut. This book, a product of the reforming ideology of the Howard League for Penal Reform, aimed to address the problems of the 'young men and women made rebels and outlaws by law' and set, as its standard, the positive and social democratic ideals of western civilisation. Youth gangs, in particular, were an item of especial concern. The authors' appeal was to an enlightened social economy, and to a preventive and welfare-oriented approach to the 'treatment of delinquency' (Garland 1985). Perhaps some emphasis is needed here. Delinquency rather than crime was the key. The upheavals of wartime (Burlingham and Freud, 1942, 1944; Bowlby 1946; Wilkins 1960), the optimism for social reform (children, the next generation, were seen as the hope for the future) and the established view that childhood was more malleable, all combined to insist that a response to 'juvenile delinquency' was an important key to social reconstruction. Delinquency, as opposed to crime, was high on the public and political agenda even before the end of the war (Carr-Saunders *et al.* 1942; Morris 1989). Even in 1950, when the first journal of academic criminology was published in Britain, it was initially titled the *British Journal of Delinquency* (only becoming the *British Journal of Criminology* in 1960).

Very much part of this reformist movement, the Howard League Committee firmly rejected the punitive and deterrent thinking of the past which only served to confirm the 'delinquent' or 'anti-social' as an 'enemy of society'. For after all, 'experience has shown, only too grimly, that a large number of older offenders begin their anti-social career in childhood or youth ... [whilst] blind severity in youth tends to produce an anti-social attitude in maturity. So that in the case of the child or adolescent the community can without great risk, set itself the task of reclaiming a potential enemy at an age when success is most likely' (p. 17).

This reconstructive approach to criminal justice (Mannheim 1946) now declared, 'we see ourselves as bound to protect the delinquent, as well as other unfortunate children, from the pressure of the community' (Fry *et al.* 1947: 18). Where punishment was called for it should only be of a kind that 'we may call an educative punishment aimed at changing the anti-social attitude of the offender' (p. 14). In Mannheim, this reconfiguring of the role of criminal justice towards a conception of 'social defence' (Ancel 1965) reiterates our point that, in postwar juvenile justice, preventive and reformist interventions were to be increasingly geared towards the more secular, flexible and pragmatic objectives of defending society (or the community) against threats posed by the 'criminal' and 'anti-social'. As Taylor has argued, 'the social democratic criminology of the 1940s was very clearly committed to the defence of a specific conception of social and moral order' (Taylor 1981: 56). In achieving this the criminal law itself became somewhat decentred, 'a shifting of emphasis from the offence to the offender, from an isolated motive to the criminal's personal situation and social background' (Fry *et al.* 1947: 32). Furthermore, 'the treatment of young offenders should be dictated by the special needs of the individual case: the "offence" where such exists will be regarded as a symptom' (ibid.: 20).

In the new era of juvenile justice, therefore, delinquency is understood in its social context and responded to for social reasons. The insight that anti-social traits can be observed (and are best responded to) early in life prompts the recognition (in a later chapter on 'prevention') that: 'it is often in the course of the nursery education that the first a-social and anti-social symptoms show themselves, and it is at that moment that they could be most effectively remedied if treated in an intelligent fashion ... [rather than waiting for] penal laws which only come into force when the damage is done' (Fry *et al.* 1947: 140). Social defence is therefore pre-emptive; it is too important to wait for the law. It identifies and anticipates, recognising where the 'anti-social' will lead if unchecked. 'The social' seeks out its antithesis, the 'anti-social' in order to ensure it will not or cannot become a 'social danger', a 'threat to society' or a 'burden on the community' (p. 142). In the Howard League's ambitions and, contra Beveridge, the whole of the postwar welfare state could be seen as an elaborate exercise in social defence and social control (Squires 1990), formal institutions of criminal justice playing only a relatively minor and peripheral part in this overall exercise of social discipline.

So even while earlier adults often complained of the activities of youth, the suggestion that they were at the same time 'anti-social' added a new dimension. Acts had been wrong, selfish, immoral, disrespectful. immature, obscene, violent, dangerous and so on, but they lacked the coherence and secular, quasi-scientific, objectivity implied by the label 'anti-social'. Yet even when ASB begins to make its first appearances in the postwar criminological literature it still remains rather vague, ambiguous and under-specified. Thus Spencer, writing in the first issue of the *British Journal of Delinquency*, argued how wartime conditions had 'intensified the anti-social nature of gang activity which would normally have been an ordinary phenomenon of adolescence' (Spencer 1950). In this light, ASB seems little more than a shade away from 'normal' youth behaviour and even that difference can be explained by the war. More intriguingly still, among the normal social activities of healthy youth, the author refers to 'street football'. Unfortunately, as we have already seen, this conception of positive social activity has not lasted so well and it now generates complaints. In the meantime, of course, the street football pitches have become on-street car parks where a stray shot might result in some expensive damage. What has not changed is the behaviour: football is football. Around it everything has changed – the perspective of the viewer/complainant, the sense of context, the physical occupancy of space, the interpretation of the behaviour and now, finally, the law.

Later in the same volume of the *British Journal of Delinquency* Warren implies that anti-social activities might be broadly continuous with a range of behaviours undertaken by normal children in his remarks regarding 'children who begin to commit anti-social acts in association with the stresses of adolescence' (Warren 1951: 166). Following his comprehensive survey of the influences upon 'conduct disordered' children, he draws no clear distinction between the 'disturbed' and the 'delinquent', acknowledging that the analysis is 'not wholly applicable for the average delinquent for whom psychological treatment is not sought' (p. 181).

Gang formation and 'anti-social' gang activities were, as we have noted, a growing focus of social concern during the war and immediate postwar years. In gangs, it was presumed, the young 'rebels and outlaws' of wartime transformed themselves into more persistent adult offenders. As Spencer noted in 1954, 'since the end of World War II, the anti-social gang has been a focus of attention in both Europe and America' (Spencer 1954). And, unless it be assumed that these preoccupations were the exclusive preserve of criminologists and other social scientists, a quick viewing of the opening moments of the 1949 Ealing Studios film *The Blue Lamp* (the film which launched the career of the eponymous PC George Dixon) reinforces the picture. The opening scenes take the form of an authentic Newsreel documentary with a voiceover warning of the youth gangs and young tearaways bringing a harder and 'more American' edge to British delinquency.

What was especially troubling about these gangs was the breaking of solidarities with family, community and society – the break with traditions of deference, authority and respect that they implied or encouraged. Delaney noted the source of the gang's appeal to individual members, 'almost without exception their individual life histories reveal failure to obtain adequate stability or security from essential parent figures; neglect and rejection have played large roles in their lives' (Delaney 1954: 35–6). While Scott depicted the consequences, 'gangs fulfil psychological needs not met by the individual's own parents … gangs need to express anti-parental or anti-social tendencies and their activities are likely to express a reversal of adult social roles' (Scott 1956: 6). It was in this breaking of social solidarities, social relationships so central to postwar reconstruction, that the threats of anti-social and youth gang behaviour lay, even though contemporaries were still experiencing some difficulty in distinguishing 'anti-social' behaviour from a range of relatively normal youth behaviours. 'Not every gang is asocial,' noted Scott (1956), whereas Delaney described a confusing array of positive and negative, inclusive and exclusive, conditions attaching to gang membership: 'Many boys who participate in the anti-social activities do not take an active role in the social structure. Boys who are not members of the gang may participate in its social activities but never in its anti-social ones' (p. 26).

There remained some uncertainty about what, exactly, the anti-social behaviour of youth – whether in or out of gangs – involved and even regarding the extent to which this behaviour might be consistently distinguished from the development of a more general youth culture in the postwar years. Other commentators, perhaps of a more liberal persuasion, voiced some scepticism about the scale and significance of these anti-social groups and suspected that media reporting had played some part in establishing these concerns (Walker 1965: 96–7). However, by the early

1960s, marked in our case by the renaming of the *British Journal of Delinquency* as the *British Journal of Criminology*, the discipline had begun to leave such vague conceptions of anti-social behaviour behind altogether. The Editorial of the first issue of the new journal expressed the editors' concern to shift its focus 'away from the whole field of anti-social behaviour' (p. 1) and towards a more practical (scientific and predictive) criminology, for

> to be sure, in the wide spectrum of human conduct, from the hypothetical normal to the criminal anti-social, lies a number of attitudes and traits which close psychological scrutiny reveals as harbingers of 'good' as well as of 'bad' (in the social sense). Nevertheless we must concentrate our attention on these larval forms of asocial behaviour which, as prediction studies are now making clear, constitute forerunners of aberrant social conduct. (p. 2)

This resolution of the future direction of British criminology certainly carried Mannheim's stamp. Crime was to be at the centre of the discipline, but studying anti-social behaviour was essential for understanding the seeds of future criminality (Mannheim 1955; Jeffrey 1960).

The immediate significance of this outlining of the trajectory for criminological science in the early 1960s for our unearthing of its preoccupation with anti-social behaviour is fourfold. In the first place it makes explicit the predictive emphasis we have referred to already. In the second place it confirms the ascendancy of a psychological and scientific 'treatment-centred' perspective geared towards normalisation within criminology. Thirdly, this sense of the criminological mission reaffirms its preoccupation with the underlying pathology of conduct and behaviour disorders. Finally, the scientific, psychological, treatment-based and predictive approaches, which in due course evolved into the administrative criminology of the Home Office (Gilling 1997; Hughes 1998) split away from the more sociological (post-Chicago School) area-based studies. Contrary to a focus upon individualised 'delinquent behaviour', these latter approaches insisted, above all, that 'analysis of delinquent and antisocial behaviour should focus upon the environmental factor of social class' (Humphries 1981: 19) – see, for example, Mays (1959).

The focus of this new criminology is evidenced by the lead articles in the first edition of the new journal: a commentary on the 'inadequate personality' (de Berker 1960), a review of 'habitual criminals' (Taylor 1960) and a discussion of 'neurotic exhibitionism' (Pollock 1960). There is no great surprise in this cluster of issues surfacing as dominant in the criminology of this period. They are, after all, among the principles towards which a diverse range of criminal justice professionals, reformers and social scientists had been working for the greater part of the twentieth century (Wootton 1959; Garland 1985; Rose 1985). It is often commented that the 1969 Children and Young Persons Act marks the 'high-watermark' of this reformist trajectory in criminal justice (for example, Rose 1989: 175). However, while 1969 may well have been the legislative high point, there is an argument to the effect that, by this point, reformism was already on the wane as some harder attitudes had begun to set in (Clarke 1980). The primary emphasis upon the pathological determinism of delinquency was eclipsed by a new 'deprived or depraved' dualism, and a relatively specialist and distinctive concern with 'anti-social personality disorders' became the more particular preserve of behavioural and developmental psychology. Prediction was still a central concern but questions about *how* one predicted, *what* was being predicted and *how accurate* (without self-fulfilling over-prediction or 'labelling') these predictions might be continued to generate much uncertainty. Looking at the ways in which criminologists grappled with these dilemmas in the 1960s helps us show how the discourses on ASB continued to evolve.

The Cambridge Study in Delinquent Development

One of the less obvious advantages of a longitudinal study such as that embarked upon by West (1967 1969) and continued by West and Farrington (1973, 1977) in the early 1960s involves not so much the tracking of a birth cohort's criminal career development but rather the shifting terrain and concerns of criminological discourse itself. The Cambridge Study, spanning over two decades, saw several changes of government and some very significant social and cultural shifts culminating, in the late 1970s, in the rightwards political shift associated with the election of the Thatcher governments in the UK (Hall et al. 1978; Hall 1979; Squires 1990).

From 1979 a new political language preoccupied with new issues (crime and disorder foremost among them) and deploying new forms of governance filtered into the criminological perspective (Garland 2001). A number of important continuities emerged from the reports of the Cambridge Study Group as their birth cohort aged, entered its teenage years, left school and then embarked into young adulthood, and the observing criminologists focused and refocused their concerns. A central concern with social deprivation, the disadvantaged backgrounds and disordered family circumstances of young people caught up in criminogenic social and cultural circumstances runs through the project. In this sense, the study was attempting to recombine the environmental and area-based perspective of sociological criminology with scientific psychological prediction (see West 1969: 1). In the study there is undoubtedly a clear focus on predicting the onset of delinquency, particularly persistent and serious offending, with generic social policies to address these problems, and with the need for early intervention. However, within the first books and their descriptions of the study, a preoccupation with the socio-pathology of the anti-social personality disorder is already slipping out of focus. Conversely, by the final two reports, in 1977 and 1982, a new more pragmatic anti-social tendency scale was being invented, a concept of the 'anti-social personality disorder' resurrected and a newer conception of 'anti-social behaviour' outlined.

Still fairly loosely defined and described, the new concept of ASB was not derived from social pathology or clinical testing but based upon rather more 'secular' and pragmatic foundations – observations of behaviour and self-reports. Relativism, judgementalism and a certain circular and self-fulfilling quality were part of the package from the start. Anti-social behaviour was what anti-social individuals did; they were anti-social because their behaviour was anti-social. Yet at the same time, we also begin to detect another shift in the discourse, a move from a conception of ASB as the special preserve of a group of 'usual suspects' – working class 'delinquents', gang members and the 'deprived or depraved' juveniles about whom the postwar social democratic reformers cared so much – and towards a more 'detached' conception of ASB, a series of performance options that any young person might choose to adopt. Largely speaking, although ASB would still primarily be found in all its old familiar haunts (a tendency rather exacerbated by our practice of looking all the harder for it there) its aetiology had subtly changed. Now, of central significance was the behaviour itself not the pathologies behind it, the unmet needs which drove it nor, ultimately, the person who performed it. The behaviour became symptomatic of nothing but the need for greater discipline and of the fears and concerns going unaddressed in a given community.

Before reporting on the study itself, it is worth reviewing West's preliminary study of the *Young Offender* which, in 1967, attempted an overview of the state of criminological knowledge of young people and crime in the mid-1960s. The tone is largely liberal, permissive and tolerant, broadly reflective of the thinking which underpinned the 1969 Children and Young Persons Act (Labour Party Study Group 1964; Home Office 1965). Thus, generally speaking, 'delinquency is typically a youthful characteristic which may be expected to clear up in later years … Like an attack of measles, a first conviction in a schoolboy, though it can be serious, does not usually portend a blighted future' (West 1967: 30). The real problem was 'the boy who goes on to become a persistent recidivist'. Furthermore with adolescence now understood as a 'transitional phase' of life and a normal feature of human development, deviance itself was also regarded as something only to be expected in youth.

A certain amount of delinquent misconduct is a normal feature of youth … delinquent behaviour has always been more or less universal … most of the young offenders who come before the courts differ from the rest of the population only in the accidental misfortune that they have been caught and prosecuted and their activities subjected to public scrutiny … like those who were not caught the great majority tended to grow out of their delinquent habits. (West 1967: 39)

Even so, this behaviour continued to trouble society: 'concern about delinquents both reflects and then feeds anxiety about the stability of our society' (ibid.: 47), but West was adamant, society's main efforts 'should be directed towards identifying and changing the ways of that small but disruptive minority of recidivists' (ibid.: 48).

According to West, the popular idea of a natural reservoir of youthful anti-social energy formed a key theme of William Golding's novel *Lord of the Flies,* first published in 1954. In West's view the book described how a band of respectably reared British schoolboys, stranded on an island, quickly regress from democratic orderliness to barbarity and tyranny (ibid.: 54). This may be one, it has to be said fairly superficial, interpreta-tion. West omits to point out the context in which the group finds itself trapped on the island. All around, a nuclear war is raging, with apparently responsible adults seemingly set upon destroying the world, civilisation and culture, eliminated at the push of a button. In this light, the descent of the group of boys into barbarism might appear little more than a regression to an adult human norm. On the island, the boys did not descend into what is commonly called 'anarchy'; rather they fell under the autocratic influence of a powerful leader (whose authority derived from his former 'civilised' existence) intent on eliminating all opposition. Golding's aim was not to criticise the anti-social delinquency of resistance but rather to expose the persecution and tyranny of which the unrestrained and powerful are capable. It might be argued that West's misreading of Golding's novel is symptomatic of an ambiguity which remained at the heart of his criminological analysis of delinquency. For, as Gillis has argued, failing to acknowledge, understand or tolerate cultural differences in working-class households and communities concerning the care and socialisation of children, the experts, 'child-savers' and social investigators of the poor invariably 'viewed the "deprived" child as the potential delinquent'. And, he continued:

This was just the kind of self-fulfilling prophecy that manages to produce the deviancy it claims to abhor, but which it must have in order to sustain the ideologies and institutions that are based upon it.

The attempt to legislate morality and restrict the independence of working-class youth naturally resulted in conflicts between the authorities and the young which could be interpreted as the latter's inherent tendency toward anti-social behaviour. (Gillis 1981: 181)

The analytical failure, described here, is, in all essentials, the same 'epistemological fallacy' (Furlong and Cartmel 1997) we discuss later in respect of the criminalisation of youth in the late 1990s. In the treatment-oriented and psychologically dominant 1960s, however, the crucial errors lay in the working assumption that the problems of adolescence were essentially psychological, rooted in the nature of the youths themselves (or in young people's reactions to the stresses of adolescence) rather than in the nature of society (West 1967: 183). For example, in West's discussion of the 'anti-social character' there remains a continuing ambiguity regarding the 'explanation of delinquency' despite his broader scepticism about the relevance of personality and conduct disorders, epilepsy, neuroses and other clinically defined abnormalities 'to the generality of delinquency' (ibid.: 105).

Criticising the emphasis placed upon prediction in many delinquency studies, West commented that, while 'the ability to predict accurately is an accepted criterion of successful science, in recent years an interest, one might say almost a craze, has developed among criminologists for trying to predict, at an early age, who will later become delinquent' (ibid.: 163). Even so, he gave credence to Stott's work (1960, 1963, 1964), rooted in psychoanalytic and personality approaches and which appeared to show how 'anti-social character traits of serious delinquents become manifest at a tender age' (West 1967: 167). Similar work in the USA based upon the Minnesota Multiphasic Personality Inventory (MMPI) (Hathaway and Monaschesi 1953) also appeared to reveal the existence of rebellious attitudes preceding actual delinquency and suggested, 'some kind of difference in the personality of delinquents as a group ... the peculiarity displayed falls in line with the aggressive, anti-social character formation described by clinical workers' (West 1967: 169). Differences from 'normal adolescents' were said to be most marked in the case of the more persistent or serious young offenders 'whose immature and anti-social attitudes are most apparent to those around them'. Often overlooked here, however, was the fact that, by the time such findings were recorded, it could well have been the case that the reactions of parents, peers and teachers – to say nothing of those of police or criminal justice system personnel – had already gone some way to harden and exacerbate the disapproved of behaviour and personality traits of the young, thereby pushing the delinquent prophecy to its fulfilment.

Concluding his discussion of the feasibility and desirability of predicting future 'delinquency' from 'anti-social' character traits in the young, West certainly eschewed the response of punitive and reformatory discipline. Unfortunately, his alternative, psychoanalytic treatment only led back to an assumption that there was something wrong with the 'delinquent' and 'anti-social' themselves – or with their reactions to their environments (Rose 1989). However, the only groups with whom this presumption might be properly tested were those under the care or supervision of state institutions. And, as has been noted, 'most youngsters who get as far as being committed to approved schools do show signs of individual maladjustment mostly in the form of some degree of anti-social or psychopathic distortion of character' (West 1967: 170). The discomforting conclusion that, hitherto, prediction had only been possible in hindsight explains the need for a longitudinal cohort study of delinquent development. In the meantime, perhaps the best that criminology could offer was a pragmatic, seemingly tautological view of the production of the worst delinquents and, in tune with the times, a renewed reminder of the dangers of gangs.

> Many persistent delinquents are anti-social characters, persons who have been damaged by social and family adversities. They are too aggressive, suspicious and impulsive to adjust to the ways of normal groups, although some may be 'pseudo-socialised' to the extent of being able to fit in with a gang of similar misfits. (West 1967: 295)

Predicting future 'delinquency'

In the first published report on the study, West spent some time detailing the social geography and composition of the working-class area, a 'crowded urban district', from which the group of 411, 8- to 9-year-old boys, was selected. Following this, a brief outline is provided of the domestic, physical and educational (intelligence and literacy) characteristics of the sample. Overall, the area and its residents are described as 'a fairly ordinary working-class urban community … where the kind of delinquent behaviour commonly encountered would probably be typical of similar areas throughout the country. The incidence of juvenile offences would be expected to be relatively high, but not particularly unusual' (West 1969: 35). However, having spent two chapters outlining a sociological portrait of the area and its inhabitants the commentary turned to consider the conduct and personality characteristics of its sample of boys, at age 8. The methods adopted drew upon the use in the USA of the MMPI by Hathaway and Monaschesi in their 1953 delinquency prediction study. The project was also modelled upon the Gluecks' (1950; Glueck

1952) delinquency study in the USA and Stott's research in the UK on identifying delinquency predictors in children's classroom behaviour (1960, 1963).

A series of tests and assessments followed considering 'conduct disorder' ratings by psychiatric social workers, 'neurotic tendency' ratings drawing upon Eysenck's (1964) work, psychomotor performance tests and peer group popularity assessments. Only in relation to Eysenck's conception of the 'neurotic extravert' is any connection to a generic notion of ASB drawn, and even this was deemed 'probably not close enough to have much practical value for prediction' (West 1969: 45). Elsewhere the signs of 'incipient delinquency' are drawn from the correlations between the various indicators achieved and emerging evidence of what is described as 'acting out' behaviours which included: lying, truanting, stealing from home or outside the home, cruelty, bad tempers, destructiveness, sexual misbehaviour, jealousy and defiance. From the point of view of prediction, the results did appear to allow the early identification of a subset of supposedly 'behaviour disordered' and 'acting out' boys: 'observation strongly suggests that ... a substantial proportion of anti-social juveniles can be picked out by their behaviour before the age of ten, when prosecutions begin' (West 1969: 140).

For West, this notion of ASB, in so far as it makes only a relatively limited appearance in the study, still retains the older conception of ASB as the particular preserve of identified 'delinquents'. ASB is what these individuals do. The variety of behaviours are never seen to coalesce into a single anti-social (AS) type. This was partly because the criminology of the time was largely preoccupied by the 'delinquencies' of the working class so that it had no professional reason to believe the middle classes capable of such behaviours and partly because it was confidently assumed that the protective features of the stable and superior middle-class household would contain the pressures towards delinquency to which the working classes were proving susceptible. In fact this was already changing. Metaphorically speaking ASB was already loosening its ties to the ghetto or the slum. Affluence and a burgeoning youth culture were driving the process. Young people were becoming the new 'dangerous class' (Davies 1986), but to begin with it was still the behaviour displayed by some of them from the lower social classes (rather than a concern about youth in general) which was the main focus of concern.

Who becomes delinquent?

The Second Report from the study in delinquent development (West and Farrington 1973) largely tended to confirm the findings of the earlier work regarding the onset of criminal offending and the related risk factors which are exhaustively analysed. However, the concept of 'anti-social behaviour' itself is entirely absent from this study. The report confines itself to considerations of delinquency based upon criminal convictions alone – even excluding some minor convictions such as truancy, disorder and breaches of the peace which today would surely figure as ASB. Even when discussing a range of self-report behaviours, and independent psychiatric social worker and teacher assessments, factors such as 'acting out', 'troublesomeness', 'daring' and 'aggression' are not seen to coalesce as ASB. Only 'anti-establishment' attitudes, seemingly passed from father to son, appear to form part of a relevant penumbra of broadly 'anti-social' characteristics related to 'delinquency' (or, in a separate study, to welfare dependency: Knight and West 1978). In most other respects it is the 'extreme degree of social pathology typified by criminal families', producing an amoral, neglectful and anti-social context in which parents, lie, cheat and steal and their offspring lie, cheat, steal, fight and truant, which is most obviously documented by the research.

For West and Farrington, the key findings seemed to lie in the predictive power of early criminal convictions – that is, actual convictions rather than more general AS traits.

> Although a relatively small group within the population, young recidivist delinquents merit first consideration. They comprise a distinctive minority of troublesome and socially disruptive individuals of unfortunate parental backgrounds, difficult personalities and inadequate scholastic and vocational backgrounds … their problems become self-perpetuating … in what has been referred to as an unending cycle of deprivation … Our research has shown that, at least by age 8, and probably before they begin to go to school, some boys are marked out as potential recidivists. (West and Farrington 1973: 201–2)

They then proceed to specify a range of characteristics of social pathology and ASB but concede that

> among boys who indulge in delinquent behaviour, those who have adverse background characteristics of a kind noticeable to authorities are likely to acquire an official juvenile conviction record. Samples of official delinquents are probably biased in the direction of an over-representation of boys with obviously unfavourable backgrounds. (ibid.: 188)

Significantly, while endorsing the principle of early prediction, the authors almost entirely dismissed the work of Eysenck who had pioneered the early identification of anti-social personality disorder (ASPD). They included a discussion of Eysenck's conception of an ASPD rooted in genetics, susceptibility to conditioning and his extroversion–introversion scale in a catch-all chapter entitled 'Miscellaneous factors of doubtful significance'. Overall, West and Farrington concluded, research results 'did not provide much support for Eysenck's theory', and a distinct ASPD syndrome 'appeared to play a relatively small part in overall levels of delinquency.' (ibid.: 113).

However, by 1977, with the publication of the third report on the Cambridge Study (West and Farrington 1977) covering the period when their boys were aged 18–19, the authors were beginning to rediscover aspects of an 'anti-social type' whose aggressiveness was a defining characteristic. 'There was a close relationship between aggressive social attitudes and delinquency ... unusually aggressive attitudes and behaviour appeared to be the most prominent and important distinguishing characteristics of the delinquent group' (West and Farrington 1977: 74, 107). Furthermore, interpretations of this behaviour now owed less to some pre-existing psychological syndrome, deprivation or social pathology; rather, the behaviour was understood as it manifested itself in violence and aggression, racism, anti-authority attitudes, heavy drinking, dishonesty, promiscuity and, more generally, a 'delinquent' style of life.

Having left psychology and social pathology behind, West and Farrington's new concept of the anti-social or deviant young person was only roughly outlined. Therefore its predictive utility was rather limited. As they noted, 'a number of features of behaviour that could be loosely described as antisocial or deviant were found to be significantly associated with delinquency' (West and Farrington 1977: 146). Accordingly they set out to attempt to produce a rating scale, 'to try to measure the degree of this antisocial tendency in each youth ... Such a scale would be strongly linked with delinquency, because each of the component features was characteristic of 'delinquents'. At the same time it would be a measure of antisocial behaviour ... which led to official delinquency' (ibid.: 146). That the researchers believed they were attempting something new here, breaking away from the psychological and pathological paradigms which had dominated earlier criminological studies, is captured in their comment, 'as far as we know, no other criminological researcher has attempted to do this.' As we have seen, such scales and diagnostic devices for measuring ASPD had tended to proliferate in psychology (Robins 1966; Moir and Jessel 1995). A purely criminological behaviour measure was a new departure.

The scale revealed a significant clustering of anti-social, aggressive and delinquent characteristics with anti-social characteristics appearing as fairly (although not entirely – there was some over-prediction) reliable precursors of delinquency. Both anti-social individuals and delinquents shared a range of deprived and adverse family and social backgrounds while, above all, early assessments of troublesomeness by teachers showed a 'surprisingly high predictive power' (West and Farrington 1977: 157). Unfortunately, this finding, like the over-prediction of delinquency on the basis of anti-social characteristics, tended to have a rather self-fulfilling quality about it, as West noted in a subsequent volume (West 1982). Accordingly, the more noticeable the anti-social and aggressive tendencies of childhood, the more likely they were to persist into later life and the more likely they were to lead to other forms of persisting anti-social (even if not criminal or delinquent) behaviour. Or perhaps put another way with the benefit of labelling theory – and acknowledging that someone has to notice 'noticeable' behaviour – we might say that the earlier the 'anti-social' labels were made to stick the more enduring their imprints might be.

The 'cycle of deprivation' and the renaissance of ASB

By 1982 and the appearance of West's fourth substantial report (West 1982) on the Cambridge Study, the concept of 'anti-social behaviour' and the related 'Anti-Social Personality Disorder' had undergone something of a renaissance. As the author acknowledged, the 1970s had seen much change and development in the theorising about and the politics of juvenile delinquency (even though the labelling perspective had seemingly gained relatively little purchase within the study). Most notably, the 'cycle of deprivation' thesis had focused attention once more upon the clustering of 'anti-social' characteristics to be found within the poorest families responsible for producing 'the minority of highly persistent delinquents with repeated convictions [who] not only pose a social problem by their frequent offences but also present a wide range of other troubles such as poor scholastic attainments, unemployment, marital disharmony and psychiatric disorder' (Rutter and Madge 1982: 162). This renewed focus upon the persistently delinquent subset of young people, in whom a variety of personality disorders were most common, in the 'transmitted deprivation' study pushed criminological attention back to a range of factors rooted in psychology (psychiatric disorder, family dysfunction, low IQ and related social pathology) which West had earlier seemed keen to leave behind.

He preferred what he called a more 'eclectic approach' and broadly criticised two alternative stereotypes which he felt clouded sensible discussion of delinquency issues. On the one hand was the stereotype of the 'delinquent' as essentially normal but just unlucky to have been caught. On the other hand was an equally misleading picture of delinquents as a 'special category of maladjusted persons lacking in restraint, primitive in their sense of right and wrong, unable or unwilling to conform to ... civilised standards of behaviour and liable to persistent trouble with the law' (West 1982: 2). As West went on to note, such exaggerated and contradictory stereotypes were responsible for the 'flux and confusion' of contemporary social policies for dealing with delinquency. At the same time, he added, in an important (and often overlooked) acknowledgement of the influence of broader cultural and political shifts, recent years 'had seen the development and hardening of ideological interpretations.' The study then went on to catalogue the patterns emerging from the Cambridge Study cohort by the age of 25.

Eysenck's work still received relatively short shrift: 'attempts to identify a crime-prone group by means of assessments of neuroticism and extraversion proved unfruitful' (West 1982: 60), but a central chapter of the report was devoted to the elaboration of a 'delinquent personality' as identified by Eysenck. Drawing upon the rating scale established five years earlier, eleven 'anti-social characteristics' were identified and found to be around three times more prevalent amongst the group of identified 'delinquents' as compared with the 'non-delinquents' (the concentration of anti-social characteristics was even greater in the 'recidivist-only' group). The characteristics included: aggressiveness, unstable job record, spending leisure time 'hanging about', involvement in anti-social groups, drinking and driving, gambling, sexual promiscuity, heavy smoking, drug misuse and anti-establishment attitudes. The findings revealed relatively little specialisation in anti-social traits:

> Youths reporting a large number of fights were particularly likely to be recidivist delinquents, to express a large number of aggressive attitudes (including hatred of racial minorities), they came from large, poor, criminal families and had other antisocial traits in addition to their aggressive propensities. [Furthermore] persistent aggression of both an 'instrumental' and 'expressive' kind was associated with persistent delinquency. (West 1982: 67)

West had identified a clustering of 'anti-social personality characteristics' at the heart of the formation of the persistent young offender. There was a 'surprising concentration of delinquent individuals, especially recidivists, among a small minority of families in our sample, and the strong tendency for criminal parents to have criminal sons' (Knight and West 1978: 173). In this way, West's work clearly helped lay some important foundations for more contemporary conceptions of serious and persistent delinquency.

Unfortunately it appears that the description of the cluster of symptoms has proven more durable than the analysis of the causes. For West, family background was the critical factor and 'the worse the background, the worse the eventual outcome' (West 1982: 116). Deprivation was an undeniable precursor of the 'anti-social lifestyle' which became evident in every stage and all aspects of a young person's life.

> Deprivation, and its aftermath, the antisociality syndrome, was associated with the hard core of persisting delinquents whose conviction careers usually started at an early age and continued into their twenties. They were predominantly lower class, poorly socialised, often impulsive and ineffectual in the crimes they committed, the kind of delinquent who is highly visible to the police, public and the media and extremely troublesome to social agencies ... Few of the boys exposed to severe early deprivation developed satisfactorily.

As West concluded, the study confirmed 'the existence of an easily identified group from problem families whose prospects of becoming contented and effective citizens are poor and who are all too likely to act as transmitters of deprivation to their own children' (West 1982: 118).

Despite this broadly materialist reading of the factors influencing the onset of juvenile criminal careers, in the hardening ideological and political climate of the mid-1980s, with record crime increases, rising fear of crime and renewed preoccupation with youth delinquency (Pitts 1988) it was the demonised image of the 'anti-social and persistent delinquent' which captured the public imagination rather more than considerations of social justice. Social control, rather than social policy was the order of the day.

Although the conception of the 'anti-social personality' was almost eclipsed for a while in mainstream academic criminology, ideological preconceptions relating to the 'cycle of deprivation' thesis breathed new life into the concept. Despite West's conclusions the concept was never entirely killed off and, instead, lay fully formed but dormant until called into action once again. There is no small irony in the fact that, when subsequently called upon, the portrait of the anti-social and persistent young offender, around which the efforts of the criminal justice system began to coalesce in the 1990s, owed so much to the work developed by West.

And then, despite the hegemony of 'left realism' in academic criminology, from the mid to late 1980s, the anti-social personality began to re-emerge, as facets of this distinctively troubling character now coincided with the ideological predilections of left realism and its values of inclusive 'community safety', reducing fear and supporting victims. Both the scale of young people's perceived 'anti-social' behaviour and the even earlier ages at which they appeared to commence it caused alarm, as did their apparently more belligerent and 'desubordinate' attitudes and the extent to which, once started, they persisted in these behaviours. Young 'delinquents', as it were, seemed not to be growing out of crime as readily as had seemed to be the case in an earlier time.

The psychological twist: anti social personality disorder

Reference has already been made to Eysenck's account of the conduct disorders he felt were detectable in childhood and which allowed the definition of an 'anti-social personality disorder'. According to Eysenck (1964), these childhood conduct disorders had neurological origins, they could be plotted on an introversion–extroversion continuum and were of significance, primarily, in so far as they appeared to influence the receptiveness of children to 'normal' socialisation or, in a treatment setting, to 'pro-social conditioning' – or discipline. Eysenck is sometimes suggested as the originator of the 'theory of anti-social behaviour' (Little 1963; Allsopp and Feldman 1976), but perhaps the best that can be said is simply that he more forcefully introduced this concept to British criminology. In fact, both the notion of ASPD and its role in helping predict delinquency precede his study *Crime and Personality* (1964) by some years. What was new in Eysenck's work, the idea that criminality is a continuous inherited trait of a similar kind as intelligence, height or weight, tended to be rejected by mainstream academic criminology. However, the notion of a criminal or anti-social personality which had its 'ultimate hereditary basis in the low conditionability and extroverted nature of the criminal' (Halleck 1971) achieved rather more widespread attention, especially in the development of diagnoses for psychopathic disorders and future dangerousness (Vold *et al.* 2002). Yet despite criminologists declaring relatively little support for Eysenck's own ideas in their findings (West and Farrington 1977; West 1982) these issues do merit some discussion because they have a direct bearing on the definition of AS behaviours and the adoption of policies and treatment 'solutions'. Equally importantly they illustrate the, sometimes coalescing, sometimes fragmenting, relationships between criminological and psychological knowledge on such questions (West 1988).

In 1947 the Minnesota Multiphasic Personality Inventory (MMPI) was developed in the USA to identify and diagnose conduct disorders in children as a precursor to the prediction of criminality and ASPDs in adults (Moir and Jessel 1995). Along with evidence of abnormal brain chemistry, low seratonin and high hormone levels as well as outward signs of aggression, impulsivity and a range of anti-social behaviours (cruelty to animals, bullying, temper tantrums, dishonesty, stealing, disobedience to teachers) such tests were used to confirm the existence of an early-age, predelinquent syndrome of anti-social conduct disorders. If left untreated, such syndromes were thought likely to persist into adult criminal careers. Not unlike the progressive, scientific and social preventive discourses developing in the UK after the Second World War, the MMPI represented the appliance of science to the disturbed and delinquent children of the USA. This new scientific discourse on children's conduct disorders marked a continuation of earlier ideologies from the American child-saving movement emphasising social pathology and 'problem families' as the source of delinquency and anti-social behaviour problems (Platt 1969). Yet again, just as in the UK, whereas in the prewar area it had been this pathology, or weakness, of youth which formed the core of the problem – and their need for salvation, in the postwar period it had become more a question of the threat that youth seemed to pose – and their need for discipline (Gilbert 1986). The problem appeared particularly acute in those sub-groups of the population where crime and social problems were especially concentrated.

Hartjen provides the following overview of the perception of the delinquency problem in the USA, the parallels with the construction of the issue in the UK being strong:

> The delinquency problem signifies the existence of a cultural clash within American society. The behaviour of children of some groups offends or poses a real or imagined threat to the interests of some other group. As these threatening groups have grown in size, visibility, activism, and the like, the behaviour of all their members poses an even greater threat. (Hartjen 1977: 234)

In postwar USA a major feature of this cultural clash centred upon race, youth and urban disorder. Piven and Cloward (1972) describe the northern migration of black populations escaping southern discrimination and in search of work in the northern industrial cities of the USA. Ghettoisation, unemployment, poverty and a loosening of family and communal social controls followed, resulting in rapidly rising levels of urban disorder and crime (Coid 2003). The authors fill out this picture of the growing threat of youthful disorder in the USA:

> The litany of urban disorders in the wake of declining occupational and family controls is by now familiar: rising rates of gang delinquency and other forms of juvenile delinquency, such as school

vandalism; spreading drug addiction; an alarming increase in serious crimes such as armed robbery and burglary ... the sharp increase in vandalism suggest not only that social controls over youth were weakening, but that youth were turning against the schools, deliberately making them a target of their anger and frustration ... Eventually, of course, disorder took the form of widespread rioting, and the rioters, too, were predominantly young, single and marginally related to the occupational structure. They were unmistakably unintegrated. (Piven and Cloward 1972: 226, 236)

The similarities with the British context, described already, cannot be overemphasised: relative deprivation, what we now call social exclusion, the emergence of an increasingly distinct youth culture and the development of gang activity (Miller 1966), generating fear and alarm and, in due course, a toughening climate of law and order politics (Singer 1996; Zimring 1998). Yet what seems especially marked in the US context is a scientific commitment to read behavioural characteristics arising from the social and structural tensions of postwar America as if they were the defining and *a priori* characteristics of individuals. Furthermore, the assumption that 'there is a heavy concentration of social pathology at the bottom of the socio-economic scale' (Wootton 1959: 51) weighed heavily upon much of the early US delinquency research. Effectively, this preponderance of pathological and deviant characteristics was taken to explain both the poverty and the deviancy of lower social groups. In turn, the anti-social characteristics of the children of the 'poor' turned out to be very reliable predictors of the even more serious criminal and anti-social personality disorders in adults. 'The essential feature of this disorder is the pattern of irresponsible and antisocial behaviour beginning in childhood or early adolescence and continuing into adulthood' (Zuckerman 1991).

Understandably, given the substantial self-fulfilling prophecy entailed, studies gave a bad prognosis for children with conduct disorders while those with an actual record of delinquency had the worst outlook:

The finding that antisocial adult behaviour virtually requires a history of child behavioural problems is well enough documented to be beyond debate ... The best predictor of post-adolescent antisocial personality disorder was the number of antisocial symptoms which had been displayed in childhood. (Moir and Jessel 1995: 311)

As significant a problem lay in the tight circularity of the definitions of ASPD provided. Thus behaviour disorders demonstrated the existence of an underlying ASPD condition, while in turn the supposed existence of this condition was taken to explain the behaviour and predict future offending.

The preoccupation with childhood ASB as a predictor of adult criminality represents one instance of the medicalised and treatment-centred criminal psychology prevalent in America (Coid 2003) and which began to find some applications in Britain (Allsopp and Feldman 1976). In the early postwar years at least, for Wootton, 'psychiatry and humanitarianism marched hand in hand' (1959: 206). It was only when the optimism that had characterised postwar social science began to dissipate, alongside evidence that being able to predict adult personality disorders and criminal traits was not the same as being able to treat them effectively, that more punitive reactions began to set in (Cohen 1985). At the same time, under the same banner of benevolence and scientific humanism, the behaviourists attempted to push further back into childhood to uncover the earliest 'pre-delinquent' warning signs, signs allowing them to independently corroborate a single syndrome of anti-social personality disorders (Rutter and Giller 1983) – based upon 'recognised symptoms' of abnormality independent of any actual misbehaviour – and prior to actual delinquency or contact with criminal justice agencies. West and Farrington's attempt in 1977 to establish an AS behaviour scale (discussed earlier) is only a relatively late British example of a type of work that had seen substantially greater development in the USA (Robins 1966; Robins and Ratcliff 1979).

Concluding his review of 'psychological contributions to criminology' in 1988, West noted how a variety of tests had been able to demonstrate a clustering of 'anti-social characteristics' in young children which were highly predictive of social problems, including crime, in adulthood. Yet, he noted, 'the stereotypical "criminal personality" is a gross over-simplification and generalisation'. It remains open to question, he added, 'how far recognisable clusters of antisocial behaviours that appear consistent over time are intrinsic to the individual, or how far they reflect environmental pressures such as poverty or family criminality' (West 1988: 81). In turn, once criminology formally ceased its quest for the 'criminal personality', the way was cleared for a more pragmatic and actuarial science of 'delinquency risk' prediction. This new penological science was largely agnostic as to causes – psychological or environmental – and was geared instead to practical prevention based upon accurate risk assessment and prediction (Feeley and Simon 1992, 1994; Young 1999). In turn, risks were to be easily read from the recorded behaviours of children, their community and social contexts, and, above all else, the child-rearing techniques of their parents (Loeber and Dishion 1983).

Rutter and Giller (1983) have argued that, despite the substantial disputes between criminology and psychology regarding the merits of 'trait' and 'situational' approaches to anti-social personality development during the late 1970s, there had recently occurred some rapprochement between these contrasting perspectives. In fact, as we have already suggested, to consider this development as only the latest twist in an alignment of psychology and criminology is to miss the most important developments and offer only a rather superficial picture of contemporary perceptions regarding ASB today. For just as administrative criminology responded to its own aetiological crisis in the 1970s with an abrupt turn towards realist and managerialist agendas (Morrison 1995), so neither criminal personalities nor (ostensibly criminogenic) social conditions are the focus of attention today. Now there is only 'anti-social behaviour', troubling for what it is and what it represents, worrying for what it might become and the best predictor we appear to have of further trouble in adulthood. In the process the, always ambiguous, language of risk has also shifted. Young people used to be 'at risk', now they have become the *source* of present and, even more serious, future risks and fears (Farrington and Coid 2003).

There is now an extensive literature on childhood risk factors relating to the onset of ASB in childhood and adolescence and persisting into adult criminal careers. If anything ASB appears to be eclipsing delinquency as a focus of concern. For instance, having previously written books about families, deprivation and juvenile delinquency, Rutter and his colleagues titled their 1998 review of the risk factors for conduct disorder and delinquency *Antisocial Behaviour by Young People* (Rutter *et al.* 1998). They justified this choice of target concept by reference to a number of good 'realist' considerations: the fact that the great majority of youthful offending never appears in criminal statistics and the need to include the behaviour of those under the age of criminal responsibility. They acknowledged the diminishing appeal of theories of causation in criminology and opted, in turn, for an essentially individualistic conception of ASB. This is behaviour made manifest by individuals and it is at this level that the behaviour has to be managed and contained. At a stroke, therefore, the book demonstrated its commitment to the new administrative criminology, embracing net-widening (ASB rather than just crime), the relativisation of the problem (problem behaviour in its own right, not that which is caused but that which is experienced), and the selective targeting of individuals in whom the risks appear greatest.

In a sense, anti-social behaviour 'came of age' when it became so useful – as a sign, a symptom, a risk predictor, a popular and universal complaint, an enforcement point, a flexible and selective rationale for intervention or inaction. But this only occurred when it had lost the ideological baggage which had preoccupied the criminological positivists for so long (the idea that the 'anti-social' were a distinctly pathological sub-class or that 'society was to blame' for the appalling living conditions they were forced to endure). It seemed to predict future risks fairly reliably, rejecting the advice of labelling theory, which urged that young people were best left to grow out of crime by themselves, by referring instead to the present fears, blighted communities, universal victims (Young 1992) and future harms if ASB were left to its own devices. After all, 'antisocial parents tend to have antisocial children' (Farrington 2003: 7) and the cycle would therefore continue (Farrington and Coid 2003). Furthermore, slipping outside the criminal law and its rules of evidence, even drawing the 'pre-delinquent' within the pale, ASB offered a much more malleable means of selectively disciplining those who caused offence.

That is, of course, those who 'caused offence' rather than those who committed offences. Their 'offensiveness' did not have to be proven any more than evidence of a pre-existing psychological or conduct disorder had to be established. The behaviour was just behaviour. ASB involved few set standards or criteria but depended largely upon a reaction from the fearful and vulnerable – this was precisely what made it so useful and so flexible. It is undoubtedly the case that the majority of perpetrators of what is now called ASB are criminology's most familiar suspects: young and male, underachieving and relatively unattached. With the invention of ASB they now find themselves surrounded by a rather more 'economic' (Foucault 1977) and efficient machinery of graduated enforcement. Whether this will 'work' is a question which is often asked but seldom satisfactorily answered. What it will achieve, and for whom, is a far more important question.

In the next chapter, turning to consider the important emerging relationship between ASB and the new youth justice, we attempt to explore these questions. In particular, we examine the wider significance of the 'dispersal of discipline' mobilised by the new machineries of 'community safety' policy and practice, ASB prevention and enforcement and youth justice management.

Chapter 4

Making links or breaking links?
ASB and the New Youth Justice

As a society we do ourselves no favours by failing to break the link between juvenile crime and disorder and the serial burglar of the future. (Jack Straw, Preface to the *No More Excuses* White Paper, Home Office 1997)

However criminal justice policies may have failed, they have nonetheless succeeded in recruiting vast numbers of people into the crime/crime control 'industry'. All this criminal justice was demonstrably ineffective at reducing crime ... becoming involved in official responses to crime could actually make continued career criminality more rather than less probable. (Hudson, 1993: 38)

The preceding chapters have sought to develop a series of arguments about the growing preoccupation with youth crime and anti-social behaviour in contemporary Britain. Chapter 1 sought to chart the emergence of this new discourse, linking current concerns about youth and ASB to wider preoccupations with the 'condition of Britain' by which New Labour in general and Tony Blair in particular have been especially energised. The unfolding narrative in the *No More Excuses* White Paper and Blair's *New Consensus on Law and Order* speech (Home Office, 1997a; Blair 2004), conveyed an essentially moral tale of Britain still exorcising the permissive demons of the 1960s (Squires forthcoming). What was needed was a firmer sense of social responsibilities, 'tougher love' and stricter discipline in our key social institutions. Many of New Labour's reforms to youth justice and youth policy were designed to bring this about.

By their very nature, politicians are, no doubt, inclined to claim credit for social changes and attribute purpose to social and political processes. In outlining what he called his 'new consensus' on law and order, the Prime Minister was doing just that. In his stance on combating the elements of anti-social disorder he perceived in contemporary Britain he was, in a very Thatcherite sense, working from moral principles, or instinct (as he put it in 2004), and adopting the role of a 'conviction' politician. There is a certain symmetry between his purposive view of governance and social change and his sense that the problems of crime and disorder in contemporary Britain are, in the last analysis, symptoms of individual irresponsibility, lack of discipline and moral failing. This, essentially conservative realist, position underpins a good deal of New Labour youth justice policy as Burney has neatly concluded. In criminological terms, New Labour may have originally lined up with 'left realism' 'in recognising that the pains of crime and disorder were sharpest in poor neighbourhoods least well-equipped to deal with them, but [it has] adopted "right realism's" zero tolerance responses' (Burney 2002: 471). In a similar fashion, Blair's undoubtedly honest recollections regarding his feelings about the scale and significance of anti-social behaviour in deprived and excluded communities are not the whole of the story. As we argued, the notion of anti-social behaviour did not arise, perfectly formed, in the mind of a rising politician in 1988. Rather, it resurfaced, or was to some extent reinvented, as a result of a more complex combination of influences.

The remainder of Chapter 1 attempted to describe this variety of influences, culminating in the current preoccupation with youthful ASB and the range of new enforcement initiatives adopted to deal with it. As we indicated, however, contemporary discourse on anti-social behaviour had its own rather overlooked history, a history that has been only rather selectively invoked where it supports the current policy thrust. In Chapter 2 we sought to review some criminological history, partly for what it might tell us about discourses of anti-social behaviour and partly in order to gain some wider perspective on the contexts in which problems of ASB and related criminal disorders surface as governmental priorities. A final reason for reviewing these earlier criminological discourses concerns the policy responses. As we have seen, a central feature of Blair's supposed 'new consensus on law and order' involves the direct repudiation of the 'liberal' and 'understanding' approach to (youth) justice which he suggests characterised the 1960s. This was, after all, the era that coined all the supposed 'excuses' for delinquent behaviour compounding our current problems, excuses which New Labour sought to sweep away in

1997–8. On the other hand, the 1960s, and the analysis of youth crime and anti-social behaviour arising then, may well provide the foundations for a series of alternative ways of viewing ASB and its youthful perpetrators. This need not involve a wholesale return to deterministic social positivism and the denial of individual agency – although the recognition of social context and of the prevailing influences under which young people make their own histories are certainly features which contemporary youth justice, in its relentless cataloguing of individualised biographical risk assessments, would do well to recall. Equally, recovering a sense of the 'juvenile delinquent' – or perpetrator of ASB – as a person, rather than just an accumulation of risk factors, someone to be understood as an individual rather than condemned and punished, might also be seen as part of the legacy of 1960s interpretative sociology. As we will go on to argue, this way of seeing stands in marked contrast to the actuarial and aggregated, increasingly programme-driven enforcement of the youth justice of today (Squires and Measor 2005).

In the chapter below, we reiterate our core argument that ASB management, prevention and enforcement activities have become central and indispensable features of contemporary youth justice. We relate this interpretation of ASB to the more general changes occurring within the youth justice field. In particular, we situate our discussion of these issues within the context provided by a series of relatively new and emerging commentaries attempting to describe, explain and evaluate recent changes in youth justice. These include the emergence of a new 'actuarial' penology and the governmentality perspective emphasising the strategy of 'responsibilisation' and new modes of exercising power. In the latter half of this chapter we develop these themes in relation to key dimensions of Cohen's (1985) 'dispersal of discipline' argument.

The shift to ASB management epitomises especially the move towards 'responsibilisation' and 'governmental' strategies of intervention that other commentators have increasingly detected throughout contemporary criminal justice. Contemporary youth justice cannot any longer be meaningfully discussed without consideration of ASB. In turn, for the youth justice system, ASB prevention and enforcement work is heralded as a solution for many of the perceived failings and dissatisfactions with the YJ system which existed before 1996. While we certainly do not seek to reduce youth justice to a simple question of ASB management, neither do we regard ASB prevention and management as but one further aspect of the new youth system; rather, the two issues have become increasingly inseparable. Youth justice in Britain is increasingly shifting to an ASB management model. In a number of ways the adult criminal justice system may be following suit. Hence our reason for devoting this chapter to the wider changes occurring within the youth justice system is, in part, to underscore the significance of the new ASB strategies to current problems of youth crime and youth justice. As we intend to show, important changes follow from this reorientation of youth justice but, as we argue while drawing upon Cohen's work (1985), there are also some important continuities.

Theoretical and empirical starting points

It is necessary, first, to offer an interpretation of the formal policy changes in the youth justice system brought about by the New Labour government after 1997 in order to connect these to the related changes in the problematisation of ASB. At the outset it is appropriate to acknowledge the perspectives from which we are approaching this issue, although we have alluded to them already in the above paragraphs. There is both a theoretical and an empirical dimension to this. To take the latter first, for three years one of the present authors was involved in the evaluation of a series of youth offending projects in South East England and London. In total we were contracted to evaluate nine separate projects (including Bail Support projects, a Restorative Justice project, a Detention and Training Order project, Mentoring projects and an Education and Skills project) for five different Youth Offending Teams in five separate local authority areas. Our experiences in undertaking this evaluation work have been written up in part (Squires and Measor 2005) and, except in one respect, we will not repeat our discussion of those issues here.

Our chief concern about the youth offending project evaluation process concerned the way the national evaluations appeared only interested in the aggregation of quantitative data about the impact of the new initiatives. Largely irrelevant from the point of view of this exercise was any qualitative data addressing how the young clients of these programmes (or, indeed, the staff running them) felt about the ways in which the interventions may have 'worked'.

This failure to engage directly with the perspective of the young offenders (to say nothing of the perspectives of experienced youthwork staff) represents a fundamental weakness in many contemporary approaches to youth offending (Squires and Stephen 2002) and a real democratic deficit in the youth offending strategy. Such an emphatic 'top-down' approach draws upon a perspective in which, at the very best, delinquency is explained rather than understood. Evaluation measures which seek to assess nothing but the impact of a given programme of interventions outside the wider social context of the young people's lives and allowing only a limited voice to the young people themselves tell us next to nothing either about young people's criminalisation or their (eventual) desistance. In any event, in the youth offending evaluations, very little at all was explained anyway, the evaluation process becoming little more than a simple cataloging of outputs. Undertaking the work one began to develop an uncomfortable sense that the data counted for rather more than the young people. Accordingly, for the range of political, sociological and ethical reasons alluded to already, we have been especially concerned to develop an approach that takes the perspectives and opinions of the young people themselves seriously in an effort to understand their choices and behaviour. We have insisted upon such an approach with the young people with whom we have worked as a matter of principle in our empirical research, as will be seen in subsequent chapters.

A critique of the New Youth Justice: theoretical foundations

Our theoretical orientation towards the changes in youth justice after 1997 draw upon a number of related themes. These include, following Foucault (1977, 1990), the work of the 'governmentality' school (Rose 1989, 1999 2000; Crawford 1997; Dean 1999; Flint 2002; Stenson and Edwards 2003; Armstrong 2004) and those commentators outlining the increasingly 'actuarial' orientation of juvenile justice processes (Feeley and Simon 1992, 1994; Kempf-Leonard and Peterson 2002). At the same time, in the development of New Labour's youth justice strategy and especially in the introduction of ASBOs and ABCs, Parenting and Curfew Orders, ISSPs and new powers to the police to break up supposedly intimidating congregations of young people there are some important illustrations of Cohen's 'dispersal of discipline' thesis (Cohen 1985) upon which we will also draw. Finally, again consistent with the critical traditions already identified, we ally our critique with the earlier work of Squires (1990) and Carlen (1996) in drawing attention to the 'anti-social' features of social and public policy, the 'demonisation' of young people (Stephen, forthcoming) and the increasing 'criminalisation' of social policy identified by authors such as Crawford (1997), Muncie (1999a) and Stenson (2000). In developing these latter themes as part of our commentary on contemporary youth justice we particularly have in mind a critique of the 'contractual' or 'exchange' ('something for something') model of citizenship articulated by New Labour – especially perhaps in its *Respect and Responsibility* White Paper of 2003 (Home Office 2003a). While this White Paper outlined the rationale for the expansion of ASB enforcement in what became the 2003 ASB Act, we question the extent to which the 'responsibilisation' strategy it embodied can be meaningfully extended to young people while, in the same vein, questioning the appropriateness of the abolition of the presumption of *doli incapax* (the effective lowering of the age of criminal responsibility).

The particular themes and issues we draw from this range of relatively recent theorising in respect of criminal justice systems include the following. At the most general level (though with some very specific implications) the argument is that, gathering momentum over the past two decades, there has been a significant change of emphasis within criminal justice systems. For example, the singling out of ASB as opposed to 'crime' as a focus for enforcement (and prevention) efforts indicates the arrival of a new priority. Moreover, anti-social behaviour has not replaced crime. Tackling ASB is not an alternative to preventing crime – it is, rather, an additional objective. ASB is, in different accounts, either a precursor to crime and a criminal career or a fellow traveller of crime (the other objectionable things that criminals do). Or, in a different sense, ASB represents an enforcement opportunity. In any event it marks a formal extension of the range of action of the criminal justice (CJ) system. In a further sense the CJ controls are extended still further by virtue of becoming also the responsibility of crime and disorder reduction partners: local authorities, social housing agencies, schools, social services departments, probation services and so on (this process being an aspect of the 'criminalisation' of social policy referred to earlier). Likewise, in Cohen's terms, this extension of control responsibilities to other agencies and organisations represents a central feature of his 'dispersal of discipline' thesis (Cohen 1985).

At a further remove, in the case of Acceptable Behaviour Contracts or Referral Orders criminal justice disciplining is delegated still further on the basis of a questionable notion of 'contract' (Wonnacott 1999) to families, members of local communities or even young people themselves. Proposals announced by the Home Office in July 2004 (Home Office 2004d) even extend an enforcement prerogative to community panels. Commentators have referred to these developments as aspects of a wider strategy of 'responsibilisation' (Rose 1989, 2000; O'Malley 1992; Crawford 1997; Garland 2001; McLaughlin 2002) in which disciplined subjects are required to assume a greater responsibility for managing their own behaviour. Such self-disciplining is directly anticipated in Foucault's account of the emerging forms of modern penality (1977) and Donzelot's account of the policing of families (1979).

A related issue forming part of the new theoretical landscape, again well represented by the recent rediscovery of and preoccupation with ASB, concerns what might be called the 'blurring' of criminal justice objectives or the emergence of a range of more flexible and relative (often politically or managerially determined) goals for criminal justice agencies. Here there is both a generic issue and a series of more specific instances. In regard to the former, a major question concerns the claim advanced by a number of critics (Muncie 1999b; Jones 2001b) to the effect that in contemporary youth justice, 'justice' itself, as a policy goal, has lately come to be compromised (or even overwhelmed) by a concentration upon 'order maintenance', 'risk management' or administrative efficiency. As Kempf-Leonard and Peterson put it, when describing the impact of managerial and actuarial techniques on contemporary systems of youth justice, 'actuarial justice presents a theoretical model of criminal justice processing in which the pursuit of efficiency and techniques that streamline case processing and offender supervision replace traditional goals of rehabilitation, punishment, deterrence and incapacitation ... *Justice*, however conceived, is not imperative' (Kempf-Leonard and Peterson 2002: 67, emphasis in original). Instead of justice, the criminal justice system has become driven by performance indicators. Garland develops a similar point. Increasingly, he argues, criminal justice agencies

seek to be evaluated by reference to internal goals over which they have near total control rather than by reference to social goals such as reducing crime rates, catching criminals or reforming inmates, which involve too many contingencies and uncertainties. The new performance indicators are designed to measure 'outputs' rather than 'outcomes, what the organisation does, rather than what, if anything, it achieves'. (Garland 2001: 119–20)

There are inevitably limits to the extent to which the new criminal justice agencies can detach their performance from the broader governmental objectives of criminal justice policy; after all the 1998 Crime and Disorder Act inaugurated a crime *reduction* strategy, and the declared overall objective of the changes to youth justice was to reduce youth offending. Furthermore, politicians, Tony Blair in particular, undoubtedly want people to *perceive* a difference in crime levels as a result of the policies adopted by government.

Of course, perceptions about levels of crime and disorder and actual rates of offending may not be the same thing at all. Commentators (Mawby and Walklate 1994; Goodey 2005) have previously drawn attention to the supposed lack of fit between the risk of criminal victimisation and the fear of crime (especially for certain groups). The issue begs the entire question of whether there is any normal or proportionate relationship between the two. Posing such questions raises the issue that the recent problematisation of ASB and the return to 'visible reassurance' systems of policing to address it (including the deployment of community support officers and neighbourhood wardens) forms part of a wider strategy to assuage people's perceptions of ASB and disorder by virtue of the fact that such incidents by their very frequency and immediacy impact upon more people than 'serious crime'. While such a 'looking after the pennies' approach to order maintenance may well bring crime reduction benefits as well, this may not be its primary purpose.

Further elements of this 'dispersal' of discipline and the expansion of criminal justice jurisdiction into new areas can also be discerned in the many aspects of 'new' actuarial penology incorporated in the new youth justice. Foremost among these would be what we might term the new 'pre-crime' intervention options now available such as the ABC and ASBO themselves, the reprimands and final warnings, the semi-formalised Referral Panels and the new 'Dispersal Order' powers to be made available to police. This new range of intervention and enforcement opportunities not only establishes a graduated continuum of discipline measures but, in addition, with the abolition of the *doli incapax* presumption (the rebuttable presumption that young people under the age of 14 were incapable of forming the required guilty intent underpinning criminal responsibility) these discipline measures become available far earlier for younger children and more marginal transgressions (Crofts 2002).

In a related sense, ease of enforcement and the lowering of evidential requirements appear to be important aspects of what attracts enforcement agencies to the ASBO (Ashworth *et al*. 1998). Following the 2002 Police Reform Act and the availability of ASBOs 'on conviction', the utility of the ASBO in applying additional levels of enforcement and heavier criminal sanctions (although, importantly, extending the purpose of the order beyond its earlier declared remit) may increase its appeal to enforcement authorities. Earlier, as Burney has noted (Burney 2002), the number of orders sought and obtained initially fell well below government expectations, Home Secretaries Jack Straw and David Blunkett each in their turn urged CDRPs to make greater use of ASBOs. During the Summer of 2004, it was announced that 'ASBO Ambassadors' would be despatched to those areas deemed not to be making sufficient use of the orders (Squires 2005). However, the significance of the ASBO in relation to 'actuarial justice', flexible enforcement options and 'discipline dispersal, is not confined to the reduced evidential thresholds required of civil justice as we have described in Chapter 1, it goes right to the heart of the definition of ASB itself. As Brown has argued, in place of a relatively well understood and (in theory at least) evidentially precise definition of crime, ASB introduces 'a rule so vague almost anything could break it' (Brown 2004: 205). Furthermore, an illusion is maintained that ASB is something new, a unique problem of the unacceptable behaviour of wayward youth in our late modernity – rather than an enduring problem of adolescence. New and special measures are required because an 'enforcement deficit' has been identified in our crime and disorder plans.

A telling illustration of the individualised and behaviourist interpret-ation of ASB can be found in Campbell's 2002 review of ASBOs for the Home Office Research Department. The supposed 'enforcement deficit' to which the ASBO was construed as a solution was said to be the limitations of existing police responses and youth justice interventions which conferred a sense of impunity on juvenile offenders. Campbell's commentary recycles precisely this idea about juvenile impunity (and the supposed licence it gave to youthful troublemakers) noting that, before 1999, the available legislation could not 'be used to deal with the behaviour of juveniles, who were therefore able to commit their anti-social behaviour in the full knowledge that there were few criminal sanctions that could touch them.' And, completing the picture, she continued, 'this situation can often cause local frustrations, as juveniles are often perceived as the cause of many anti-social behaviour problems, and anti-social behaviour is often used as a synonym for problems with young people' (Campbell 2002: 2).

Finally, the fact that much of the 'pre-criminal' risk assessment, profiling and targeting is now undertaken by agencies falling outside the traditional criminal justice system illustrates to some degree the emergence of the 'seamless web of discipline' anticipated by Cohen in 1985. The particular role here of New Deal for Communities projects is also worthy of consideration. Established in the most deprived and dis-advantaged areas to tackle problems of social exclusion, the rationale behind the projects clearly acknowledged the ways in which persistent problems of crime and disorder could compound and exacerbate the difficulties faced by such communities (Social Exclusion Unit 1998). In this sense, tackling crime and disorder was always an inseparable priority for New Deal projects and, in order to deliver upon this priority, the projects established their own multi-agency community safety teams to address these issues. In effect, therefore, in a broader sense, the New Deal teams established a kind of *a priori* area-based targeting of the usual suspects in the poorest areas – a first tier of the disciplinary continuum.

As we have argued earlier (Chapter 2), the identification of chronically crime-prone areas has a long history. More recently, realist criminology's renewed attention to communities and to victims has refocused political attention on these high and rising crime areas with the result that in selected areas, therefore, new forms of enforcement intervention have increased the likelihood that a range of 'target' behaviours and activities will be identified, reported and recorded. The New Deal initiatives after 1998 have reinforced this trend and, what is more, as we show later, with their own enforcement and performance targets to meet, they have further institutionalised this pre-emptive targeting of the crimes and disorders of selected people in selected areas through initiatives such as 'acceptable behaviour' contracts and 'youth inclusion' projects. As the 2004 BCS analysis itself shows, people living in such areas do appear to be significantly more sensitised to crime, disorder and anti-social behaviour issues (Thorpe and Wood 2004).

Cavadino and Dignan (1997) have described a surprisingly similar process of problem definition occurring in official accounts of the origins of control and disorder problems within prison establishments. According to Cavadino and Dignan, conventional accounts typically look largely to the interior of the prison, placing often especial focus upon what they refer to as the 'toxic mix' of prisoners which sparks an underlying crisis. It often appears not to matter especially which combination of offenders creates the supposed 'toxic mix' (an imbalance of young or old prisoners, long- or short-sentence inmates, or racist, drug dependent or politically motivated inmates) for the real issue concerns the fact that, in combination, they provoke a particular crisis of order and control within the prison establishment. The point is that in many conventional and managerialist discussions of anti-social behaviour, similar 'toxic mix' arguments appear to prevail. ASB problems are attributed to the characteristics of the particular families, groups and individuals who live in a given set of neighbourhoods (for example, Campbell's (2002a) discussion of the wilful youthful troublemakers committing criminal and disorderly acts with apparent impunity, referred to earlier).

Just as Cavadino and Dignan attempted to construct an alternative account of prison disorders drawing upon wider social, economic and ideological factors lying beyond the walls of the prison, so our understanding of ASB has to encompass the wider contextual factors, social forces and urban processes generating the particular problems and the ways these are perceived and intervened upon in selected environments. Part of this critical reinterpretation of the social construction of ASB has to examine the relationship between what has earlier been called 'anti-social policy' (Squires 1990), what Carlen (1996) has termed 'anti-social control' and what is now known as 'anti-social behaviour'. In developing this point we need to develop a wider analysis of contemporary concerns about youth, moving beyond immediate manifestations of ASB, youth crime and disorder, in order to better appreciate the contexts and cultures in which these emerge (or are identified), the social relationships they are said to threaten and the prevailing discourses – the law, citizenship, social justice and governance – within which these issues are framed.

Respect, responsibility and social control

For Carlen, as indeed for New Labour, the exercise of social control is related directly to contractual notions of citizenship. For New Labour in particular such a contract and the 'responsibilisation' strategy we have referred to earlier was precisely articulated in the White Paper *Respect and Responsibility – Taking a Stand Against Anti-Social behaviour* (Home Office, 2003a) which preceded the 2003 Anti-Social Behaviour Act. The Ministerial Foreword to the White Paper spelled out a broad conception of responsible inclusive citizenship. The government clearly aspires to a deeper philosophical justification of its youth justice and anti-social behaviour strategies and, in commenting upon them, we must necessarily address this.

> Our aim is a 'something for something' society where we treat one another with respect and where we all share responsibility for taking a stand against what is unacceptable. But some people and some families undermine this. The anti-social behaviour of a few, damages the lives of many. (Home Office 2003a: Ministerial Foreword)

This is an idea that is not always consistently applied with young people in mind. Edwards and Hatch (2003) are certainly not the only commentators to discern some confusingly mixed messages in the way that contemporary social and public policies engage with young people. At times, they argue, young people 'are depicted as vulnerable and in desperate need of protection and at other times they are characterised as thugs and potential thugs whose actions infringe on the rest of the community' (p. 5). What Edwards and Hatch term the 'mixed messages' relating to youth are seen in a more critical light by other commentators (e.g. Worpole 2002). R. Smith (2003), for instance, also complains about what he sees as an essentially managerial and enforcement-driven attempt to discipline youth where 'containment' and, in some cases, 'treatment' are prioritised over and above the broader social and welfare needs of young people. Likewise, as Goldson has noted, the new arrangements for youth justice appeared to treat young people in trouble as offenders first and children second (Goldson 2000b). This is a point reiterated by Walsh with her argument, entirely consistent with our view of ASB, that 'the Government's youth justice policy is more concerned with maintaining order within the community than with the welfare of the child' (Walsh 1999: 138).

Nonetheless, it is to this contractual theme – something for young people – that we now turn in order to cast some light upon the level and nature of social provision for young people. We need to consider the contexts in which they are allowed to develop in order to help understand the competing perceptions placed upon their behaviour. To begin with, available research suggests that 'provision for teenagers can be patchy, unreliable and inconsistent' (Edwards and Hatch 2003). A MORI survey in 2002 found that adult respondents consistently prioritised more 'activities for teenagers' as the major need in their area, a finding repeated in the 2002–3 Survey of English Housing (MORI 2002; ODPM 2003). In many respects, services and provisions for young people have come to be associated with crime prevention or 'diversion' activities rather than as forms of service delivery that are important in their own right. This more selective targeting of youth services can have consequences for the take-up of such opportunities. Even so 'modern youth clubs that combine activity with support and advice are in short supply [and] no national strategy is in place to revive the often tired and out-of-date centres that are currently available' (Edwards and Hatch 2003: 6). Hallsworth, drawing upon evidence from youth services support in one (unnamed) London Borough notes:

> Like many boroughs in London, the state of the youth service in the borough and, not least, its contribution to community safety effort remains questionable. It is certainly not able in its current form to actively perform the crime prevention role … There are a number of reasons … first … the idea of a youth service organised around the comprehensive provision of youth clubs has been questioned and abandoned. Second, this questioning has moved hand in hand with a series of sustained budget cuts that have literally decimated the forms of provision the council did operate or support. Third, in the face of financial retrenchment, the local state has responded by effectively off-loading responsibility for youth provision onto a voluntary sector, ill-equipped to undertake the infrastructural support role now being foisted upon it. Fourth, given access to inherently limited and precarious funding regimes, those seeking to work productively with young people are forced to engage in what amounts to a series of ugly beauty competitions with each other in order to sustain often minimal funding for their activities. (Hallsworth 2002: 207)

Not surprisingly then, according to Worpole, 'two thirds of 9–11 year olds in the UK are dissatisfied with the quality of outdoor play facilities where they live. For 15–16 year olds this rose to 81%, higher than any other European country' (Worpole 2002). He connects this perception with a wider critique of the quality of parks and public environments in many – especially urban – areas. 'Neglected and unattractive environments not only send messages to people that their quality of life does not count very much … they can also be breeding grounds for vandalism and anti-social behaviour especially amongst children and young people' (ibid.). An important corollary of this he omits to mention, however, is that the fact that such environments are precisely the contexts in which fear and intolerance (especially of young people) appear to be magnified. As we have already seen in work by Finney (2004), and Thorpe and Wood's (2004) analysis of the 2003–3 BCS data, an apparent lack of guardianship over public space, a build-up of litter, of vandalism or signs of neighbourhood decline, low estimations of or perceived inadequacies in local service delivery and criminal justice system effectiveness all appear to promote a set of fears and concerns centring upon the behaviour and activities of children and young people. If a key feature of Worpole's argument is that 'good quality public space is vital to the health and emotional well-being of children and young people' (p. 3), then it is also pretty clear that it is no less important for adults and older people.

In 2002 a UNESCO funded project 'Growing Up in an Urbanised World' identified the kinds of social and spatial requirements necessary to enable children and young people to learn and develop in a positive and rounded fashion. These comprised:

- a sense of integration and acceptance within communities;
- varied and interesting activity settings;
- peer gathering places;
- a sense of safety and freedom of movement;
- cohesive community identities;
- green areas for informal play and exploration as well as organised sports.

On the other hand, there was another range of factors which impinged heavily upon children and young people's sense of freedom and opportunity and, in turn, their ability to grow and develop within their communities. These included:

- a sense of social exclusion and stigma;
- boredom: a sense of 'nothing to do, nowhere to go';
- fear of crime, intimidation, bullying or harassment;
- heavy traffic;
- an untidy and neglected environment, uncollected rubbish and litter. (Chawla 2001).

The argument from the research reiterates a view that, where the form and nature of local environments fail to respect the social and developmental needs of children and young people then it is hardly reasonable to demand responsibility from those forced to inhabit such unsatisfactory environments. In a direct sense, young people are not, themselves, responsible for the shortcomings of their environments and, in a wider sense, the adjustments they might have to make in such environments (or their 'delinquent solutions' to adopt Downes's (1966) concept) need to be understood in this light. The *Respect and Responsibility* White Paper promised 'something for something' but, while it demands respect and insists on responsibility, its *quid pro quo* chiefly consists in the withholding of disciplinary or enforcement interventions rather than the distribution of tangible benefits or support.

In many respects this discussion of children and young people's rights and opportunities takes us close to Carlen's notion of 'anti-social control' (Carlen 1996, but see also Squires 1990). Both Carlen and Squires connect the premise of free and equal citizenship subsequently adopted by New Labour and which underpins the *Respect and Responsibility* White Paper with the liberal ideological tradition of 'social contract'. In this tradition, according to Doyal and Gough, citizens conform to the legal order of the state and, in return, they have a right to expect the state will protect their lives and property. In democratic societies the state agencies are themselves expected to be subject to due legal process. In welfare states, moreover, an expectation has also been raised that citizens will receive 'minimal need satisfaction' (Doyal and Gough 1991: 92). In this way a moral reciprocity is set up – as the White Paper puts it, 'something for something.' However, as Doyal and Gough continue, in such a culture, 'it must follow that a precondition for blaming anyone ... for acting immorally and expecting them to do better in the future is respecting their right to the minimum level of need-satisfaction to enable them to do so' (Doyal and Gough,1991: 96). Employing this critique, Carlen's objective is to reveal how, during the 1980s and 1990s, 'the British state failed to meet the minimum needs of increasing numbers of young citizens at the same time as targeting them for receipt of tighter disciplinary controls and even harsher punishments' (Carlen 1996).

Furthermore, she continued:

> Instead of a moral reciprocity of citizen rights, there is an asymmetry of citizenship, with young people being punished for not fulfilling their citizenship obligations even though the state fails to fulfil its duties of nurturance and protection towards them ... Citizens forced to pay their penal dues without receiving any citizen dividends are likely to experience many state controls as anti-social and therefore illegitimate. For, whereas legitimate social control is comprised of a variety of benign institutionalized practices designed to set limits to individual action in the interests of the collectivity's ideals (as instanced in law and dominant ideologies), anti-social controls set

limits to individual action by exploiting asymmetries of citizenship and thereby atrophying the subjugated citizenry's social contribution even more. (Carlen 1996)

It may not be a great leap of imagination from 'anti-social control' or 'anti-social' public policy to anti-social behaviour. The former are, perhaps, the seedbed for the latter. If Chawla's (2002) analysis of the social environments in which the optimum conditions for the growth and development of children and young people is correct, and the indications drawn from the 2002–3 BCS are accurate, we not only deprive children and young people of the spaces and opportunities they need, we also engineer the situations in which adults are the least able, or least willing, to cope with or tolerate them.

Reeves (2003) has also described the detachment of broader society from responsibilities towards children. Instead the role is being ever more privatised onto parents alone – until such time as they may fail. 'Raising children is being privatised into the hands of their parents; it is seen as a job only for them, not for all of us. This erosion of collective responsibility for children represents perhaps the greatest threat of all to our hopes for a space for childhood' (Reeves, 2003: 18–19).

Symptomatic of this broader failure in our conceptions of supporting children and young people is the fact that public support for parents tends to be only available in certain types of areas and in certain types of ways. These tend to be the poorest and most disadvantaged areas and the most problematic or least competent of parents. As Edwards and Hatch remark, 'there is real danger that state intervention in parenting is only considered appropriate and necessary for those who live in such areas rather than being seen as a universally needed and available resource' (p. 51). Furthermore, it is support which is needed, not just punitive stigmatising and disciplinary enforcement action such as fixed penalty notices, compulsory 'Parenting Orders' or 'Acceptable Behaviour Contracts' which threaten the entire household with eviction or similar consequences. As these authors argue, support for parenting and for children and young people has to amount to substantially more than sticks with which to beat them after their failings have become apparent. In many cases, as our recent research has suggested, if many of the resources devoted to after-the-event enforcement were instead deployed earlier in support, many of the worst anti-social and disorder problems might have been avoided to begin with (Stephen and Squires 2003a).

Respect and responsibility is a two-way street – it cannot be demanded of children (or of adults too for that matter) who have not the wherewithal or the opportunities to demonstrate responsibility. Childhood and adolescence are steep learning curves – it is unreasonable to expect responsibility and to withhold respect from young people who have had neither the opportunity nor the means to learn or earn either. The sharply contrasting images of youth we have considered so far also reflect the ways in which young people become disengaged from local policy-making processes.

> Young people tend to feel on the peripheries of decision-making and the receivers rather than the shapers of services. At times their opinions and ideas are clearly at odds with those of local service providers. The most obvious example is the mismatch between young people's accounts of their behaviour and the way that they felt that the police respond to anti-social behaviour such as street drinking and gathering in groups. (Edwards and Hatch 2003: 52)

The authors go on to argue for the creation of opportunities for more effective dialogue between such groups and 'the authorities'. This is not a new request and we have encountered similar arguments before (Measor and Squires 2000). Perhaps more fundamental than simple consultation, however, are questions about citizenship, community and inter-generational obligations. Our question is whether the seemingly contractual model of citizenship implied by the government's talk of a 'something for something' society is an appropriate basis upon which to model relationships with young people or from which to discern hard and fast definitions of anti-social behaviour.

On a number of dimensions, emotionally, intellectually, psychologically and certainly legally, youth – or adolescence – comprises a series of complex transitions between the statuses of child and adult. This process is not complete until maturity is attained and full adulthood achieved. This is a social, not biological nor chronological process through which different people will progress at different speeds and complete at different ages. Yet until this process is completed it seems clear that the broader community does owe some significant non-reciprocal obligations to its younger members (DfES 2003). However the 1998 Crime and Disorder legislation lowered the age of criminal responsibility to ten years (barring Ireland, the lowest in Europe and contrary to the UN Beijing charter).

Unfortunately, the principle of equal criminal responsibility is fundamentally out of kilter with more widely accepted contemporary notions of child growth, development and maturation. Youth is a time to learn, to develop, to make choices, to become socialised and, inevitably, to make mistakes without having these condemn one for life (Christie 2004). In other European legal cultures this learning and developmental approach to youth, youth as a developmental space, is more explicitly recognised in youth and criminal justice policies (Crofts 2002). For other writers, this recognition of youth developmental needs has to be underpinned by further investments at the level of the environment and social ecology. For instance, Katz (1998) has argued that 'young people's growth and development depends upon environments that provide stimulation, allow autonomy, offer possibilities for exploration, and promote independent learning and peer group socialising. These criteria are important in all settings, not just those designed specifically for teens such as schools, leisure environments and teen centres' (p. 141).

To return to our point of departure in this discussion, a brief summary of the developing argument suggests itself. Before we come to dwell too closely upon the allegedly 'toxic' behaviours of 'neighbours from hell', 'mindless hooligans', lager louts, vandals and (supposedly) 'feral' children in the marginal communities, depressed areas and disadvantaged housing estates of contemporary Britain, perhaps we should attempt to understand how these 'toxic' or 'anti-social' contexts came to be created in the first place. Of course, to understand contexts and causes is not to exonerate all resulting behaviour: people still have choices and not everyone makes those that are criminal or anti-social. But, above all, we should not be too surprised to find people making 'anti-social' choices in 'anti-social', unpleasant, excluding or oppressive environments. Children and young people, after all, did not create the environments in which they are forced to live. In later chapters we argue that this fairly obvious fact needs to influence both our interpretations of the behaviour and choices of young people and be reflected in the policies adopted for tackling youth-related problems. Before turning to these issues, however, we need to draw together our critique of the contemporary youth justice system.

The dispersal of social control

The third major theoretical influence upon our critique of contemporary youth justice and ASB enforcement activity concerns the work of Stan Cohen (1985). In many ways, New Labour's efforts to impose a strategy of 'responsibilisation' upon those considered disorderly and 'anti-social' corresponds closely to Cohen's account of the 'destructuring movements' occurring within criminal justice systems from the late 1960s. For Cohen, these 'destructuring movements' amounted to 'master transformations' of entire systems of western criminal justice, akin to the institution-building and 'great incarcerations' described by Foucault (1967) or Garland (1985) regarding earlier phases of penal history. The change processes described by Cohen included decarceration, diversion, decategorisation, delegalisation and deprofessionalisation, all of which underlay a new conception of decentralised community control. The argument is not that these changes were uniformly or smoothly accomplished, nor even that there have not been partial reversals and changes of direction, but simply that, from the late 1960s onwards, a number of trends were set in motion that have begun to reshape the practice, promise and performance of criminal justice systems. The changes are closely bound up with a number of the issues we have referred to already: the increasingly managerialist ethos of criminal justice policy, the growing consumerist orientation to criminal justice services and, connecting to both, the rise of actuarialism (risk assessment and management) in criminal justice strategies, all of which have been commented upon by the 'governmentality' writers referred to already. Our argument is that so many of these changing characteristics of contemporary criminal justice, perhaps none more so than Cohen's depiction of the dispersal of discipline, are embodied in Britain's new Youth Justice policies. In this regard, some might consider it deeply ironic that a decade (the 1960s) that politicians (e.g. Blair 2004) are prone to castigate as the source of many of our current problems is itself, on another reading, the watershed for an equivalent range of 'post-liberal' criminal justice interventions that these same politicians, despite their aversion to the consequences of that significant decade, have little hesitation in employing in pursuit of law and order.

A starting point for Cohen was the fact that the new forms of discipline were not solutions for the emerging problems of criminal justice nor alternatives to existing largely punitive measures. On the contrary, any new measures seldom replaced anything, they were largely an addition to what preceded them offering new control, discipline or management opportunities or intervention rationales. Above all, he argued, any new measures were best seen as further symptoms of the wider crisis of criminal justice (Cohen 1985: 35–9).

Cohen spelt out, in 1985, a series of key developments underpinning the changes in criminal justice he was then considering and, in our following commentary, we review these in turn, indicating how they relate, often very directly, to new youth justice strategies. Following this we turn to consider a range of further developments in the 'dispersal of discipline' before concluding by discussing some key features of contemporary youth justice policy, illustrating the critique by reference to evidence from our research and evaluation of a number of local youth justice projects.

I. Reforms and alternatives have been supported for non-progressive reasons

In 1985, Cohen's first issue was more directly concerned with a critique of decarceration, substantially associated with the work of Scull (1977), in which so-called 'community alternatives' to custody were encouraged and supported, not for any intrinsic merits (for instance that they might be any more humane or effective) but simply because they were confidently expected to be cheaper. By way of fairly direct comparison, it will be recalled that it was, after all, the Audit Commission report of 1996, *Misspent Youth*, which largely began the process culminating in the new youth justice strategy after 1998. The Commission's originating concern was that so much (over one billion pounds) was being spent on managing the youth justice problem but to so little apparent overall effect. The subsequent reforms, therefore, were driven by a concern for efficiency – rather than justice, or the welfare of young people 'at risk'. In any event, as Jones has effectively demonstrated, many of the judgements reached by the Audit Commission do not stand up to rigorous examination. He cites examples of the selective use of evidence, the cavalier use of crime statistics, a lack of understanding of youth justice processes, confusion over average and marginal costs, judgements arrived at not based upon sufficient evidence and conclusions and recommendations which were 'more political than actuarial' (Jones 2001a: 378).

Most telling of all, however, concerns what Jones has called the 'undercurrent of objectification and dehumanisation of young people' to be found throughout the reports. A far cry from 'progressive reasons' for youth justice reforms, such attitudes reflect the 'punitive populism' and 'soundbite politics' that commentators have identified elsewhere in new youth justice reforms (Muncie 1999, 2000a; Pitts 2000; Smith, R. 2003). A case in point here would be the particular focus upon 'fast-tracking' (avoiding delays and speeding up the process of prosecution) to be found in the Audit Commission Report and the subsequent White Paper, *No More Excuses* (Home Office 1997a). While the familiar adage that 'justice delayed is justice denied' might underpin a general case for avoiding unnecessary delays in prosecuting young people it is difficult in such instances to see the young people in question as the real recipients of the justice on offer. What fast-tracking actually amounts to is quicker punishment. The White Paper makes it clear (para. 7.2, page 23) fast-tracking is important for victims, for ensuring the law does not fall into disrepute and for the sake of the efficiency of the criminal justice system itself (reducing the risk of further offences being committed while on bail), but not for the young offender. The White Paper made the point that, delays in prosecution postpone the opportunity to commence inter-ventions to address a young person's offending behaviour. Yet when such 'opportunities' arise only on a finding of guilt, we might have grounds to question the streamlining of due process to achieve 'guilt' more quickly. Perhaps a finding of 'guilt' alone ought not to be the sole arbiter of whether young people 'at risk' (of offending) receive appropriate support. In fact, even in a youth justice system now more oriented around punishment than welfare and support, it is not the case that supportive interventions have to await a guilty verdict, New Labour's youth justice strategy also involved the introduction of a range of bail support and remand management projects. Justice delayed may be justice denied but, equally, perhaps social justice should not have to wait upon criminal justice. Or, in the terms of the government's own 'rights and responsibility' discourse, in the case of children and young people especially, the right to welfare and support ought not to wait upon punishment. This brings us to Cohen's second issue.

2. Alternatives have been co-opted and absorbed

A central criticism of the 'dispersal of discipline' argument has been the fact that supposed 'alternatives' to custody, or to punishment, have seldom functioned as alternatives but have instead become additional forms of discipline and control, applied to a rather larger population and working to filter people into the wider social control system rather than divert them from it – in other words, a classic case of net-widening (Austin and Krisberg 1981). Such net-widening is often treated as the dominant characteristic of the 'destructuration' process described by Cohen. Concluding our discussion of Cohen's first point (in the previous paragraph) it was clear that, even there, the issues were largely framed within the welfare/justice or treatment/punishment dualism that has long characterised this issue. Thus treatment (or diversion) is posed as an alternative to punishment and justified as more humane and constructive, but because it is delivered as a condition and consequence of a finding of guilt and, therefore, continues to serve the interests of the criminal justice system it is invariably experienced as a burden and an imposition by those subjected to it. Thus as 'welfare alternatives' are made to do the work of the criminal justice system and serve the purposes of punishment it is of little surprise that they come to resemble and be experienced as punishments.

As we discovered while undertaking an evaluation of a Detention and Training Order project for a local Youth Offending Team (YOT) and the YJB, young people clearly resented the 'community' training elements of the orders. In a fairly typical comment, one young man we interviewed put it this way:

> This is all bollocks, why do we have to do this, it's not fair. We did our time, and that ... but why do we have to do this crap as well?

The 'crap' referred to involved an education and training project addressing numeracy and literacy needs and providing basic computing skills. The programme appeared to be resented by many of those required to undertake it. During their time in custody, the education classes were appreciated as an opportunity to get out of their cells. After custody education and training were perceived as a burden, the young people's resentment growing when they discovered that the training classes followed because they were part of an evaluation project. In their eyes, education and training had become part of the punishment; in the eyes of the court and the youth justice planners it had become part of a sentence. The supposed 'alternative' had become absorbed.

The Detention and Training Order is far from being the only instance of 'alternatives' subverted by the discipline process. In a much broader sense the 'toughening up' of community penalties in the wake of the 1991 Criminal Justice Act, particularly the attachment of more stringent breach conditions to community orders (Raynor and Vanstone 2002), represents an underlying trend here. The problem is one of interventions which are almost inevitably destined to fail, and when they do, a return to punishment follows. As Haines and Drakeford have noted, 'highly interventionist programmes of treatment often do more harm than good ... because once a young person had tried and failed at treatment, then punishment was the inevitable outcome of further criminal justice involvement' (Haines and Drakeford 1999: 42).

In the case of the New Youth Justice system, the replacement of the police practice of cautioning a significant number of (first-time or less serious) young offenders (thereby diverting them from formal criminal justice processing) by the introduction of reprimands and final warnings also embodies Cohen's point.

Even so, well before the early 1990s, a debate had grown up surrounding the question of whether the police cautioning of juveniles really amounted to 'diversion' (Farrington and Bennett 1981; Goldson 2000b). Because the administration of a caution effectively involves the police acting in the roles of 'investigator, prosecutor, judge and jury' and, acknowledging that the police may be 'poor judges of the quality of their own evidence' (Bell 1999: 202), a question often arises as to whether the evidence sustaining the caution would have been sufficient to support a prosecution or whether the caution is seen as a simple and quick low-cost resolution acceptable, though for different reasons, to parents, police and young person alike. Yet, low-cost is not the same as no-cost and, however compelling the pressure to 'own up, and get it over with' by a caution rather than run the risk of a prosecution, a criminal record is still created – especially with the formalisation of cautioning during the 1980s (Smith 2003). In a national evaluation of final warning projects for the YJB, researchers found evidence that despite police officers' assurances that the guidance was clear, well understood and adhered to, that guilt must be admitted before a caution could be given, in fact some 'admissions of guilt could be contentious'. In three cases young offenders denied admitting offences to the police and in another case 'the offender and his parents traded an admission of guilt to escape a risky and stressful appearance in court' (Holdaway and Desborough 2004: 19).

During the 1980s and early 1990s, while the police and youth justice practitioners (firmly supported by the Home Office) continued to operate a fairly liberal and flexible approach to cautioning, effectively diverting a large number of young offenders from formal criminal justice processing, court appearances and custody, the practice was largely regarded by practitioners and academics alike as tolerant, progressive and fairly benign (Rutherford 1992; Bateman 2003). Home Office Circulars (14/1985 and 59/1990) firmly endorsed and promoted the practice of cautioning and as recently as 1993, most young offenders, 90 per cent of boys and 97 per cent of girls, were diverted by formal and informal cautions (Goldson 2000b). Butler and Drakeford went so far as to describe youth cautioning as 'the one demonstrable success of youth justice in the United Kingdom since the war' (1997: 218). For Smith it was the paradox that was of particular note: the Thatcher government, 'an ostensibly right wing and authoritarian government [had] presided over one of the most benign and liberal periods ever witnessed in the history of youth justice' (Smith, R. 2003: 2).

However, in the increasingly punitive climate developing after 1993, the year in which 2-year-old James Bulger was abducted and murdered by two pre-adolescent boys, cautioning came to attract growing criticism. It was said to be too lenient or was said to have little impact upon a growing 'yob culture' (creating, it was claimed, an impression of juvenile impunity). Singer describes a parallel process of 'recriminalizing delinquency' occurring within the New York juvenile justice system (Singer 1996). In due course the practice of repeat cautioning was effectively abolished (in 1994) in England and Wales (Smith, R. 2003: 33, 47 192). And later, at the Labour Party conference in 1997, the new Home Secretary, Jack Straw, criticised the diversion approach which had underpinned youth justice policy and practice during the postwar era as one of 'endless cautions and no action' grounded upon a fantasy that 'they will grow out of it' (Brownlee 1998). Furthermore, the informalism of cautioning gave rise to complaints about discriminatory decision-making and inconsistency (Pitts 1990; Evans and Ellis 1997; Reid 1997; Goldson and Chigwada-Bailey 1999). At a time when victims' rights were in the ascendancy, diversion was said to neglect victims (Davis *et al.* 1989) and, in certain cases, it was also said to represent a missed opportunity to make some potentially decisive intervention in the life of a child or young person 'at risk'. To fill this supposed gap, projects referred to as 'Caution Plus' began to appear. These were championed in particular by the Chief

Constable of Thames Valley Police, Charles Pollard. They offered a programme of activities, sometimes incorporating elements of restorative justice, for young offenders having accepted a caution. Such programmes were rather more in tune with the broadly preventive orientation which was then gaining ground as a key criminal justice priority and supplanting the earlier, more offender-focused, policies. The police were a significant pressure for changing cautioning practice in another sense. Faulkner argues, for instance, that around 1993 'the police conducted a sophisticated and mostly successful campaign for more punitive action to be taken against persistent juvenile offenders' (Faulkner 2001: 122).

An impression was created that police action in respect of juveniles was especially time-consuming and largely a waste of resources when it resulted in nothing more than a caution: a proverbial 'slap on the wrist'. This was said to leave both victims and the police dissatisfied and de-motivated while allowing the 'yob element' to believe itself 'untouchable'. We have encountered this perception before, specifically regarding the supposed youth disorder 'enforcement deficit' to which the ASBO was construed as a solution. As we have already seen (Chapter 2), Campbell's (2002) analysis of the policing of ASB recycles exactly this idea about juvenile impunity (and the supposed licence it gave to youthful troublemakers).

Building upon this analysis of the problems associated with cautioning, the *No More Excuses* White Paper argued:

> The trouble with the current cautioning system is that ... too often it does not result in any follow-up action, so the opportunity is lost for any follow-up action to turn young offenders away from crime ... Inconsistent and ineffective cautioning has allowed some children and young people to feel they can offend with impunity. (Home Office 1997a, para. 5, pp. 10–12)

We will not, at this point, engage in the debate about the effectiveness, or not, of cautioning (for this, see our final chapter) except to note, in passing, Goldson's remark, having reviewed a range of the evidence, that New Labour's commitment to early intervention and its abolition of 'diversion approaches' (specifically cautioning) was 'at odds with established theory, research findings and practical experience' (Goldson 2000b: 42; Bateman 2003). In the event New Labour abolished cautioning, replacing it with a system of reprimands and final warnings. Whereas decisions about cautions had often been decided upon by an inter-agency panel, decisions about final warnings were to be solely a matter for the police. Aside from issues concerning whether the police, acting alone, were equipped to reach appropriate decisions in such cases, the Audit Commission reported, in

2004, that most police decision-makers had received no special training in final warning procedures (Audit Commission 2004). As Bell has suggested, the reduced discretion now available to decision-makers created a 'two strikes and you're in court' rule. 'The new system of reprimands and final warnings will lead to a significant increase in the number of children and young people appearing before the Youth Court, in many cases for alleged minor infringements of the criminal law' (Bell 1999: 203). And as Kemp *et al.* have reported, drawing upon their research findings:

> Prosecution at any stage has no beneficial effect in preventing reoffending. On the contrary prosecution seems likely to increase the likelihood of reoffending ... Erring on the side of informality in responding to youth offending seems both to reduce subsequent offending by young people who come into contact with youth justice officials and to keep associated intervention costs down. (Kemp *et al.* 2002: 4, 11)

The loss of discretion, the direct and intended consequence of a *final* warning scheme, acts to propel young people into court for prosecution earlier in their delinquent 'careers', there to undergo punishment. The government's consultation paper *Tackling Youth Crime*, published in 1997, had made this quite plain: 'If they ignore the warning and offend again, they can expect significant punishment from the courts' (Home Office 1997b: 5). The outcome of this, therefore, is that what appeared to a broad constituency of delinquency researchers, practitioners and commentators to be an effective diversionary alternative has, first, become subsumed within the broader criminal justice processing and, second, it has ultimately come to serve the purposes of punishment. As we have seen, whereas, informed by the social reaction and labelling perspectives, diversion was precisely intended to serve as a preventive measure, it is now the case that its precise opposite, early intervention, is promoted to achieve the very same purpose. As we have noted before, both *Misspent Youth* and *No More Excuses* claimed to be out to 'break the link' between anti-social behaviour and crime. Our argument to the contrary, in keeping with a wealth of research that is now dismissed and overlooked rather than disproven, is that these links are not being broken but reinforced. Early intervention serves to fashion criminal careers rather than terminate them. As West argued in 1982, 'processing delinquents thorough the juvenile justice system, especially if it involves any substantial period of detention within penal establishments, is more likely to exacerbate than reduce anti-social behaviour' (p. 143). More generally, echoing Cohen's (and before him Foucault's) original critique of the significance of supposed 'alternatives to punishment', Hudson has remarked that in whatever ways criminal justice policies might be considered to have failed, 'they have nonetheless succeeded in recruiting vast numbers of people into the crime/crime control "industry". Yet all this criminal justice was demonstrably ineffective ... becoming involved in official responses to crime could actually make continued career criminality more rather than less probable' (Hudson 1993: 38).

3. The old structures (prison, juvenile institutions, professional monopolies) still remain and their position and significance may even be strengthened

There are already indications that some of the central structures and institutions of youth justice have become vested with a new power and significance within the new youth justice. As we have seen, the police are confirmed as having primary responsibility for making initial decisions about reprimands and final warnings while the Detention and Training Order gives, ostensibly, renewed purpose and legitimacy to the institution of youth custody. In fact, in many ways, because youth custody still sits at the end point of the youth justice system, it continues to exert a symbolic influence beyond its strictly numerical impact, in the manner originally described by Foucault (1977), wherein 'all roads lead to prison'. But given the broader significance of custody within the youth justice system and the Youth Justice Board's declared ambition of ensuring that the system functioned as a consistent and coherent whole working to a common set of principles and standards, it was instructive, at least in the first year of the new youth justice projects, to find YOT workers describing Young Offender Institutions (YOI) as 'largely outside the loop' when it came to shared assumptions and partnership working. At meetings of a regional association of youth justice workers responsible for remand management or detention and training order projects, numerous instances were described in which YOI performance fell way below the expectations of the YOT workers. Information was often not passed on because communication relationships were poor. YOIs were often said to lack facilities to undertake meaningful education and training, appointments were cancelled at short notice (and sometimes only after YOT workers had already travelled long distances to meet with their clients) while adequate facilities for holding contact and assessment meetings with young people within YOIs were said to be rare or non-existent.

In truth the YJB were already aware of many of these deficiencies of the custodial arrangements for young people. A report by the YJB in 1998 on the *Juvenile Secure Estate* found

little positive to say about the present arrangements for providing secure accommodation for remanded and sentenced children and

young people. Regime standards are inconsistent and often poor...
there is no effective oversight or long-term planning ... Fundamental
change is needed if it is to meet the aim of providing accommodation
and regimes appropriate to the age and maturity of the young people
held in custody on remand and under sentence and which addresses
their offending behaviour and wider developmental needs. (YJB
1998: 7)

Only the year before, a thematic report on young prisoners from HM
Inspectorate of Prisons had broadly condemned the principle of holding
people under 18 in prison conditions. The report stated that prison
conditions fell well below the minimum standards required of social
services secure accommodation by the Children Act 1989 and the UN
Convention on the Rights of the Child (HMIP 1997: 6). The Report found
'no evidence that the Prison Service has acknowledged the Children Act
1989 as having any relevance to children held in Prison Service
establishments.' So, far from any spuriously confident rhetoric that 'Prison
Works', the Inspectorate Report found clear evidence – in high
reconviction rates, complaints and disorders, instances of bullying, self-
harming and psychological maladjustment – that 'if regimes are not needs
based and effective, custody can do more harm than good' (HMIP 1997:
12). Furthermore, the report concluded, pressures of overcrowding and
reduced operating budgets had lately tended to 'reduce those elements of
regimes which bring about positive change in young people' (ibid. 13).

Undoubtedly, the YJB is committed to exerting greater influence over
the Prison Service performance, partly through its responsibility for
providing overall management and direction of the 'juvenile secure estate'
but also through its role in commissioning and purchasing custodial places
for young persons on remand or sentenced to custody (Moore 2000;
National Audit Office 2004). As we have discovered, however, in a related
project on health promotion and youth custody, while it is possible for
outside agencies to 'lever in' some positive changes in respect of custodial
regime conditions and performance, the barriers to progress can still
appear immense (Squires and Measor 2001).

Nevertheless, during the second half of the 1990s, it was into these
custodial conditions, deemed so unacceptable by Prison Inspectors and
academic researchers alike, that an increasing number of young offenders
found their way. Rather like the rejection of diversion policies in respect of
young people's entry to the criminal justice process discussed earlier,
diversion from custody also appeared to succumb to the increasingly
punitive rhetoric of politicians, media and public alike (Moore 2000). The
establishment of the 'secure training order' in 1994 reflected this
increasingly punitive climate by effectively reintroducing imprisonment

for 12 year olds (Goldson 1999), although the first specialist 'secure training centre' was not actually opened until 1998 (under Labour). Two further centres have been opened and two more are planned. The overall number of 15–20 year olds given custodial sentences rose by 42 per cent between 1992 and 1998, with the incarceration rate for offenders in the youngest age range, 15–17 year olds, increasing most of all, by as much as 79 per cent. Most dramatic of all, the figure for the total number of 15–17 year olds in custody on 30 June 1999, compared with the corresponding date in 1993, showed a 122 per cent increase (Howard League 1999a, 1999b). According to evidence collated by the Home Office, the chief explanation for these increases in the number of young prisoners concerned the increasing frequency with which the courts were imposing custodial sentences and the increasing length of these sentences; it was not a reflection of larger numbers of young offenders appearing before the courts (White 1999).

Once the new Youth Justice arrangements began to operate the overall percentage of 15–17 year olds receiving custodial sentences appeared to stabilise at around 14–15 per cent but there was a doubling of the numbers of 10–14 year olds getting custody between 1999 and 2001 (Audit Commission 2004). For the most recent period for which Youth Justice Board data are available, the total youth custody population has remained fairly stable at around 3,300 to 3,500 (with around 6,000 to 7,000 custodial disposals a year), although the majority of these (just under two-thirds) are held on Detention and Training Orders and an overwhelming majority (around 85 per cent) are held in Young Offender Institutions (as opposed to secure training centres or secure local authority accommodation) where conditions are generally agreed to be worst and least capable of meeting the educational, support and welfare needs of young people (Youth Justice Board 2004; Audit Commission 2004).

Evidence from a variety of recent sources (for instance those drawn upon by the most recent Audit Commission Report) reveals a number of difficulties in drawing firm conclusions about the performance of the new Youth Justice system. These include, first, the difficulty, in a rapidly changing institutional field, with new arrangements and orders coming on stream at different times, of drawing clear conclusions about what the figures might tell us. This can be compounded by the different ways of compiling the data showing either the total custodial population (with or without custodial remands), annual custody sentencing rates and breakdowns of the figures by age, sentence type or institution type. For instance, during 2002 there was a sharp increase, peaking in August, of section 90–92 custodial sentencing, the most serious of custodial sentences, but which is all but obscured by the overall trends. The increase is attributed to the effects of the government's 'Street Crime' initiative and new sentencing guidance from the Lord Chief Justice on robbery offences (Audit Commission 2004).

A second difficulty relates to the very complexity of the institutional arrangements and multiple decision stages comprising the youth justice system itself. One aim of the YJB was undoubtedly to try to bring a greater consistency, unity of purpose and coherence to the disparate agencies making up the youth justice system. However, there is plenty of evidence in the recent reports of the Audit Commission and National Audit Office (NAO) that there is still some way to go on this: it represents more than just a question of unforeseen or unintended consequences. Indeed, even if the YJB were able to bring a greater unity and consistency of purpose to the overall working of the youth justice system there are grounds for wondering whether this would be a good thing. Given the political spotlight now shining upon youth justice policy and practice and the worrying tendency of criminal justice processes at times to act like a lightning conductor of punitive populism, we might be grateful for inconsistencies and resistances. Thus the practice of many youth justice workers (in over a third of YOT areas) of never recommending a custodial sentence may result in frustration for many magistrates, but it might also help to keep the rate of custodial sentencing down (Audit Commission 2004). At times the youth justice 'system' may not really resemble a system, but rather a series of discrete and almost unrelated 'decision stages' such as described by Bottomley (1973 – although Pitts (2004) employs a telling 'plumbing' metaphor). This can also make firm and clear conclusions difficult to draw.

That said, the following points, germane to our present discussion of the ways in which what Cohen termed 'old structures' (the prison, juvenile institutions, the juvenile court and professional monopolies) retain their position and significance (and may even be strengthened) seem fairly clear. The lion's share of youth justice resources (around three-quarters) are taken up by costs associated with custody. This creates a strong motive for the YJB to reduce the number of custodial remands or sentences. However, except for the fact that younger offenders are being spared the 'rush to custody' currently affecting the adult criminal justice system, it is still scarcely happening. Although Rutherford (2002) has argued that the YJB can still be seen to be acting as a 'shield' on the youth justice system, standing between 'law and order' politics and the youth justice system, protecting the latter from the worst excesses of punitive populism.

Numbers on remand fell significantly into 2001 but have been climbing again through 2002 and 2003. Overall the youth custody population is fairly stable but there are trends that cause particular concern: the growth in custodial sentencing of 10–14-year-olds, an increase in 'serious' custodial sentences (section 90–92 offences) and a seemingly growing disproportion in the custodial sentencing of black and mixed-race young offenders compared to white young offenders (Audit Commission 2004). A considerable majority of the youth custody population is held in the least fit for purpose institutions while pressures on available space, especially in London and the South East, have necessitated a large number of disruptive inmate transfers (thereby impeding the development of effective education and support programmes: National Audit Office 2004). Furthermore, the custody population remains relatively stable despite the introduction of the Intensive Supervision and Surveillance Programmes (ISSPs) (surprisingly the proportion of young offenders sentenced to custody fell more in YOT areas without an ISSP). The ISSP is intended as a 'tough' new community penalty designed to occupy and 'manage' young offenders while meeting their education, development and support needs in the community. Here, as Cohen has earlier argued, alternatives to custody have to be designed to be 'tough' in order to achieve credibility with sentencers and the public alike. Yet very often, it is this 'toughness' which can undermine the effectiveness of the measure and cause it to fail. When it fails, sentencers often feel they then have little option but to employ custodial measures. As the NAO's Report summary put it, 'in some areas over half the young offenders did not complete [the ISSP programme] and some had to be resentenced to custody' (NAO, 2004: Report Summary, p. 2).

What is true of prison custody, an 'old institution' retaining a potent significance within the new system of youth justice despite repeated criticism of its almost inherent unsuitability for meeting the needs of young offenders and which for much of contemporary youth justice is construed as an alternative, is also largely true of the youth court. According to the Audit Commission (2004), the percentage of young offenders receiving a pre-court disposal has been falling fairly consistently over the previous six years. Such a trend might be explained by the significant turn against pre-court diversion, discussed earlier, and the resulting restriction in the discretion available to pre-court decision-makers ('two strikes and you're in court'), yet this is so despite the availability of evidence regarding the effectiveness of pre-court diversion and the Audit Commission's expressed concern that 'too many minor offences are taking up valuable court time and require YOTs and courts to deal with a high volume of low risk young people' (Audit Commission 2004: 7/37, para. 30). With the further point that pre-court diversion, in the form of decisions about reprimands and final warning, is now more firmly in the hands of the police then a picture begins to emerge of the continuing central role of the 'old institutions' – police, courts and custodial institutions in the reformed youth justice of New Labour.

That said, it was an explicit ambition of the government that the YJB bring some considerable influence to bear upon the working of the youth justice system. Recent reports from the Audit Commission and National Audit Office undoubtedly confirm that this has been achieved in a number of ways but herein lies a further issue. For notwithstanding the continuing significance of certain older features of the youth justice system, one clear objective of the government was to achieve some further centralised control over the system. Youth crime is undoubtedly a major political priority of the present government. Accordingly the government is keen to be seen taking an appropriate lead on reforming youth justice. In turn, it undoubtedly wants to be associated with any successes on this score. In Garland's sense, the youth justice strategy retains many 'sovereign' features even as key aspects of its management have been dispersed to a variety of agencies and institutions (Garland 2001). While there may be important differences in the ways by which the government has secured its more centralised control over youth justice – or the means by which problems of youth crime are now managed, what we might call the 'governmentalisation' of youth justice (Pratt 1989), it is nevertheless abundantly clear that another 'old institution', in this case the state, is now playing a far firmer hand in the management of youth crime. Smith alludes to this issue in what he refers to as the 'ideological function' of the Youth Justice Board in prescribing particular forms of intervention, setting standards and dictating precise performance measures. As a direct consequence, he argues, youth justice practitioners are now required to undertake a narrowly bureaucratic form of 'korrectional karaoke' employing 'one-size fits all' interventions and having significantly less discretion to exercise their own professional judgements (Smith, R. 2003: 113–15). When undertaking our own evaluations of youth justice projects, as outlined earlier, many similar criticisms were voiced by youth justice practitioners (Eadie and Canton 2002; Squires and Measor 2005).

It is arguable that we now have a stronger and more centralised system of youth justice than at any previous time since the first introduction of the juvenile court in the early twentieth century. Moreover, key institutions have not been by-passed and decentred by virtue of the creation of more 'effective' alternatives. They have, on the contrary, become even more tightly combined within a more purposive and directive system of youth justice processing, more closely resembling an actuarial model of justice (Feeley and Simon 1992, 1994; Kempf-Leonard and Peterson 2002) geared primarily to the exercise of control (the production of responsibility, the distribution of sanctions and the maintenance of surveillance) rather than the achievement of justice. As Cohen originally argued, this is not necessarily any cheaper, more humane, more just or more effective.

4. The new structures are not necessarily any cheaper, more humane, more just or more effective

We have already referred to the proportion of the YJB budget absorbed by 'custody costs' (Audit Commission 2004: para. 90, 27/37) and indicated some of the many misgivings voiced (some even from within the prison service itself) regarding the inhumane and largely counter-productive custodial confinement of young offenders (HMIP 1997; Moore 2000; Smith 2000; Squires and Measor 2001). With those issues addressed, the following commentary will concentrate upon 'justice' and 'effectiveness' issues.

There have been many criticisms made of the undermining of traditional principles of justice and due process arising within the new youth justice. To begin, perhaps most appropriately, with the core concerns of this book, there have been many criticisms made of the Anti-Social Behaviour Order (ASBO). In the following critique we reiterate our main argument that the ASBO has become a central feature of contemporary youth justice. Likewise, contemporary youth justice cannot any longer be meaningfully discussed without consideration of ASB.

Some of the chief criticisms of ASB enforcement work have been referred to already. A particular criticism we have mentioned concerns the very definition of the behaviour itself (something acknowledged by the Home Office). Then there are questions of intentions and consequences. ASB concerns an alleged perpetrator 'acting in a manner that caused or was likely to cause harassment, alarm or distress'. Here, perceptions are everything, and yet, even as the scope of action for ASB enforcement expands (with new powers outlined in October 2004: Home Office 2004e) definitions become less clear. It may not be necessary to *intend* to cause 'harassment, alarm or distress', nor are any complaints or consequences strictly necessary; it is simply that the behaviour is *likely* to cause such offence. Likewise it is enough that a range of 'environmental offences' are thought to be 'detrimental' to an area or its amenities or that groups of young people gathering on street corners (prior to being required to disperse) are likely to cause alarm and distress. As Brown has argued, ASB introduced 'a rule so vague almost anything could break it' (Brown 2004: 205). Furthermore, as we have also noted, the legal test originally envisaged for these behaviours was not the more familiar 'beyond reasonable doubt', but the rather lower evidential threshold, the 'balance of probabilities' applied in the civil courts (Ashworth *et al.* 1998). Subsequently, however, a House of Lords ruling has held that for consideration of an ASBO, courts should apply the criminal standard of proof although the admissibility of hearsay evidence has been confirmed

(Grier and Thomas 2003; McDonald 2003). Cases may be determined without the defendant necessarily being heard – and, in the case of Interim Orders, without the defendant even being notified (Stone 2004) – and where behaviour which is otherwise entirely legal may be prohibited. A consequence, according to Jones, is that ASBOs are 'likely to be used in a discriminatory way' (Jones 2001b).

On the other hand a more generic question of injustice concerns the decision to overturn the presumption of *doli incapax* and effectively lower the age of criminal responsibility to 10. We will not repeat here the more general discussion (to be found earlier in this chapter) nor debate the specifically legal point that it is only the *presumption* of *doli incapax* that has been abolished (Walker 1999; Crofts 2002). A case could still be defended on the basis that a young offender did not appreciate the serious criminal significance of his or her actions, but no doubt such defences will be much harder to make and few and far between. A number of critics of what is described as an increasing tendency to criminalise children anticipate serious negative consequences, both for children and for justice, arising from this effective lowering of the age of criminal responsibility (Ashford 1998; Bandalli 1998, 2000). However, it is a remark from the Family Policy Studies Centre (1998) which connects these reactions to a number of further concerns expressed in relation to potential injustices associated with a number of other youth justice provisions: Child Safety Orders, Referral Orders, Curfews and Acceptable Behaviour Contracts (ABCs). As the Family Policy Studies Centre put it, 'society has not reached a particularly high degree of sophistication if it regards a criminal conviction as an appropriate way of illustrating the consequences of doing wrong to a child as young as ten' (FPSC 1998: 61).

However, as the recent history of children's criminal responsibility shows, social change is not a one-way street – gains secured can be later reversed, and for a variety of reasons. The Child Safety Order is a case in point. This order was introduced to deal with occasions in which a child under the age of 10 committed an act that, if the child had been aged over 10, would have constituted an offence. The orders were considered in relation to the child curfew schemes designed to keep young children off the streets at night-time. As R. Smith (2003: 61) has argued, along with Acceptable Behaviour Contracts, Child Safety Orders (CSOs) and curfews ushered in new conceptions of 'pre-delinquency' and the 'pre-delinquent' – or in other words 'pre-crime', an idea with an uncanny air of science fiction about it (Fox 2002).

The new orders and the curfews blurred important distinctions between prevention, social support and crime control, conflating rights and responsibilities in ways reminiscent of the intrusive welfarism which characterised an earlier generation of delinquency management (Donzelot

1979; Burchell 1981; Rose, 1989). For Fionda (1999) such orders, schemes and contracts abandon any conception of a minimum age of criminal responsibility 'by the back door', while confusing children 'in need' and 'at risk' with those posing threats and risks to others. Furthermore, the new measures appear to conflict with the principles of the 1989 Children Act which had sought to prioritise the needs of children while abolishing the criminalisation of the needy or the victims of neglect (Hayes and Williams 1999; Walsh 1999). Instead, the CSO, while neglecting certain legal and procedural rights which might be due to a child conventionally charged with a criminal offence (either a *guardian ad litem* or a right to speak), envisages the introduction of a punitive form of care triggered by minor offending behaviour undertaken by children well below established international norms defining an 'age of responsibility' (Crofts 2002).

Gelsthorpe and Morris (1998), in a comment criticising curfew schemes which could equally well be applied to the new Dispersal Orders, remark on the ways in which the new powers, 'penalise the "normal" behaviour of ordinary children' by viewing the normal – 'hangin' about' and 'doin' nuthin'' (Corrigan 1979) – as suspicious or positively harmful. As Walsh notes, the new curfew and dispersal orders go much further than simply seeking to control the criminal or anti-social behaviour of young people; rather they aim 'to control their behaviour completely … [and] seek to ban groups of young people congregating in public at night, regardless of whether or not their intent is criminal, or indeed, antisocial' (Walsh 2002: 73). Furthermore, dispersing groups of young people, or sending them home, does tend to assume that these are safe and appropriate courses of action, and that the young person's home is a safe place. It may not be. As we argue in a later chapter, when discussing our research findings on the use of ABCs, the practice in some families of imposing virtual house arrest upon children subjected to an ABC for fear that the child may get in further trouble and thereby jeopardise the family's social housing tenancy can create enormous pressures, sometimes resulting in violence, within the household. As Goldson has argued, the apparently benign sounding and seemingly consensual characteristics of the ABC certainly embody the 'responsibilisation' strategy of 'governing through the family' endorsed by New Labour (Goldson 1999). Unfortunately they also tend to conceal both the punitive sanctions upon which the intervention may ultimately rest and appear to eschew any public responsibility (oversight and accountability) for the ways in which some families might deal with these issues, whether via house arrest, domestic exile or fear and intimidation.

A number of the issues already identified apply equally to another new order worth mentioning here, the Referral Order (RO) (established by the Youth Justice and Criminal Evidence Act 1999). This order involves Youth Court magistrates referring a young offender at a first conviction to a new decision-making entity, a Youth Offender Panel. The purpose of this panel, comprising (trained) volunteer members of the public, was to engage directly with the young offender and his or her parents in conjunction with victims and/or other relevant persons in order to agree a form of contract guided by notions of restorative justice, reintegration and responsibility which set out how the young person might seek to make amends for their offending behaviour and stipulating a course of future action. The contract arrived at could be similar in form and content to an ABC and contain things a young offender should do (letters of apology, direct or 'community' reparation, attendance at counselling or guidance sessions) as well as what he or she should not (avoiding certain behaviours, places or people). Haines has criticised Referral Orders for, among other issues, their attempt to graft an artificial and apparently inadequately conceived notion of restorative justice onto an enforcement process (Haines 2000). Other criticism of the order, rather like our criticisms of the ABC, relate especially to the spurious form of contract upon which it is said to rest. Wonnacott (1999) has argued that the supposed contract upon which the order rests is false, being based upon compulsion (the order of the Youth Court) and the basic imbalance in power (between the young person on the one hand and the alliance of youth justice workers, community representatives, panel members and victims on the other).

Although Newburn and his colleagues, having undertaken an evaluation of the introduction of Referral Orders into the youth justice system (Newburn *et al.* 2002), concluded that 'Referral Orders seem to come remarkably close to providing the basis for a constructive and thoughtful youth justice' (Earle *et al.* 2003: 148) many commentators remain very critical. Because the panels are designed to engineer a direct engagement between young offenders and the above 'alliance' of interests, young people are disallowed any legal representation before the panel when coming to agree the content of their 'contracts'. This could lead to 'institutionalised bullying' (Wedd 2000) and, for a young person, irresistible pressure to consent to sign an agreement stipulating fairly intensive (or unreasonable) levels of behavioural compliance for many relatively minor and first-time offenders. Yet where the conditions are too demanding and the contract is breached, a return to court and further punishment could result. Finally, Goldson (2000) argues that the RO may prove to be incompatible with a number of international rules and treaties relating to youth justice, adding (a point also relevant to the ABCs) that there is something rather unethical about expecting a child as young as ten to sign and adhere to a contract. For example, despite assurances about how ABC 'contracts' were very carefully compiled in full discussion with the young people destined to be subjected to them, we still found examples of young people who either could not remember what their contracts said or did not understand what they meant. There may well be many such issues of principle at stake here, yet a good deal may still rest upon how ROs are implemented *in practice* and the roles that Youth Offending Panels actually come to play. Much criticism of the New Youth Justice has centred upon its 'top-heavy' and bureaucratic nature (Jones 2001; Pitts 2001; Smith 2003; Squires and Measor 2005), the loss of professional and local discretion and its narrow focus upon justice and offending to the exclusion of the wider needs and welfare of young people. A question remains regarding the extent to which YOPs can offer some counter-balancing influence to all of this. Optimists such as Newburn see 'the successful integration of a large number of volunteers into the system' (2002: 568) as a real opportunity for a critical exterior voice to influence the adoption of restorative principles and thereby positively influence the shape of youth justice. Other commentators (Burnett and Appleton 2004) find evidence to pin their optimism on a resurgence of the inclusive and welfare-oriented values of the professional culture of social work.

Thus far, although our discussion of this, the fourth of Cohen's critical themes, has focused upon the question of 'justice', there is also the question of 'effectiveness'. Clearly effectiveness can imply a number of things depending upon the stated objectives of a policy. In the case of the new youth justice system we have already alluded to some emerging and interim conclusions about the impact and effectiveness of the new measures (some of which are related to containing costs and improving internal management processes), although undoubtedly reducing offending and especially lowering reconviction rates were the more obviously outward-facing policy objectives. Unfortunately, simple measures of effectiveness are difficult to arrive at given the competing and often inconsistent pressures placed upon the youth justice system: for example, the pressure for more demanding community punishments yet, simultaneously, pressure to reduce the number of community orders breached. Equally, there is the emphasis upon making decisive early interventions to 'nip youth crime in the bud' and dispel notions of 'youthful immunity' while, at the same time, avoiding cluttering the system with low-risk minor cases which might be suitably and successfully diverted.

In our commentary here we can only provide a fairly broad overview of the 'effectiveness' of the new youth justice initiatives but, at the outset, it seems appropriate to distinguish between what we might call 'overall' outcomes and the particular outcomes of specific initiatives. In respect of the former, we are returned directly to the Audit Commission's concerns about the overall performance of the youth justice system and what we might call the 'political utility' of anti-social behaviour. The Commission began from a concern regarding the seemingly minimal purchase of the youth justice system on youth offending. Thus, it claimed, of an estimated seven million offences committed by young people each year, only around 19 per cent were recorded by police and only 5 per cent were subsequently 'cleared up' by police. Finally, only 3 per cent overall entered the youth justice system via arrest and further action, over half of these receiving a caution and just over a third being charged and subsequently appearing in court (Audit Commission 1996: 13). Jones (2001) has rightly called into question the derivation of these figures which may well dramatically inflate the proportion of offending behaviour attributed to the young. But as we have seen, the sense of youthful impunity which these figures appeared to bear out corresponded closely to an emerging public mood. The seeming majority of offences (95 per cent in the Audit Commission's figures) did not represent victimless crimes with no wider social impacts but, rather, the very things about which a growing volume of complaint was being registered, especially in urban residential areas (Girling *et al.* 2001). In the Audit Commission's eyes, the role of youth justice would be to deal decisively, effectively and appropriately with the (relatively small) proportion of young offenders referred to it, discriminating effectively between those who could be diverted with more minimal interventions and those whose serious or persistent offending called for more robust interventions. It is, accordingly, at this level that more subtle considerations of youth justice 'effectiveness' might be called into question. As regards the bigger picture, however, a different question applies.

It was not the intention of the Audit Commission or the government that a huge expansion of youth justice capacity should result from the implementation of the new arrangements after 1998 – this was neither planned for nor resourced. Nor was it feasible. The public were not likely to increase their rate of reporting youth crime and, even if they did, the police would be swamped by the demand. Rather, with the new youth justice system managing (hopefully, more effectively) the relatively small proportion of young offenders channelled into it, another means had to be found for addressing the wider youth problems and the resulting public concerns referred to by the Audit Commission. Thus the parallel system of ASB enforcement now established in the wake of the 2003 ASB Act, standing, in many ways, outside the formal YJ system, has become a vital precondition for the YJ system performing its own role effectively – that is without costly and unsustainable expansion and without being swamped by less serious cases. Somewhat paradoxically, of course, all of this has been achieved through a huge expansion of youth-related enforcement work, in the form of action against ASB. The fact that tackling ASB still carries a broadly preventive ethos, 'nipping crime in the bud', as it were, also contributes to its positive image and legitimacy – provided one overlooks the unsettling questions regarding whether we are merely widening existing nets, intensifying the surveillance, intervening harder and earlier, tolerating less, targeting more and ultimately exposing more young people to the risks associated with criminalisation.

Looking, then, at the overall YJ outcomes we can see that, as the 2004 Audit Commission Report notes, 'although young people are not committing significantly more crime today than five years ago, public spending and activity on youth justice have increased considerably.' In particular, over this period the YJB's budget alone (excluding special grants and additional project funding) has increased by over two-thirds (Audit Commission 2004: para.19, 3/37). In the light of this we are entitled to ask a question dear to the heart of the Audit Commission itself. Given that the total of youth offending has not increased significantly over this period, what has been achieved by this additional funding and activity? Consistent with the YJB's ambitions for more 'early intervention' there has been a significant reduction, from 22 per cent to 9 per cent of arrested young offenders, who said that nothing happened to them following the arrest. In a similar vein, as we have seen, there has been a continuing decline in pre-court diversion. Perhaps as a consequence of this, too many low-risk offenders facing minor charges are finding their way into court. These expansionist trends can be observed if we consider the two most recent years for which YJB data is available, 2002–3 and 2003–4. Between these two years we saw an increase (7 per cent) in the total number of offences dealt with, a 14 per cent increase in the number of cases going before a court but a 2 per cent reduction in the proportion of cases diverted from a court appearance. This is one reason for the Audit Commission suggesting that the CPS might itself divert cases direct to a Youth Offender Panel, thereby avoiding a formal court appearance (offences would have to be admitted) but like the Final Warning and the Referral Order such a process might raise further issues.

On a positive note there is a slight reduction in the overall proportion of cases receiving a custodial disposal (falling to 6.5 per cent of court outcomes, approaching the YJB's own performance target of 6 per cent). A rather less positive outcome concerns the increase in secure remands, moving further away from and now some 50 per cent above the YJB target (YJB Annual Reports 2002–3 and 2003–4).

Such aggregated trends reflect the outcomes of many quite disparate decisions, processes and their consequences. Some of these we have already alluded to: for example the 'tariff-jump' effect of a single 'Final Warning', the net-widening consequence of a tough, so-called, 'community alternative' (such as the ISSP) with stringent breach conditions which many will fail (leading to increased custody rates), and the intensified scrutiny and surveillance ('mesh-thinning') applied at lower levels (ABCs, ASBOs and Referral orders) leading to further enforcement action – as over one-third (36 per cent) of ASBOs result in breaches (Armitage 2002; Home Office 2004g). Understandably these are not the aspects of effectiveness that the YJB has set itself. With one or two exceptions, YJB performance indicators involve simple measurements of its own activities (for example, the proportion of Final Warnings followed up by interventions, the proportion of Pre-Sentence Reports completed on time, the relative use of restorative justice processes and victim satisfaction).

However, as Jennings argues, 'the Home Office's success in its fight to reduce crime will be judged on outcomes' (Jennings 2003: 1). Yet only two of the YJB performance indicators genuinely measure *outcomes* (as opposed to outputs), the impact and effectiveness of all this youth justice activity on patterns of youth offending. The first concerns crime prevention and the second recidivism (or rate of reconviction). The first real measure of youth justice effectiveness assesses the extent to which young people are involved in three forms of criminal activity: vehicle crime, domestic burglary and robbery. However, this can only be measured in relation to recorded offences for which a person was apprehended by the police and for whom a youth justice 'outcome' is recorded. As we have already noted, this can be a fairly small proportion of the total number of each type of offence. The YJB performance target aims to reduce young people's involvement in each offence type by 30 per cent, 25 per cent and 15 per cent (compared to 2001) respectively. The available figures only allow us to conclude that during 2003 the youth justice system dealt with less young offenders in each category of offence than it did in 2001 (YJB Annual Report 2003–4). In effect, all three YJB targets have been comfortably met, but what this allows us to conclude about actual crime prevention effects is rather less clear cut. Both the British Crime Survey and offences recorded by the police show that each of these types of offences have fallen by around 7–10 per cent year on year (and, in the case of burglary and car crime, falling fairly consistently since the mid-1990s) (Ringham and Wood 2004). The fall in recorded offending clearly began prior to the youth justice reforms so they alone cannot be credited with this 'prevention' effect and, in the case of vehicle-related offences, a survey of motorists (in Autoglass 2004) suggested that less than half now report theft from or damage to vehicles. Concurrent with recent changes to the youth justice system and the reproblematisation of anti-social behaviour we are perhaps witnessing a shift in perceptions and responses whereby a range of less serious vehicle-related crimes is no longer being processed through the YJ system but diverted via ASB interventions. A number of questions would follow and the wider implications may be interesting but it is too early to draw clear conclusions. Either way, the issue underscores our wider argument regarding the centrality of ASB – and strategies to address it – to recent changes in youth justice.

Turning to the other YJB performance indicator, reconviction rates, the situation is even less clear cut. The performance target involves achieving a modest 5 per cent reduction in rates of reconviction for the following four groups of offenders dealt with: those receiving pre-court diversions, those receiving 'first-tier' disposals (such as discharges, fines, referral or reparation orders), those receiving community penalties and those receiving custodial sentences. Unfortunately, although making the data here available to YOTs for purposes of comparison, the YJB does not make this information public. There are, as the YJB acknowledges, a number of difficulties associated with the use of reconviction data. For example, control group type experiments are considered unethical and unsuitable in this field yet differences between reconviction cohorts may skew results in a number of directions. There is the related difficulty of ensuring the establishment of satisfactory original baselines against which subsequent reconviction rates might be compared. To avoid such problems comparisons can be made between actual and predicted reconviction rates (as described below) although such methods bring their own problems. It is important to clarify whether 'raw' reconviction data (simple 'before and after' studies) are being compared or whether current reconviction rates are being compared with rather more artificially constructed 'predicted' reconviction rates (established by taking the known reconviction rates of a former sample, including all variations for age, gender, race, number of previous convictions, etc.) and comparing these rates to the present sample. Then any difference between the present sample's actual rate of reconvictions is compared to the predicted rate (Jennings 2003). Notwithstanding these complexities, one could still be forgiven for thinking that, if the results had been more positive, the YJB would have published them. As it is we have to look elsewhere for this reconviction information.

Accordingly, the *National Evaluation of YJB Final Warning Projects* (Holdaway and Desborough 2004) compared Final Warning reconviction rates with reconviction rates from a 1997 Home Office reconviction study. Having acknowledged some significant differences between the relevant cohorts (age, offending histories) the findings revealed that, taken overall, more of those undergoing Final Warning interventions were found to have reoffended within one year (31 per cent) than in the 1997 Home Office Study (25 per cent). By contrast, a study by researchers at the University of Sheffield (Hine and Celnick 2001) found Final Warnings resulting in a rate of reconviction 6 per cent lower (after one year) than might have been expected. Here, however, much hangs on the construction of a somewhat artificial 'expected reconviction rate' based upon the frequency of reconviction of a cohort of earlier cautioned offenders.

Findings from a national study of YJB Restorative Justice Projects undertaken by the YJB (Wilcox and Hoyle 2004) raise similar questions. Here the young offenders completing restorative justice (RJ) projects were compared to a Home Office sample sentenced in 2000. The one-year RJ reconviction rate was 46.6 per cent compared with a simple rate of 26.4 per cent for the Home Office sample but almost all of this difference could be attributed to the numbers of previous convictions of the respective samples. On the positive side, there were slight reductions in seriousness and frequency of reoffending in the RJ group but also an increase in the custodial sentencing of those reconvicted. Turning to a national evaluation of YJB Mentoring Projects (Tarling *et al.* 2004), 55 per cent of young people had reoffended within one year of joining the programme (approximately twice the rate of reconviction compared to Home Office reconviction cohorts with which the project made comparisons). Again, however, the differences are largely explained by the proportions of young offenders with previous convictions in the respective samples. On YJB Cognitive Behaviour Projects, one-year reconviction rates varied between 58 per cent for those on education projects, 75 per cent for those on sex offender projects but 80 per cent of those on persistent offender projects (falling to 71 per cent of those who actually completed the projects satisfactorily) (Feilzer *et al.* 2004). On Education, Training and Employment Projects, there was a 29 per cent reduction in the overall rate of offending by project participants in the year following the commencement of the project, although 59 per cent of project participants were reconvicted within one year (Hurry and Moriarty 2004). In both these latter project evaluations, high reconviction rates are explained by the fairly serious criminal records of the participants. For instance, the average number of previous convictions of those on Education, Training and Employment Projects was nine.

Finally, considering the reconviction of young people on Intensive Supervision and Surveillance Programmes (ISSP) the evaluation suggests that 85 per cent of young people on ISSP were reconvicted 'at some point' (YJB 2004). Similarly almost 60 per cent of programme participants were breached at some point although many were allowed to continue with the programmes, eventually completing them satisfactorily. These findings have to be set alongside the relatively high-risk target group for whom the ISSP was designed – as an alternative to custody – and the fact that, comparing the years before and after the programme, both frequency of reoffending and offence seriousness appeared to fall. Indeed, Little *et al.* (2004) persuasively argue that the ISSP ought not to be evaluated simply by reference to reconviction rates but by reference to demonstrable

reductions in the volume and seriousness of offending by ISSP participants. Their research, examining a pioneering ISSP scheme in Kent,
concluded that ISSP cases (young offenders) were arrested between 30 per
cent and 50 per cent less than young offenders in two control groups. It
might follow, therefore, that an effective intervention achieving a
demonstrable crime reduction effect ought not to be terminated by
reconviction alone. Too rigid an application of breach rules could nullify
the impact of the programme if all participants were to be transferred to
custody simply for reoffending. Clearly this is an area where professional
discretion and programme integrity might clash with established
sentencing principles. There was some evidence in the YJB evaluation of
ISSP (YJB 2004: 32) that some discretion was being applied, thus 39 per
cent of ISSPs 'completed successfully' had been breached at some stage.

Taking together these various outcomes relating to crime reduction and
reconvictions, a number of important issues emerge. The first is the
observation that although demonstrable crime reduction impacts (crime
prevention and reduced reconviction rates) represent the 'Holy Grail' of
youth justice evaluation they are no less difficult to find and no simple
matter to demonstrate. In 2003, Jennings's analysis of *One Year Juvenile
Reconviction Rates* (Jennings 2003) was confidently reporting that the YJB
target of a 5 per cent reduction in reconviction rates 'has already been
exceeded' before proceeding to present data indicating that, compared
with an 'adjusted predicted' reconviction rate based upon 1997 figures
2000–1 overall reconviction rates had fallen by 7.7 percentage points (26.4
per cent of young offenders dealt with in 2000 were dealt with for subsequent offences within one year). This represented a 22.5 per cent
reduction in reoffending compared to the 'adjusted predicted' reconviction rate. Clearly, a great deal hangs upon the calculation of this
'adjusted predicted' reconviction rate. It can take into account differences
in the composition of the respective cohorts (age, previous convictions and
other assessed 'risk factors') as well as control for the 'speeding up' of
youth justice processing, but may be less able to reflect wider more
broadly based changes in the social and cultural environments inhabited
by young people. As we have seen, young people's involvement in at least
two of the YJB targeted crimes was falling before the new youth justice
measures came onstream. Perhaps this is not such an unfamiliar scenario –
everyone likes a share of success and, when crime is falling, there is
usually enough success to go around. This, despite the existence of a minor
industry devoted to the identification and dissemination of 'best practice'
and in marked contrast to when crime is rising, tends to disincline people
from making too rigorous a search for the reasons.

That said, judged in their own terms many of the youth justice projects,
whose national evaluation outcomes we have referred to above,

demonstrate the difficulty of achieving successful outcomes with young offenders already demonstrating signs of persistence in their offending patterns. Many of the relatively high tariff community projects (Cognitive Behaviour Projects, Education, Training and Employment Projects and Intensive Supervision and Surveillance Programmes) had relatively high – though not unexpected – failure rates (through reconviction on breach). There are a number of ways of looking at this. It can be taken as evidence that these programmes were properly engaging with the appropriate high-risk target groups for whom they offered a genuine (although in many cases only a temporary) alternative to custody. On the other hand, when such programmes fail to divert offenders, custody is often the next step, therefore this reinforces the point that project managers need to be free to exercise some discretion in managing their offenders and should not be confined by over-stringent breach conditions which produce high failure rates and render such projects little more than stepping stones to custody.

These project evaluation results suggest that it is important to ensure that 'tougher' community penalties are not brought into play too early, although the Audit Commission (2004) noted that the proportion of young offenders given 'higher tariff' community sentences has increased. In contrast, the role of such measures as 'alternatives to custody' should be protected and, in their management, discretion should be optimised in order to avoid the 'tariff-jumping' effects, creating an artificially steep and slippery slope into custody, that we have referred to earlier. There is a suggestion in the 2004 Audit Commission Report that these issues have been recognised. The Commission acknowledged a need to 'shift away from the vertical tariff' towards a more flexible package of community or 'action-plan' orders comprising a 'horizontal' or 'sloping' tariff and rejecting the idea that 'if a previous sentence has not worked then a more punitive one should be used' (Audit Commission 2004: para. 92, 27/37). Instead, a greater variety of orders are intended to facilitate the more specific tailoring of programmes to individual young offenders. It remains to be seen whether this flexible diversity of programmes can be delivered in practice and whether sentencers (and the wider sentencing culture) respond by employing the new orders as intended.

Above all, however, the most important conclusion to be drawn from the evaluation of YJB projects rather takes us back to our original point of departure. The most effective response to youth offending is, and always has been, pre-court diversion. The fact that such diversion is now occurring less frequently and is now governed by a more inflexible decision-making framework – the *Final* Warning – may suggest the new YJ system is undermining its own effectiveness and its chances of success. Thus as the most recent YJB statistics have shown a 7 per cent increase in the number of offences dealt with turns into a 14 per cent increase in the number of young offenders going before a court and reflects a 2 per cent reduction in pre-court diversions (YJB Annual Reports 2002–3 and 2003–4). To this more disappointing commentary upon YJ system impact and effectiveness we should also add the impact of establishing a parallel system of ASB enforcement alongside the main YJ system. Although it is a central part of our argument that the parallel systems for ASB and YJ management need to be considered very much in relation to one another, the processes for ASB enforcement contribute a number of their own net-widening and tariff-jumping characteristics which, we suggest, will compound many of those already referred to. With this in mind, we now turn to consider some further aspects of Cohen's dispersal of social control reflected in the new youth justice and, especially, ASB enforcement action.

5.The criminal justice system has expanded and drawn more people into its net

6. Entire (non-criminalised) populations are both subjected to increased surveillance and regulation and also drawn into acting as control agents

We have chosen to consider these two aspects of Cohen's analysis of the dispersal of social control together. In part this is because they are closely related and refer to two aspects of the same process. Primarily, though, it is because, when taken together, they define the core relationship between youth justice and ASB enforcement action which lies at the centre of our argument. Many of the issues to be addressed here have already been referred to so we can afford to address them with greater brevity. To begin with, the YJ system has certainly undergone some significant expansion and development while, through ASB enforcement, ABCs, Curfews, Dispersal Orders, Parenting Orders and Child Safety Orders, a wider range of hitherto non-criminalised populations are drawn into tighter relations of surveillance and regulation. In fact, these relationships of surveillance and regulation do not only comprise free-standing and quasi-criminal enforcement processes, they are often embedded in other social policy relationships. Perhaps especially one could mention social security and unemployment benefit administration and the work of the Child Support Agency. At times it might appear that as much administrative effort is being devoted to ensuring that fraudulent claims are not successful or that the unemployed are 'genuine' as opposed to paying benefits to those who need them or finding employment for those seeking work (Andrews and Jacobs 1990; Bryson and Jacobs 1992; Jones and Novak 1999).

Confirming Cohen's further point about the public at large being drawn into acting as control agents, it is worth noting that one of the most public faces of the Benefits Agency is now its dartboard-like 'Targeting Fraud' logo appearing regularly in newspaper and TV advertising, and on a range of sites from billboards to bus shelters, inviting concerned citizens to call the benefit fraud hotline. In a further sense, the development of additional tagging, scanning or tracking initiatives, including situational crime prevention measures such as CCTV, as well as ASB 'name and shame' initiatives, has exposed significantly wider populations to hitherto unknown levels of surveillance (Lyon 1994, 2001).

At the more intrusive end of all this work of scrutiny and surveillance where the capacity for the individualisation of subjects is greatest, we find the range of direct behaviour management orders (ASBOs, ABCs and Parenting Orders) referred to already. Collectively, such initiatives, along with those referred to above such as the Benefit Agency Targeting Fraud initiative, reflect the broader strategy of 'responsibilisation' identified by Garland (2001) which we have discussed earlier. The central paradox of this strategy, alluded to in that earlier discussion, concerned the premature and seemingly 'compulsory responsibilisation' of young people who may have had relatively little opportunity or encouragement to acquire 'responsible habits'. This anomaly at the heart of New Labour's contract of citizenship seeks to find responsible social behaviour flourishing in often quite anti-social circumstances. Yet the fundamental mistake of harbouring such assumptions was exposed over 60 years ago by Sir Alexander Paterson, formerly a Prison Service Commissioner and generally credited as the architect of the reformed Borstal system in the 1930s. He remarked upon how, when visiting youth offender institutions in the 1930s, 'I have frequently called the attention of prison governors and doctors to the fact that an unusually high proportion of their prisoners have bowlegs ... the truth is, of course, that the two phenomena of bow-leggedness and burglarious habits are apt to emerge from the same environment' (Ruck 1951: 30). Furthermore, Paterson continued, a poverty-stricken and overcrowded home resulted in a poor diet and rickets and, in such a home, 'habits of honesty are with most difficulty taught' (ibid.). So when it came to addressing the factors responsible for the vast majority of the depressing case histories represented by the inhabitants of the penal system, Paterson turned first to the problem of disadvantaged social conditions.

> The problem of recidivism is in the first place met by an improvement in social conditions. A housing system which provides a decent home life, an education which is ... a preparation for a complete life, and assignment to work on leaving school that offers a reasonable chance of regular and appropriate employment – these are the three

main desiderata for a generation of good citizens, and a reduction of crime to the exceptional individual. (Ruck 1951: 58)

Roughly half a century later, Newburn (1998) and Goldson and Jamieson (2002) have questioned the compatibility of contemporary Parenting Orders with the main thrust of New Labour's policies on social exclusion. Recent years have witnessed a veritable explosion of books, manuals, articles and guidance, framing a new discourse on 'positive parenting' (an aspect of a wider responsibilisation strategy) all aimed at helping modern parents cope. We are entitled to ask about the new needs, problems or anxieties that this new literature addresses (Furedi 2001). The full spectrum of the 'guidance' runs from the purely voluntary and 'aspirational' to the increasingly punitive. The new guidance has seemingly 'raised the stakes' on the question of satisfactory parenting but, somewhere along the spectrum, the motivations attributed to parents seem to shift. At the top end of the market, purchasers of the latest glossy manuals are regarded as discerning parents wanting only the best for their offspring – indeed their purchasing power can often deliver the best. At the other end of the scale, parents struggling to cope or lacking resources, 'raising children within the poorest and most disadvantaged estates, neighbourhoods and communities in a divided, starkly polarised and profoundly unequal land' (Goldson and Jamieson 2002: 95), are publicly vilified for their failings. Newburn notes how 'poor parenting' is 'viewed as the consequence of wilfulness – requiring parents to be disciplined – rather than the product of multiple social disadvantage' (1998: 209).

Yet, as we report in a later chapter, in our work on ABC enforcement, wilful neglect never featured as an issue in the families to which we gained access. Rather more often, the parents (more particularly the mothers) appeared overwhelmed by circumstances. This could include the burden of meeting their children's needs, domestic violence and/or the difficulty of soliciting help and support from relevant local authority or statutory services. More often than not, parents (again, almost entirely the mothers) could produce reams of correspondence documenting their efforts, often to little avail, to engage the help and support of a range of agencies.

We can describe the attempt to operationalise the notion of responsibilisation in one case from our ABC sample. It was the one case which also involved a Parenting Order against a single mother of eight children, herself the victim of an earlier sexual assault and repeated domestic violence who had needed to obtain an injunction to prevent her abusive former partner from returning. Her children, ranging in age from the early teens to three years old, were alleged to be the source of a great deal of nuisance and harassment to neighbours, but were also the victims of bullying by groups of other children on the estate. One of the children was the subject of an ABC, and community safety officers had provided neighbours with a video camera which was mounted in the bedroom window of a house facing the family home. Through this relationship neighbours exerted a responsibilising influence while also gathering evidence to support the enforcement process. At the same time the mother was required to attend parenting classes. When we first interviewed her she explained that she found attending the classes very difficult because she had no transport to get there and no one to supervise her younger children while she was away from the home. The Parenting Order added to her difficulties rather more than it enabled her to solve them. Much as Hunter and Nixon (2001) have described how ASB enforcement work chiefly targets women, as mothers, so this is more explicitly the case with the Parenting Order. According to Gelsthorpe (1999), through the Parenting Order the 'war on crime' may become a war upon selected parents, while the stigma and resentment felt by parents concerning the orders might exacerbate rather than alleviate their problems. In particular, she argues, the orders are likely to discriminate against women.

Similar criticisms regarding the discriminatory implementation of legal powers or decision-making (sometimes known as 'selective targeting') can be made of Dispersal Orders and Curfews. It is appropriate to discuss the aptly named 'Dispersal Order' in the context of a review of the 'dispersal of discipline' (although Walsh [2003] also speaks of a 'dispersal of rights') through ASB enforcement. There is a marked sense in which the Dispersal Order recreates a new type of discriminatory 'status offence' (such as 'vagrant' or 'common prostitute'). Such laws, by virtue of the way they have been seen to undermine the rights and citizen status of selected groups of the public – and empower the police (Waddington 1999: 24; Reiner 2000: 95) – have been considered essentially contrary to a culture of civil rights and social justice. However, even though they appear quite incompatible with today's language of social inclusion (Walsh 2002), they are nevertheless becoming more familiar. Thus the Dispersal Order virtually reinvents the old 'sus' laws whereby simply being a certain type of person in a certain place constituted, in the eyes of enforcement officers (or, more generally, the 'responsibilised' citizens who may have raised an initial complaint) grounds for intervention. Given the long-standing police tradition of 'moving on' groups of young people alleged to be causing nuisance (Anderson *et al.* 1994; Loader 1996; Measor and Squires 2000), there is a sense in which the Dispersal Order may simply represent the law being brought into line with existing police practice, although now with added emphasis and tougher sanctions in the event of non-compliance. According to a Home Office Report on the 'Together: Tackling ASB' campaign, there were 416 dispersal orders issued in the first nine months of 2004 (Home Office 2004g). As we have already seen in respect of reprimands and final warnings, police-only decision-making can give rise to a number questions. Just as in police operational practice regarding stop and search, enforcement discretion and discrimination may be at issue in respect of the use of dispersal orders (Walsh 2003).

There remains one further aspect of the 'dispersal of responsibilisation' implicit within governmental ASB strategies we think it appropriate to mention at this point. It concerns both the opinion polling and victim surveying and the assessment of 'community perceptions' which have become so central a feature of contemporary crime prevention and community safety planning. A number of commentators (e.g. Tonry 2004) have argued that New Labour virtually 'invented' the notion of ASB. We have shown that there is rather more to this, but certainly over recent years the Prime Minister, many senior government ministers and the Home Office itself have gone to considerable lengths to raise the profile of ASB. In many respects this follows directly in the tracks of New Labour's crime and disorder strategy. This strategy, rolled out after 1998, involved the development of three-yearly 'crime audits' to be followed by local crime and disorder reduction plans which involved CDRP consultations with a range of local groups and interests.

Nationally, the British Crime Survey has given particular emphasis to analysing and understanding respondents' perceptions of crime and disorder (Finney 2004; Thorpe and Wood 2004) and, with the rise of ASB, local and regional government has increasingly come to do likewise as a means of setting local and regional targets and priorities (Flint *et al.* 2003; Association of London Government; 2004; Squires *et al.* 2004). The purpose of these new consultation and survey exercises is not simply to inform government about the impact of crime reduction programmes; they have become rather more instrumental in shaping the very discourses of crime and disorder management themselves. Not unlike the manner in which evaluation processes can become increasingly tailored to management and implementation priorities (Wilcox 2003; Squires and Measor 2005) rather than the assessment of outcomes and effectiveness, so the broad array of surveys and 'perceptions' studies undertaken into ASB, nuisance and disorder tend to establish and reinforce the very phenomena they are meant to be examining. In this sense, they have become central aspects of the discourse of crime and disorder governance itself rather than commentaries upon it. Local surveys may throw up a wide range of complaints about factors impinging upon a community's right to a 'quiet life' but not all of these will be attributable to individual or collective behaviour problems and not all are the responsibility of young people.

Actual complaints may feature issues such as fly-posting, abandoned motor vehicles, noise, litter, dog-fouling, speeding and obstructive parking as well as ASB by groups of young people but it is often the latter which commands most attention. Problems may be attributable to local authority enforcement deficits, policy failures, business malpractices and inconsiderate motorists but young people often prove to be the enforcement point of least resistance. For example, on the very day the Together Campaign *One Year On* report was launched at a press conference featuring both the Prime Minister and Home Secretary, the *Guardian* ran an article by the Labour MP for Mitcham and Morden, Siobhan McDonagh, featuring an issue of ASB by adolescent moped, goped or motorcycle riders (McDonagh 2004). The article called for stronger powers to confiscate these offending vehicles from the 'yobs' riding them although it was silent on speeding by car drivers, other dangerous and inconsiderate driving and obstructive parking, all fairly common causes of complaints and disputes in urban residential areas.

As we have already seen, ASB is deliberately defined in a particularly open-ended and flexible manner as a range of actions and behaviours. The merit of this definition is supposed to be the scope that it allows local communities and CDRP agencies to set priorities and targets according to local problems and concerns. Yet the disadvantage of this approach is precisely the implicit prior specification of a stereotypically 'yob'-centred set of priorities and youthful 'usual suspects'. For instance, Camden's decision, during the summer of 2004, to use ASB powers against the executives of music publishing companies in an effort to curtail fly-posting within the borough is the exception rather than the rule. Tonry (2004) may be right to argue that the government's establishment of the ASB agenda is a 'high-risk strategy' but it is equally clear that they have done much to minimise that risk by prioritising enforcement action against the softest, most familiar, typically poorest (and frequently the youngest) targets, and vindicating these enforcement priorities by reference to survey and perceptions data recycling a familiar series of 'respectable fears' (Pearson 1983; Brown 1998). It may seem a misnomer to refer to this process, the recycling of perceptions, as a dispersal of 'responsibilisation' but it is no less a component of a broader process. In seemingly ever decreasing circles, the cycle of problem definition, intervention and evaluation, forming the core of modern governance, intensifies its enforcement action around the 'anti-social minority' but seldom gets to grips with the causes, definitions or conditions of emergence of these problems – in other words, 'tough on crime, but not on the causes of crime'.

Finally, this extended deployment enforcement action, as reflected in Dispersal Orders and, for example, ABCs, Curfews and Fixed Penalty Notices, embody a further dimension of Cohen's dispersal of discipline analysis. This is characterised in the following observations.

7. Petty offenders are subject to more intrusive and hidden forms of control, and serious offenders are subject to increased degradation as their position is redefined as being 'hard core' and 'irredeemable'

Many features of the developments in youth justice and ASB enforcement that we have already catalogued entail more intrusive and early interventionist forms of discipline and control against petty offenders. Often these measures are applied to even younger 'offenders'. We have seen this as an aspect of ABCs, ASBOs, Child Safety Orders, Reprimands, Referral Orders, Dispersal Orders and Curfews and, in the much wider sense, in the abolition of the presumption of *doli incapax*, lowering the effective age of criminal responsibility to 10 years. All such early interventions addressing less serious or 'entry-level' forms of delinquent or anti-social behaviour flow from the government's core ambition to 'nip youth crime in the bud' (Muncie 2002). Notwithstanding this, as the ASB enforcement strategy has developed, the utility of the ASBO has come to be recognised and the orders adopted in ways which transcend their original stated rationales. We can see such cases as further illustrations of the 'blurring' and 'widening' of politically and procedurally useful criminal justice interventions described by Cohen (1979). A case in point would be the introduction of ASBOs 'on conviction' after 2002. Thus an ASBO can be used to increase the conditions, enforcement profile and sanctions attaching to certain chronic or persistent offenders in ways which would not be possible under other sentencing options.

Yet, in a parallel sense, just as more intrusive forms of discipline come to bear upon young people at the shallow end of the youth justice system, so other young people, perhaps the 'stigmatised others' of ASB discourse, the 'mindless thugs', 'feral children' or the 'neighbours from hell' and especially 'persistent young offenders' emerge as a hard core against whom rather special measures are required. There is an important sense in which the persistent young offender (PYO) problem was instrumental in laying the foundations of the new youth justice. After all, intervening early and 'nipping offending in the bud' were predicated upon preventing young offenders graduating into more persistently delinquent 'careers'. Roger Tarling made the point succinctly: 'If the small group of chronic offenders could be identified early in their criminal careers and targeted for some form of successful intervention to reduce their offending, this could have a significant impact on crime' (Tarling 1993). By contrast, while Faulkner (2001) has argued that the PYO was a largely fabricated identity, we have tended to suggest that rather than breaking the links between minor delinquency and serious offending, recent policies have further reinforced them. While researchers have had relatively little success in pinpointing this group, or even agreeing upon a common definition of 'persistence' (Hagell and Newburn 1994) the notion that a large proportion of crime was committed by a small percentage of young offenders – 5 per cent of young offenders responsible for two-thirds of all youth offending, as cited by the Audit Commission (1996: 12) – became enshrined in official discourse. Indeed, this idea stuck firm, despite evidence that, for even the most persistent of young offenders, high rates of offending were typically of fairly short duration. Nevertheless, as the rationale for a new youth offending strategy, the 'persistent young offender problem' opened doors through which the pro-interventionist New Labour government were only too willing to march.

In turn, the tougher penalties available to youth courts (ISSPs, DTOs) are justified by the apparently more serious and persistent young offenders. As the Audit Commission (2004: exhibit 14) noted, 'the likelihood of being sentenced to custody has increased for those aged ten to fourteen.' Likewise, further corroborating our arguments about the net-widening effect of tougher community penalties, the Commission also noted that ISSPs 'may be drawing in young offenders who would otherwise have received community sentences,' while 'some young offenders are receiving DTOs who do not reach the eligibility threshold for an ISSP' (ibid.: para. 88). In other words, there is some confusion of aims and outcomes which, bearing in mind the reconviction profiles of both the 'more substantial' community penalties and of custodial sentences, tends to suggest that 'toughness' carries a certain self-defeating quality and is not the same thing as effectiveness.

Yet running across the presentation and discussion of youth justice policies and the wider public and political debates about them is the demeaning and dehumanising rhetoric of vilification referred to above. In Garland's (2001) terms, such language helps establish the 'otherness' of these offenders which, in turn, supports and condones our punitive treatment of them. The Home Office 'Together: Tackling Anti-Social Behaviour' campaign is a case in point. The first annual report of the campaign, *One Year On*, catalogues the work of the campaign in broadly positive and constructive terms (Home Office, 2004g). Its introduction even speaks of tolerance and respect for young people who have, it says, just as much right to use public space as any other members of a community (but then drawing a line where this use of public space causes concern for others). But when it comes to the ministerial press release launching the report, the language reverts to tabloid-speak and references to thugs, loutish behaviour, yobs and 'yob culture'.

Developing this theme, Goldson (2000b), R. Smith (2003) and Stephen and Squires, (2004), among others, have argued that the new youth justice provisions reveal a marked tendency to treat young people as offenders first and children second. It is as if the most significant things about them were the risks they are presumed to represent and the offences they have committed. Smith, in particular, finds a great deal to criticise in the key analysis instrument the YJ professionals are required to use to make assessments of the young offenders with whom they work: the ASSET form. This document is positioned as a key document, the central feature of a 'micro-politics of social control' (Smith, R. 2003: 63). The information provided by it formed the core database information, eventually to be held electronically, for every young person with whom a YOT came into contact. In addition it comprised a criminological profile, served as a risk assessment tool and a record of decisions made regarding actions to be taken by the young person (or interventions to be made by others). For these reasons the ASSET assessment profile was a central document in the YOT's administrative system. In ASSET, each young person became a *case* and, in a very real sense, became reduced to the sum of offences committed, a series of social and psychological predispositions, behaviours and inferred motives, risks presented, interventions attempted – in short, reduced to a set of manageable descriptive factors and eventually, as we have seen, to a number, their assessment profile score.

Yet while this form aims to establish a truth about young offenders in order to determine a course of action to address the young person's offending behaviour, Smith concludes that, based upon standardised actuarial principles of risk management, 'the form is of little value in identifying needs or assisting in the construction of supportive intervention strategies – welfare is written out of its remit' (Smith, R. 2003: 192). Furthermore, to focus almost exclusively upon the criminalised behaviour of the young person while neglecting the needs and contexts in which the criminal behaviour arose effectively separates the crime itself from the 'causes' of crime – which had originally been New Labour's 'big idea' (ibid.: 188). Thus the standardised approach contained within ASSET overlooks many of the factors that are important to young people themselves, concentrates upon the risks and the offences rather than the person, fails to address needs or contexts and remains preoccupied with the criminal event rather than justice or welfare. Such a narrowing of the YJ system's frame of reference suggests to Pitts (2001) that the new system will not be able to deliver the new 'holistic' approach originally anticipated. For R. Smith, such limitations also extend to the range of orders available for young offenders. For example, in the case of the ISSP, he notes, 'there is a strong sense that surveillance and containment dominates at the expense of any underlying factors linked to the young person's offending, and there is no recognition of the importance of addressing need' (2003: 68).

The final element of Cohen's critique of the 'dispersal of discipline' takes us back to these broader questions relating to social welfare, needs, social exclusion and deprivation. It concerns both the conditions of emergence of ASB itself and our increasing preoccupation with it.

8. The neglected and deprived have been abandoned

Cohen's final theme connects to far wider critique of social disadvantage and exclusion than we can adequately deal with here. In a sense it is not simply that the poorest have been abandoned for there have been a wide range of 'joined-up' New Labour policy initiatives, in particular the New Deal for Communities programme targeted upon the most deprived communities. However, there remains a profound sense in which these 'multi-agency problem-solving initiatives' are just that, an attempt to respond to manifest problems rather than more long-term structural and material changes. To borrow an analogy from the policing and crime prevention fields, at worst they are a responsive form of firefighting, crisis interventions, filling gaps, knocking agency heads together or fighting for marginal adjustments in the composition of local budgets. Precisely this point came up in an interview we conducted with a member of a community safety (CS) team in a New Deal area in which we were working on one of the projects described in a later chapter.

> At the moment we're really just responding to what comes up, this is pretty much what we have been doing for the past year. But then there's a real backlog of problems which have been just left. We've got to get the other agencies on board and keep them at it. A lot of my time is spent on the phone with other parts of the council or the health trust to find out what they are doing or why something hasn't been done. A lot of it is just coping with what comes up. I think we are making progress, but if we are still doing this kind of firefighting five years down the line we'll have failed. (interview with CS team member, fieldwork notes)

Moving beyond simply coping, at best such 'multi-agency problem-solving initiatives' represent a kind of *situational* social policy (SSP) targeting local risks and problem hotspots, using sound actuarial and evaluation criteria. Yet, just as situational crime prevention (SCP) is typically said to be uninterested in the alleged *causes* of crime – or is at best agnostic – so situational social policies are relatively untroubled by (and largely incapable of doing anything about) the underlying causes of poverty, youth unemployment, educational failure, racism or family dysfunction. Or, at least, in so far as the policies adopted *imply* some pattern of causation for these problems, structural conditions are read as relational, behavioural or personal failings, that is to say they are individualised. Poverty is understood not as a lack of income or wealth, or a consequence of broader social inequalities, but rather as the result of poor spending decisions. Youth unemployment is not a result of the collapse of a youth labour market but the consequence of laziness and unemployability, and educational failure is not a problem of schooling but, largely, a consequence of pupil and parental indifference just as, as we have seen in our discussion of Parenting Orders, parental failure is understood as wilful and deliberate neglect.

The parallels between SCP and what we have called SSP go further. Thus it is sometimes argued, drawing upon neoclassical and control theory perspectives in criminology (Felson 1994), that 'opportunity ... plays a role in causing all crime' (Downes and Rock 2002: 252). As with SCP, so with SSP, social problems are reduced to questions of opportunity and choice, and victims of circumstance are held responsible for their predicament, something which is all the easier to do with a ready-made demonology of 'the other' available in populist discourse. The key policy (or crime prevention) interventions become confined to influencing people's choices rather than the circumstances under which they make them. In like fashion, Garland has written of the emergence of a supply-side criminology (2001: 129) in which the *consumers* of criminal opportunities become subjected to ever more disciplinary and coercive disincentives. By contrast, the *supply* of criminal opportunities (or the actions of those supplying criminal opportunities) are regarded as the fixed, inevitable and unalterable laws of nature – or, more typically, of the marketplace. Thus the criminogenic conditions resulting from the residualisation of social housing, the collapse of youth employment opportunities or the creation of a leisure economy based upon marketing alcohol to teenagers may be acknowledged but are seldom reversed. Likewise, social policies creating problematic social conditions, school exclusion policies, housing allocation policies, spending limits and service cuts can create precisely the kinds of anti-social contexts in which ASB is only to be expected. As Scraton and Haydon (2002: 325) have argued, 'children's offending and anti-social behaviour, like their other life experiences and personal opportunities, are located in powerful, structural determining contexts. We return, therefore, to a conception of anti-social policy (Squires 1990), the context in which ASB manifests itself.

It is all the more disappointing that our perspectives on contexts and behaviour or opportunities and choices have become so polarised (and, having done so, given rise to such behaviourally focused and individual-ised interventions) because there are alternative approaches which draw upon solid research evidence. In this vein, Pitts (2003) discusses work by Hagan (1993) and Wikstrom and Loeber (1997) which points to the developmental effect of neighbourhood deprivation upon young people's growth and socialisation, their accumulation of 'risk factors' and their patterns of offending. Thus 'the relation between risk factors and serious offending breaks down for those living in the most disadvantaged communities' (Pitts 2003: 119). In other words, neighbourhood deprivation factors appeared to overwhelm personal and familial protection factors (Beinart *et al.* 2002) for those in the poorest neighbourhoods. As Pitts concluded, 'the causal significance of neighbourhood socio-economic status has been seriously under-estimated in both mainstream criminological theory and contemporary criminal justice policy' (2003: 119). In this light, the failure to address the criminogenic factors associated with deprived neighbourhoods is compounded when they are effectively replaced by social control and enforcement policies. Less social crime prevention and more offender targeting and enforcement action seem bound to create more criminalisation. This issue seems rather less a simple question of net-widening and, instead, something more akin to the production of crime and disorder. These are issues we return to in the final chapter.

These issues lead us to a final aspect of the new 'situational' social policies. This concerns the priority afforded to crime and disorder management within them. Elsewhere we have referred to this as the 'criminalisation of social policy' or, in Cohen's own terms, the 'dispersal of discipline'. Even though the broad rationale informing New Labour social policy remains one of social inclusion, it is a highly disciplined form of inclusion (Levitas 1996) involving a profound individualisation of the delinquent. It shows, according to Garland, that New Labour in both its penal policy and its welfare, 'has rediscovered market discipline and [the] purity of economic disincentives' (2001: 130). Burney states the apparent contradiction more directly as a result of New Labour's attempt to combine sounding tough (for the benefit of middle England and the tabloid press) while trying to be effective. Thus, 'in criminological terms [New Labour] had lined up with "left realism" in recognising that the pains of crime and disorder were sharpest in poor neighbourhoods least well-equipped to deal with them, but adopted "right realism's" zero tolerance responses' (Burney 2002: 471). In fact, as we have argued earlier, it appears increasingly that the punitive and enforcement driven responses are now eclipsing the more progressive ambitions of 'community safety'. In its place we have inherited community enforcement, and this, as we have argued, is where ASB enters.

It may be objected that this is not what Cohen meant, when he referred to the abandonment of the 'neglected and deprived'. The question is undoubtedly one of social exclusion and yet New Labour have evidently prioritised inclusion as a policy goal. We would argue that this is a question of what these communities are being abandoned to or included within. Certainly the most troublesome among them are scrutinised, surveyed, tracked, tagged, curfewed and monitored more than ever before. This is not neglect, but rather more akin to what Foucault described as a new system of discipline reflecting the 'reversal of the political axis of individualisation' (1977: 192). In this system, 'the child is more individualised than the adult, the patient more than the healthy man, the madman and the delinquent more than the normal and the non-delinquent' (ibid.: 193). To follow Foucault here, the new systems of discipline both constitute the 'deviant behaviour' as activities contrary to some ideological conception of social order and individualise certain prototypical exponents of this behaviour. One aspect of this has involved the debate, in the case of ASBO proceedings, about whether the usual protection from public disclosure applied in juvenile justice proceedings should be waived. The case for suspending this protection (originating in the 1933 CYPA) is based upon both 'public interest' and 'enforcement' considerations. Thus 'naming and shaming' is said to be more effectively achieved where the public are informed about who may be subject to a given order (Stone 2003). Equally, considerations of enforcement are also employed to justify a more purposive stigmatisation of selected offenders: the community needs to know who is subject to an ASBO in order to report them if they are not complying with it. As Grier and Thomas (2003) note, there is some irony in the fact that recipients of ASBOs (who may be responsible for lower-level disorderly behaviour) may be denied a protection available to more serious juvenile offenders. A more cynical interpretation may be that the government welcomes such ASBO publicity because it communicates to the public that 'something is being done'.

A similar, although more generic point applies to the Youth Inclusion Projects (YIPs). In many areas, appropriately named Youth Inclusion Projects compiled a list of their top 50 most troublesome (or most anti-social) young people in order to target these for special measures to reduce their offending risk and associated anti-social behaviours. Interestingly, the choice of lists of 50 was loosely derived from the self-report and offence profiling work of Graham and Bowling (1995) and subsequently reported in *Misspent Youth* (Audit Commission 1996). Thus, around two-thirds of youth offending is attributed to some 5 per cent of young offenders. Hence the putative 'solution' almost speaks for itself. The infamous 5 per cent are to be identified and targeted accordingly – even 'nipped in the bud'. Notwithstanding Jones's concise dissection of what he called the Audit Commission's 'numerical sleight of hand' (Jones 2001a: 364), the 5 per cent of offenders is translated into the nicely rounded target of 50 'persistent young offenders' for each CDRP's Youth Inclusion Project. For each young person, a substantial dossier is then compiled although, in one of the few efforts to rigorously evaluate the attempt to operationalise the 5 per cent persistent young offender equation Little *et al.* found that 'the incidence of persistent offenders is not as high as agencies had planned for' (Little *et al.* 2004: 231). A proportion of 2.5 per cent seemed closer to the mark, suggesting that YIPs targeting a 5 per cent proportion were themselves contributing to the kind of net-widening effects we have earlier discussed.

Yet this net-widening is not abandonment and neither is enrolment into a Youth Inclusion Project or the intensive scrutiny package that comes with ISSP. However, they do mark a significant change in the terms of engagement of many young people with public policy institutions. Grier and Thomas (2003) refer to this as the 'disappearance of welfare' while rather earlier it has been referred to as the 'fragmentation' and 'secularisation' of the 'welfare ideal' (Squires 1990: 42) or, elsewhere, as the 'death' or 'crisis' of 'the social' (Rose 1996; McLaughlin 2002). Equally, it represents the increasing criminalisation of social policy or the substitution of 'criminal' for 'social' justice: the attempt to close the social justice gap with criminal justice interventions.

In the UK we have tended to react with a mixture of disbelief and disapproval at US evidence to the effect that over a third of young African-Americans are either in prison, on parole or taking part in some form of probation or community corrections programme (Tonry 1995; Currie 1996). The evidence points to a situation in which the primary relationship between racially marginalised minorities and the state becomes one dominated by punishment and social control (Wacquant 2001). It is not our suggestion that UK conditions even remotely approach the scale of the USA's problems in this regard, but simply that both net-widening and the criminalisation of social policy contribute to a trend leading in that direction. At this level our argument is simply that it is important that the primary contacts that young people have with public institutions are not those driven (exclusively or primarily) by punitive and social control imperatives (Beckett and Western 2001). Thus the 'abandonment' referred to relates to the 'manufacture of criminal careers' (Ruggiero 1997) and the related ostracism, exclusion, stigmatisation and progressive disengagement of relatively deprived young people from more inclusive and supportive forms of social policy. In Pitts's terms this means the abandonment of solidaristic social policies and the resort to discipline (Pitts 2003). Prior to that, it implies abandonment and exposure to market-led, globalising economic and social processes which have rendered certain skills, classes of people and even whole communities increasingly redundant (Bauman 1982, 2004; MacDonald 1997; Byrne 1999).

In the next chapter, by way of illustrating Pitt's arguments, we describe and analyse the use of new disciplinary measures to impose invidious standards of behaviour upon marginalised communities.

Chapter 5

The enforcement of acceptable behaviour

The publication of the Five-Year Plan *Confident Communities in a Secure Britain* (Home Office 2004c) addresses the government's 'commitments to law-abiding citizens' to enable this majority to feel safe in their homes and local environments through the fostering of 'strong and cohesive communities'. The Prime Minister, Tony Blair, concludes his foreword:

> Our target is another 15 per cent reduction in crime by 2008, safer streets and stronger communities. It is a tough challenge. But with the continued overhaul and modernisation of the criminal justice system which the government has outlined today, I believe that we can and will achieve. Investing more, acting more effectively and getting tougher with the hard core of criminals and troublemakers, we can build a new partnership with the decent law-abiding citizens to improve the quality of life in every neighbourhood. (Home Office 2004c: Foreword by the Prime Minister)

Tackling anti-social behaviour is a key aspect of this strategy (see Home Office 2004c: section 2.4). The quantified costs of this 'low-level criminality' superimposes upon the recounted wider social costs to local communities. In explicitly setting out to create a 'culture of intolerance', the government advocates the greater use of 'swift' measures to deal with anti-social behaviour, notably Acceptable Behaviour Contracts and Agreements (ABC/As), Parenting Contracts and Fixed Penalty Notices

(Home Office 2004c: 49). The term 'swift' peppers this section of the Plan – this 'swift' response will be backed up by greater responsiveness from a 'more effective' criminal justice system in processing cases since delays 'cause misery for the law-abiding majority' (Home Office 2004c: 51).

For reasons to be explained in this chapter, our research with young people subject to already extant anti-social behaviour measures (Stephen and Squires 2003a) and their families raises profound concerns about the emphasis on 'swift justice', the 'culture of intolerance' and the cementing of *Otherness* contained within this Plan. This Plan further reveals the extent to which, despite long-standing government rhetoric that, as well as 'being tough on crime', they seek to be 'tough on the causes of crime', this latter, sadly increasingly shallow, sentiment appears to have today become merely an interpretation of 'causes of crime' as the minor incivilities that may (at some possible time in the future) eventually lead to crime, instead of tackling the circumstances within which anti-social behaviour, or criminal agency, develops and proceeds. The 'investing more' of which the Prime Minister speaks appears to be investment in the ever growing anti-social industry rather than wholehearted commitment to fundamental issues of equity and social justice for all citizens, not just the seemingly unproblematic 'law-abiding'. Yet why should we be surprised as we have been forewarned of such trends for some time:

> Intervention comes earlier, it sweeps in more deviates, is extended to those not yet formally adjudicated and it becomes more intensive. (Cohen 1985: 53)

Alas there is no surprise, but certainly grave disappointment that a Labour *(sic)* government is championing acute social divisions through Draconian measures, particularly against young people, that potentially criminalises commonplace youth activities. Objectification, surveillance and 'swift' intervention are set to become routine *rites de passage* for young people in contemporary Britain. The Plan focuses upon efficiency and effectiveness, thus in progressively extending the parameters of intervention, as with the wider justice system, it further illustrates the most notable shift in youth justice: the advent of managerialist practices, or, more explicitly, the management of danger through 'actuarial justice' which Feeley and Simon (1994: 173) describe lucidly:

> It is concerned with techniques for identifying, classifying and managing groups assorted by levels of dangerousness.

In contemporary youth justice this shift is grounded in the 'hyper-politicization of youth crime' (McLaughlin *et al.* 2001: 303) and the consequential 'essentialization' of young people as 'Other' (see Young 1999). Such shifts have not been without their detractors, but David Smith (2003), correctly, bemoans the shortage of empirical assessment of the criticisms directed at New Labour, notably that the target of critical commentators is 'the language of New labour's policies rather than their effects' (Smith, D. 2003: 230). Although undoubtedly interconnected, and developing core concerns outlined in the preceding chapters, this chapter will, therefore, draw upon our empirical research with so-called 'anti-social' young people and their families. It shall be shown that empirically-grounded critiques must be offered for, as Kempf-Leonard and Peterson (2002) contend, this new model of 'justice' has less to do with traditional liberal notions and more to do with formal mechanisms of social control; indeed, in his accompanying speech, the Prime Minister hailed the launch of the government's initiatives as the end of some seeming 'liberal consensus'. It is this extension of social control, through the net-widening activities (Cohen 1985) inherent in the new 'civilianized' (Hope 1998b) youth justice measure of Acceptable Behaviour Contracts (ABCs), that must, and will, be exposed. Yet, it is not easy to challenge the realities faced by many communities subject to acts of anti-social behaviour by young people as characterised in governmental pronouncements:

> Anti-social behaviour can sometimes seem like minor crime in a courtroom. Vandalism, graffiti and harassment may seem trivial on a charge sheet. But behind those charges is often a community living in fear besieged by a reckless and out of control minority of thugs. (David Blunkett, in Home Office 2004a)

Notwithstanding these concerns, 'thugs' and 'yobs' (e.g. Home Office 2004b, 2004c, 2004d), commonly used populist adjectives in anti-social behaviour discourses, serve to reinforce notions of *dangerous Other* and cement ready acceptance of another, exponentially intrusive, measure to contain 'out of control' youngsters (*cf.* Garland 1996). Facilitated by left realism and fortified by media hyperbole of 'neighbours from hell', such representations have become almost self-evident truths. Yet, anti-social behaviour measures, underpinned by a growing 'institutionalized mistrust' (Kelly 2003) of marginalised youth, and a positivistic and somewhat narrow notion of 'victim', have failed to offer any insight or understanding of these *dangerous Others* (*cf.* Smith, R. 2003), let alone acknowledge their versions of this 'truth' (Stephen and Squires 2004). In illustrating the vacuous nature of pejorative constructs and responses by the accounts presented in this chapter, the consequences of ill-considered Acceptable Behaviour Contracts (ABCs) upon marginalised young people and their families will be revealed as unintelligible and deleterious to fostering any sense of inclusion and social justice in their lives (Stephen and Squires 2004). In offering the young people and their families nothing in return for compliance, ABCs appear to serve only to extend objectification, surveillance, control and marginalisation of this particularly vulnerable population.

Garland (2001) highlights the changes that have occurred within criminal justice, not least the relative impotence of criminal justice agencies and actors in the face of increasing political intervention. Contemporary populist punitiveness has led to a situation whereby

> A new relationship between politicians, the public and penal experts has emerged in which politicians are more directive, penal experts are less influential, and public opinion becomes a key reference point for evaluating options. (Garland 2001: 172)

This undoubtedly has electoral benefits (*cf.* Garland, 2001). It is, therefore, imperative to understand this increasing political intervention in youth justice. McLaughlin *et al.* (2001) outline the centrality of 'managerialisation' and command of 'the central ground of law and order politics' to New Labour's success in the 1997 General Election; these authors show that at the core were the 'communitarian values of mutual obligation, self-discipline and individual responsibility' to foster safer communities (McLaughlin *et al.* 2001: 303).

Thus, through the rhetoric and categories associated with Community Safety young people, especially, were to become 'the universal symbol of disorder' (Burney 2002: 473), the 'essentialized Other' (Young, 1999). As such, the apparently innocuous responses of 'civilianized' (Hope 1998b) crime prevention measures have become increasingly oppressive (Smith, R., 2003) with concomitant adverse consequences upon young people's rights (Fox 2002; Smith, R. 2003; Stephen and Squires 2004 (Stephen, forthcoming)). Rather than being severed, the links between 'anti-social behaviour', 'non-criminal disorder' and crime have become more and more entangled; as Kempf-Leonard and Peterson (2002) show there is an exponential effect of seemingly benign surveillance and intervention and subsequent chances of detection and sanction, with attendant repercussions for future life chances (e.g. Davies and Tanner 2003). This vital issue will be developed in Chapter 6.

A realist solution?

It is totally unacceptable that people are having to tolerate this type and level of anti-social behaviour in their communities day in and day out. It causes untold misery, corrodes communal life, undermines public services and forces people to live in fear in their own homes, afraid to go out and enjoy the public space in their community. (David Blunkett, in Home Office 2003d)

Supporting long-standing left realist concerns (e.g. Lea and Young 1984) and such populist governmental sentiments, research has long demonstrated the high priority the public accord to the need to tackle various anti-social behaviours and quality-of-life issues as well as more serious offences (e.g. Bland 1997). However, despite high levels of expressed concerns, what actually constitutes 'anti-social behaviour' is unclear and perceptions are influenced by a number of factors (see Wood 2004). Although, as also acknowledged in *Confident Communities in a Secure Britain* (Home Office 2004c), fear of crime and anti-social behaviour often seems to exceed the risk or experience of victimisation (Squires and Measor 1996), there have been calls for some years to accord public concerns about crime and fear reduction a much higher priority (Donnison 1997).

As part of New Labour's response, the Crime and Disorder Act 1998 marked a significant watershed in what has been described as 'the civilianization of crime prevention' (Hope 1998b: 6), if not also 'a Foucauldian strategy for classifying and controlling the problematic behaviour of the young' (Smith, R. 2003: 159). This Act makes specific provision for the tackling of anti-social behaviour through Anti-Social Behaviour Orders (see Home Office 2000, 2002b for guidance; see Burney, 2002 for fuller discussion). Of particular significance to this chapter was the inception of the Acceptable Behaviour Contract (ABC) which was said to be 'a useful alternative to Anti-Social Behaviour Orders (ASBO) where the latter are not considered justified' (Home Office 2000: Appendix G). The main difference between an ASBO and ABC is that the former is a civil order carrying legal force, while the latter is a more informal procedure. ABCs are not without some teeth, however, as they can lead to legal action in the form of an ASBO or Possession Order (if living in social housing) as consequences of any breach. The perceived advantage of the ABC was that it could be effected much more quickly and at much less cost (Home Office 2000: Appendix G); this certainly finds clearer resonance in more contemporary priorities of 'swift justice' (see Home Office 2004c).

The ABC was designed to tackle acts of anti-social behaviour by 10 to 18 year olds, though can be applied to a young person aged over 18 if they still reside in the parental home. The ABC is an individual written agreement between a young person and a partner agency (usually housing) and the police to desist from behaviour deemed 'anti-social' (Home Office 2004c: 49). Where the young person is under the age of 10 years, a similarly orientated Parenting Contract has been used where the parents adopt full responsibility for their child's behaviour (Home Office 2004c: 49). The ABC is usually in force for up to six months and can be extended; its effectiveness is monitored by the partner agency and the police through regular reviews (Home Office 2000, 2002b).

The family and its place in Community Safety

> The predictive element in targeting 'at risk' families exemplifies actuarial justice strategies, as do the net-widening activities of including families in the first place. (Kempf-Leonard and Peterson 2002: 445)

As the accounts offered shortly will show, the ABC does not just have consequences for the young person – there are knock-on effects for the whole family. This reflects wider policy trends of recent years where there has been an important shift towards intervention in the private sphere of the family. This is particularly so with regard to family breakdown and failure and breaking the cycle of disadvantage through multi-agency, preventive interventions (see Bayley 1999), especially, as shown below, in the light of the, real or perceived, association between the family and crime.

> Strong families are at the centre of peaceful and safe communities. Parents have a critical role in teaching their children the difference between right and wrong, and giving them the confidence to grow up to be proud of themselves, their family, their friends and their community. Respect is all-important, and this is missing in families that behave dysfunctionally. (David Blunkett, in Home Office 2003b: 8)

In New Labour's rather functionalist vision, 'the family' plays a central role in society's well-being and progress (see Barlow and Duncan 2000a, 2000b) and, through increasingly value-laden discourses as typified above, the government have been seeking to use policy to encourage 'good' family forms and practices, for example by the Parenting Order incepted in the Crime and Disorder Act 1998. Certainly, the White Paper *No More Excuses* (Home Office 1997a) presented clear predisposing factors for youth crime: living in a family with multiple problems and/or having criminal parents and poor parental discipline, alongside being male, associating with delinquent peers and school exclusion. Such findings provide fertile rationale for regarding the family as 'a site for expert invasion' (Cohen 1985: 79) in order to engender 'a new, disciplined capacity for self-regulation' (Pitts 2000: 10).

This focus upon the role of the family, however, masks the wider factors that produce anti-social or criminogenic outcomes, and, indeed, belies this government's own well-meaning attempts to tackle social exclusion through a range of initiatives such as the *New Deal for Communities*, *Sure Start* or *Youth Inclusion Project* (see Home Office 2004c), and hereby upholding their continuing commitment to the recommendations of The Morgan Report (Home Office 1991). In this latter respect, local Community Safety Partnerships are encouraged to adopt a holistic, problem-solving approach when dealing with anti-social behaviour (Campbell 2002b). Correspondingly, however, other research highlights a serious lack of support for children and families in socially excluded estates (Page 2000) which is supported in our own research with marginalised young people and their families (e.g. Stephen and Squires 2001; Stephen and Squires 2003a) as will now be shown.

Outline of sample and methods

During 2002 research relationships were fostered with ten families in a New Deal Area in a city on the south coast of England. This New Deal for Communities (NDC) Community Safety Team was one of the first projects to be developed by the local NDC Community Partnership; at the time of research the project had funding for three years and this has since been extended. This Team aimed to take effective action to reduce anti-social behaviour and crime through a co-ordinated approach to:

- support victims and build community confidence in local services to address local concerns;
- bring together a range of services to reduce anti-social behaviour and the incidences of crime;
- deal with all serious cases of anti-social behaviour;
- provide opportunities for people to change their behaviour;
- work with mainstream services to prevent problems;
- use legal powers to stop anti-social behaviour;
- coordinate projects.

The core team comprised a Team Leader and an administrator, the Neighbourhood Warden Leader, a Community Beat Sergeant, Housing Officers, community representatives, a solicitor and a Youth Inclusion Project Manager. The team liaised with wider agencies that contribute to community safety: the police, housing management, environmental health, youth services, cleansing and highways, education, health, probation, Youth Offending Team and Social Services, all of whom, purportedly, had named personnel for this purpose, but, in practice, commitment was highly variable (Stephen and Squires 2003a).

Commissioned by the Community Safety Team, the qualitative research remit was to elicit the families' feelings about their experience of the ABC process (Stephen and Squires 2003a). The 13 young people subject to contracts within these families comprised 11 males and 2 females who were aged between 9 and 16 years. Twelve were, or had been, subject to ABCs and one was under 10 years, so a Parenting Contract applied. The young people had been placed on contracts for a range of 'anti-social behaviours' that encompassed swearing, stone-throwing, harassment and bullying, and, in a couple of cases, fire-setting. Research encounters with the young people and their families comprised pre-interview informal telephone calls and meetings, at least one loosely structured qualitative interview as a family group and/or individually, follow-up telephone calls and letters, and a final meeting. All research participants were invited to evaluate the findings before the final draft.

Overview of the key data

The key opening question asked of the participants at the start of each interview was: 'How did you come to be involved with the Community Safety Team?' Tensions with neighbours and other local residents emerged as the foremost response and, in these cases, the participants provided names and extensive details of those whom they believed had made the complaints. Most participants questioned the credibility of those complainants and the evidence against them. This was especially so where the complaint seemed to have been made by someone with whom a parent had had a previous disagreement and, frequently, participants commented along the lines of 'if we'd known how easy it was to report [person] we'd have done so before they reported us'.

Naturally, as researchers, we had to remain objective about the families' claims, but one of us was to be present during an 'incident' which seemed to lend some veracity to a particular family's situation. When reviewing the casenotes for one of the families, it was noted that the neighbour had recorded a complaint about the young person's behaviour on the very date and time of the main family interview. In the light of the researcher's observations throughout that particular evening, this complainant's account must be questioned. This is not to undermine the extensive, albeit 'grey', intelligence collated by the Community Safety Team, but to provide an introduction to the sense of injustice and frustration expressed by many of the participants in respect of the problematic notions of 'evidence' and 'anti-social behaviour'.

The Crime and Disorder Act 1998 defines 'anti-social behaviour' as 'behaviour which causes or is likely to cause harassment, alarm or distress to one or more people who are not in the same household as the perpetrator'. Concerns have been directed at these developments since not only can almost any behaviour potentially be regarded as 'anti-social', but there is a much lower standard of proof (see Burney 2002; Fox 2002). Indeed, among the research participants, the notion of 'anti-social behaviour' itself produced the greatest discontent; they felt that the young people had been 'singled out' for behaviour that was often very little different from that of their friends in the same age groups:

> How can you explain to a boy that we'll lose our house if he doesn't behave when he doesn't know what he's done different to all the other kids around here ... He knows right from wrong, but they'd made him out to be really bad.

> It was all a battle for dominance amongst peers to become leader of the gang. Some of his mates were worse ... where we're from you get respect for being a good bank robber, if you come from an affluent area, you get respect from good qualifications, here, it's the same, you need to prove yourself to be leader of the pack ...

> It was all just boy things that went too far.

As indicated, relativity was the key factor the families wished to highlight. This related to what they regarded as the relatively minor nature of the young people's behaviour when compared to the much more serious crimes apparently going unpunished within these marginalised estates. As such, parents and youngsters frequently alluded to the severity of the contract vis-à-vis the young people's behaviour.

As mentioned earlier, an ABC can lead to legal action in the form of an ASBO or Possession Order (if living in social housing) as consequences of any breach. The Guidance on drafting ASBO Protocols applicable at the time, however, made a not insignificant statement, in that 'an ABC is *not legally binding* but it can be cited in proceedings such as for an Anti-Social Behaviour Order' (Home Office 2000: Appendix G, emphasis added). Not only were the families not informed of the dubious legality of the contracts at the time of inception, but, significantly, one of the families who participated in this project resided in their own private house and even this did not delimit the threat of eviction because an old local authority by-law had been found relating to their property. This threat of eviction weighed heavily on most of the research participants' minds and they simply could not understand why they faced eviction for the behaviour of their child and, indeed, for behaviour that was often (as will be shown) rooted in mental health problems or learning difficulties.

[ABC subject]'s dyslexic, he can't read or write and the eviction really played on his mind. What kind of responsibility is that for a boy knowing that his family will lose their home if he doesn't behave.

I thought it was bullshit cause we didn't do half the things that goes on in this estate. Yes, I was worried that we'd be evicted, but it seemed completely over the top for a couple of things when you see what other families're doing ... but with me, they'd be straight in on my case. No it ain't fair is it, but that's just the way the world is.

I can't read or write ... They got me to sign this contract saying my family'd be evicted if I didn't behave ... I had to ask Mum after what that meant.

Most of the families felt they had been offered no choice but to sign the contracts which contained terms already decided upon. They felt that, contrary to English law and human rights, they had been afforded no opportunity to demonstrate innocence or challenge the (questionable) 'evidence' against them. These contracts were, most felt, more to do with the Community Safety Team's requirements and less to do with their own family needs. The young people's, and many of the parents', general inability to recall the terms of their contracts or the specific reasons why they, or their children, had been placed on a contract highlights the extent to which they felt subject to, rather than involved in, the ABC process.

They'd built up this dossier, there was no warning

No names were supplied so I had no opportunity to question the honesty or accuracy. You have no choice not to sign ... I never had a chance to say 'prove it', you can't when you're faced with losing your home.

The contract was just sitting there, we'd no choice, had to sign it. The first meeting was scary, we just walked in and they told us ... that they had evidence.

They gave us the impression they were out to stick the knife in.

I wouldn't have signed the contract if I didn't feel it was a threat.

Although the key concern is to prevent anti-social behaviour through a range of initiatives (e.g. Boys and Warburton 2000; Smith, D., 2003), there has been a growing trend for social landlords to exclude tenants on these grounds (Hunter *et al.* 2000). It has been shown that evictions serve to weaken housing demand in unpopular areas and transplant problems elsewhere (Hunter *et al.* 2000). Of particular relevance, the Policy Action Team 8 report (Social Exclusion Unit 2001) highlights more than the social and financial costs to the local communities, it addresses the impact of eviction and exclusion on persistent perpetrators and their families which can include:

- loss of contact with service providers, family and friends;
- the effects upon children in terms of education and health and the increased likelihood that they will be taken into care;
- alienation from society;
- imprisonment.

As indicated here, it has been shown that exclusion from social housing can undermine initiatives to tackle social exclusion by denying housing to those who may need it most (Butler 1998), as this mother explains:

> But they don't realise they'll split the whole family up if we're evicted, I've been looking for houses and it's all 'no DSS', so [oldest child] will end up in prison, [youngest child] will end up in care because they don't put special needs kids into B and B and [middle child] and me'll be in homeless accommodation cause they said they wouldn't re-house us cause we'll be making ourselves intentionally homeless … It's going to cost the government more to kick me out than keep me here.

Despite such sentiments, others suggested that feelings about the status of the ABCs had been mixed and they were not prepared to accept the possibility of eviction without a fight

> I felt it was a threat, but I didn't actually feel threatened, I feel there's anti-social behaviour and there's anti-social behaviour, but what they were doing wasn't actually illegal, they were just being little sods … It would take a lot more than my kids doing a few verbals to get me out of my house, I'd've got a solicitor onto it.

Nonetheless, the ABC appeared to provide fertile ground for abuses given the much lower burden of proof required. A few of the families reported the influence of what they believed were pre-existing biases against them.

Most believed they had not been given a 'fair hearing' and questioned the presumption of 'guilt'. They felt they had been given little or no opportunity to present their 'side'. The families, therefore, suggested that all parties should be listened to on an equal basis and mediation attempted before the application of an ABC.

> They only picked him up because he was there, he was a 'known face' from a 'known family', that's all it comes down to really.

> We're a well known family mostly through our oldest son, he's not liked by the police, [eldest son] is considered by the police as dangerous ... they won't go near him ... it's not like we get preferential treatment like the Krays when we go to Asda, but we're known to be not a nice family, so everything [ABC subject] does is watched, he's the most prominent child at his age of his generation just 'cause of our family, he got a lot of stick at school 'cause of his brother ... so they read the Riot Act to [him].

> It was the same as taking him to court, but the difference was that [son]'d already been tried and convicted, they'd made up their mind about us 'cause of our relations, but we're not like them ... We already knew they'd made their minds up about us (explains his sibling's situation) ... that's different, [sibling's] kids were getting into real trouble, but what [son] was doing was minor, so why was he given the same treatment? It could all have been sorted if they'd just spoken to us before going so far ... 'Cause've my family, I think, 'cause they said 'we're not going to tar you with the same brush as your [sibling]', but they said that, so we knew they'd made up their minds about us, they didn't give us a chance to tell our side of the story, it was worse than going to court, 'cause we were guilty from the start ...

Despite these concerns, the families stressed they had believed they would receive something in return for compliance with the contracts and it is these expectations of the contractual process that provide a way of understanding the families' feelings about 'success' or 'failure' of the ABCs. Basically, where expectations that very real and long-standing support needs would begin to be addressed, implicit in the families' understanding of the mutual obligations associated with the term 'contract', but were not, evaluations were least favourable. The notion of 'contract' raised expectations that something concrete would be received in return and is particularly significant where mainstream services were perceived to have failed the families in the past. For the majority of families involvement with the Community Safety Team reinforced rather than redressed existing feelings of disengagement with, if not alienation from, wider agencies.

> What's the point of this contract if they're not giving us any support? It's the same for all the kids round here on them, they need support, but there's nothing. The kids are left to get on with things, but they've no future.

> That visit once a month is what they give. Just had to get on with it ourselves 'cause that's the way it's always been with [son].

Instead of 'contract' being a relationship of mutual obligations, as they had anticipated, the families were left feeling this was merely a further stick with which to beat them. From their world-view, contracts, underpinned by the moralistic rhetoric of 'responsibilisation' (e.g. Flint 2002) and enforced by threat of eviction, revealed the extent to which they had become almost 'ideal types' of that great 'epistemological fallacy' (Furlong and Cartmel 1997) of late modernity in that they were being coerced into formulating individual solutions for problems that, for them, were almost entirely of a structural nature.

> When he was in infants school I was told he was a spoilt child … Everyone's just called him a 'problem child'.

Over half of the young people associated with this research project had rather serious mental health or significant personality disorder problems and related learning difficulties, although learning difficulties were also reported among those who did not have specific mental health problems too. Where mental health problems were diagnosed, most of the young people were receiving psychological/psychiatric support.

> I'm concerned why [son] was put on it, he'd only two cases, wasn't a long history … [named police officer] said there had been a discussion about what kids should be on it, who was vulnerable, she didn't think he should be on it, but [more senior police officer] did. I was asked if I could attend housing to see about the ABC. I wasn't happy with that, he's not as bad as other kids, he was just stupid about a year ago. I said I'm not signing that, my husband neither, he's still not happy. [Son]'s had a few problems since birth so he's not responsible for what he does and now we have to be responsible for what happens. Told them I'm not signing it. It's not a legal document but then I thought since he'd been in no trouble since on police bail

this might help him with the issues about his mental health ... They've had information after information about his mental health, he can't read or write, but it's all ignored.

While three of the young people were receiving support for depression-related illnesses, two being related to past experiences of domestic violence and abuse, officially diagnosed Attention Deficit Hyperactivity Disorder (ADHD), for which psychological support and medication (mostly Ritalin) was being received, emerged as the central mental health issue. The parents whose children were thus diagnosed were adamant that those in authority needed to recognise the effects of ADHD on family life. This mother describes her sense of relief on receiving this diagnosis:

When the doctor started describing his symptoms I just listened, amazed, I couldn't believe it. I thought to myself, 'that's not just [son]'s symptoms,' he was describing the exact same symptoms as I'd seen in my older three children. It was astonishing, I didn't know what to say ... But afterwards it really helped, we knew then that there was something really wrong, it wasn't that they were just naughty or that we'd done something wrong to them ... When he went onto Ritalin, then suddenly he became a normal boy again, a normal three and half year old boy. You could begin to hold a conversation with him, he could ask for what he wanted, without getting really frustrated that he couldn't get the words out. It was completely different, he was just a normal boy from then.

Ritalin, however, was not the complete answer to the family's problems:

At times when he's got really wound up, like when his pills have been wearing off, he's stabbed his dad in the stomach, he's thrown bottles at me when I've been holding the baby in my arms, so I talk to him to try and defuse the situation, get him to calm down and think about what he's doing. He'll shout, rant and rage at you, calling you all the things under the sun, but he'll never look you in the eye. All you can do is try to get him to calm down.

Those parents also stressed that, once their children had reached their teens, they were not able to impose this 'medicinal cosh', as typified in this Father's conversation with one of his older sons:

Father: Why won't you take your Ritalin any more now?
Son: Because it makes me be good.
Father (to the researchers): What can you say to that?

Parents were very eager to explain the consequences of such mental health problems for their children

> The kids at the school know he has to take the pills, so they all get onto him about being a drug addict, so that's not very nice is it. They also know that by about lunchtime he'll be coming off the Ritalin, and they know they can wind him up about then. He takes his pill before lunch but it can take 20–30 minutes to start to work. So they wind him up then, trip him up, push him out of the dinner queue, nothing that much really but they know they can get a reaction from him … and he kicks off. We've told him that if other boys bully him he can fight back to defend himself, but there's been a few incidents where he's got upset and it has taken four teachers to hold him down. So now they've made him leave at 12.30 and he only does the mornings. It's as if he's the cause of all the trouble. And because he misses the afternoons, he doesn't get to do sports and games or go swimming, it is not fair.

Parents also wished to explain that this sense of exclusion extended far beyond the school into their wider social relations

> At home we've tended not to let him out, as far as we can. We don't want him to be a prisoner in his own home though. Mostly he doesn't want to go out very much, he can't really street play. ADHD kids often get bullied or manipulated by the other kids who think it is funny to wind them up. When they're on the Ritalin, they can be very calm, but also very suggestible and other kids tend to take advantage.

> They can be very excluded … they don't get invited to any other children's birthday parties. It's not easy explaining to your children why they've not been invited. They know, for instance, that there will have been invitations going around in the classroom, but they never get one.

It is, therefore, imperative to underline the omnipresent sense of anger and frustration expressed by parents whose children were diagnosed with ADHD and subject to ABCs.

> I was angry, [son]'s got ADHD and they [Community Safety Team] were punishing him for something he's got, he couldn't help … it was like a punishment, they were using him as a scapegoat, like an experiment … I'm not just angry with how [he]'s been treated, but all

these kids on the estate, there are hundreds with ADHD, but they [the authorities] are doing nothing for them, they don't understand the condition.

You can't treat a whole family as responsible for the behaviour of a 12-year-old – especially when he's got ADHD. It just isn't right … They are punishing these children … they're punishing them for an illness that they can't control.

Perhaps surprisingly in the light of what has just been said, the ABCs were deemed to have 'worked' with 10 of 13 young people involved in this project. What this actually means is that the young people finished their contracts to the satisfaction of the Community Safety Team. However, there existed a range of conflicting ideas about what actually counts as 'success' between the Community Safety Team and the families:

He lets it build up, but he still comes in here and kicks off throwing and breaking things. He's had to learn to control it in the house … He still loses it, but he has to come in here and break things, he wants to murder people, but it all kicks off in here … He is so angry he can't do anything about it. I tell the kids [other family members] to let him do it 'he's doing it in here and not out there'.

I've had to do night work to be here if he kicks off during the day, it's hard, we don't have qualifications to look after a child like [name], but we're left to cope on our own … I don't have time to fill, or for the other kids 'cause I'm always protecting [ABC subject]. It really affects your nerves, every time I hear I siren, even if I know he's in the house, I sit and worry.

These differing notions of success reveal, starkly, the lacuna between qualitative lived outcomes for the families and the managerialist outputs of 'actuarial justice' (Feeley and Simon 1994) inherent in the 'management of danger' through ABC enforcement. This new form of 'economic government' (Kelly 2003: 167) was certainly reducing visible acts of anti-social behaviour by those young people in their local community, but this came at increased risk and cost to the well-being of already fragile family units.

As shown earlier, current government rhetoric focuses upon the importance of 'strong families' to community safety. However, in contrast, the families' accounts revealed that the ABC served to undermine the integrity of their families. The ABC caused tensions between parents and children, among parents themselves and created intra-familial marginalisation through resentment from siblings of the young person subject to the ABC:

Don't see why we'll all get punished for [brother]'s behaviour, s'not fair, this is our house.

He's got [siblings] breathing down his back, they're scared too, they don't see why they should lose their home because of him, so they've been breathing down his back all the time ... It's not just him that's on the ABC, but the whole family ...

But they didn't just put him on it, they put us all on it, that puts you under a lot of stress, it affected the other kids most, they knew if he didn't behave they'd lose their house. Why should we be punished for his ADHD?

I'm on anti-depressants. It's not doing the rest of the family any good either, they're all blaming [son], they're all arguing

It all put a lot of strain on [wife] ... they were giving us unnecessary grief ... [asked how they cope] ... We don't cope, its as simple as that. [Wife]'s on tranquillisers and anti-depressants and I'm about to lose my job.

Parents did not expect much, they simply wanted their children to have a 'fair chance', especially in terms of education, and a few had shown great resourcefulness and tenacity in securing some limited opportunities themselves, but the contracts achieved nothing in respect of such fundamental concerns. The young people and their families needed more positive reasons for change than the threat of eviction, but the Community Safety Team were impotent in their ability to deliver concrete opportunities due to poor partnership engagement and wider resource constraints.

Various agencies are expected to work in partnership to effect Community Safety policies in practice, but there are major tensions between enforcement and support, and barriers to full partnership working (Stephen and Squires 2003a). Nonetheless, if employed in an anti-oppressive (e.g. Braye and Preston-Shoot 1995) manner, ABCs could offer new opportunities for family support by opening up opportunities to re-establish relationships between agencies and marginalised young people and their families by enabling access to wider resources. One of the two mothers who supported the contracts explains:

I felt I'd been dumped when it was over. They've been there ... It's like the ambulance service, you never need an ambulance, but you know it's there... I know if I want to speak to [Community Safety Officer] she's there. They're like the fourth emergency service. I feel quite grateful to them ... it was all positive, nothing but positive, they broke the barrier down I had in dealing with people ... the contract saved us a job and helped us, it made life easier for us.

The two mothers who felt the ABCs had been a success were united by common elements. In both cases, older children were in prison and neither mother wished their younger children to follow in their siblings' footsteps. The mothers had experienced past domestic violence and were now in new, more supportive, relationships. Although the older siblings had been affected by this, the age differences meant that the younger children had largely escaped the adverse effects experienced by their older siblings and did not have mental health problems or special educational needs; neither mother reported current mental health problems either. Although those mothers reported that their initial feelings about the ABCs had been entirely negative and confrontational, they said they came to appreciate having been made aware of their children's behaviour and welcomed the supportive relations with the community safety and police officers whom they held in common. Both had wished the supportive relationship to continue on a more formal basis when the contracts were completed. Arising from their earlier experiences with enforcement agencies, their initial expectations of any workable relationship had been very low. However, the significant factor to note is that the young people in these families had not been in need of wider support resources, unlike the rest of the young people subject to the contracts.

In stark contrast to such positive sentiments, wider resources, or rather their absence, are what the majority of families believed lay at the root of their children's difficulties and there was a strong feeling that they were being punished for failings in the wider system. The research participants all focused upon two main agencies: education and social services. Despite the pressing educational needs recounted, only four of the young research participants attended school on a routine basis (one of whom, with severe emotional problems, was truanting regularly).

I don't think that these half-day schools are any good. If they're said to have special educational needs, what kind of sense does it make to give them less education than other kids get?

Like this mother, young people and their parents were quick to mention what they perceived as a completely absurd situation: that young people with special educational needs receive less education than their mainstream counterparts. Parents expressed a desperate desire for specialist provision for their children and, even where this had been possible, they regarded it as too little to be at all effective in the long term.

He was at [named specialist school], he got on alright there, came home with lots of certificates, but it was only for three months and that wasn't long enough, they wanted to mainstream him, and that all went wrong. If he'd've stayed there [specialist school] he'd've been alright ...

In most of the cases where specialist provision had been found, the parents usually said they had organised this themselves. The parents whose children had learning difficulties compounded by mental health problems expressed the greatest resentment towards the educational system and they all attributed this to a fundamental lack of provision for, and awareness of, their children's problems:

He's always been a hyperactive kid and since the age of eleven years I've been asking to have him statemented, but nothing happened. If he'd've got help then, this wouldn't be happening now. [Junior school] said he'd have problems going to the big school and he did, he was thrown out of [senior school] for fighting and verbal abuse.

Why did they take him out of [special school]? Why didn't they give him a residential place when I asked? He's got literacy problems and no one's helping him. I've been crying out for help, but nobody wants to know.

This lack of educational provision was superimposed upon a long-standing dearth of support from wider welfare agencies:

Education are the worst offenders, but none of them have any insights into what's happening. Social services suggested locking him in a room, but how can I do that, he's no fear so he'll just jump out the window.

I've been trying to get a social worker for [son], but no one ever gets back to you. I've even said it to the police, what can I do about [him] that I'm going to try social services again, but they did nothing. The police've said to me that that's common in [this estate] ...

I asked for help from social services and all they offered me was family therapy, but the rest of the family objected 'what do we need to see a family therapist for?' I wanted respite care so I could take the other kids away, because they're the ones who lose out in all of this, but no, they said they 'had no money'. Some of us wanted to set up a special club for these kids, but they told us they didn't have the money or the qualified staff. No one wants to take any responsibility for it [ADHD] ... The doctor's not offering any hope either, just prescribes pills [anti-depressants for the mother and Ritalin for her son].

Community Safety is supposed to be about keeping the community safe and the rhetoric and policy documents suggest that it is easy to identify victims and perpetrators. The accounts offered show that no such objective categories exist. Indeed very many people in the neighbourhoods within which those young people's anti-social behaviour was enacted suffered and residents have every right to expect protection, but do these sentiments not apply to the young people and their families too? Anti-social behaviour enforcement is opening up highly complex situations for which the community safety practitioners are relatively ill-equipped by virtue of their housing backgrounds, as one parent indicated:

But they're limited in what they can do ... they are only allowed to do so much.

The Community Safety Officers' roles appeared to have had very fluid edges and, from the discussions with the families and practitioners themselves, it was clear that they offered more support to the families than might have been expected. Significantly, the extent to which they were able to empathise with the families' situations was very apparent; they seemed to be able to balance the enforcement/support line in a commendable manner. However, the families believed that the so-called 'partner agencies', if not also government, needed to adopt much more responsibility than they had been. It was interesting to note that the families' concerns were to be supported in the priorities identified by one of the key specialist project professionals who worked closely with the Community Safety Team. These were

- the need to look at the young people's situations holistically;
- the needs for empowering support for the families;
- the need for respite care;
- the need for someone outside of the home whom young people can talk to.

The following outline, therefore, demonstrates the means through which the families believed such imperatives encompassed in their almost unanimous appeal for 'support not punishment' might be realised. Most of the young people and families focused upon wider organisations than the Community Safety Team. Firstly though, almost all highlighted their alienation from local neighbourhood developments.

A few questioned contemporary managerialism and the New Deal priorities. For them, there was no sense of inclusion in the multi-millions of pounds being invested in their neighbourhood:

> It seems that it's [ABC] just given out to put the numbers up for their statistics. When we went to court, the police told the court official that the arrest 'had to be marked up as a New Deal arrest' and when the court official asked why they explained 'it was to do with government numbers'.

> *Father*: That's why I think it's unfair about the contract. I think it was all about them trying to make a name for themselves … It felt like a strong threat, very strong. It's all government funded, they're advertising jobs at £32,000, so they're serious about it, so they're all trying to make a name for themselves cause they were just starting … *Mother*: They knew all the trouble we were in and they just added more. We were their guinea pigs.

> The whole problem in this area is the youth and anti-social behaviour, but it's just 'cause there's nothing for the kids to do. The New Deal is all out of touch with what people really need, but they're not listening … no, all they're interested in is buying and selling and becoming landlords.

For those young people aged 13 to 16 years who could attend the Youth Inclusion Project, even the most reticent among this age group expressed the benefits of the project, highlighting particularly the relevance of the activities to their lives and the lack of condescension from the staff. The apparent success of the Youth Inclusion Project (YIP) to engage those young people was marred by its exclusivity; the young people under the age of 13 expressed a desire to partake in such activities and were denied by virtue of their age. One of the government's 'commitments to law abiding citizens' is that YIP funding will increase by 50 per cent (Home Office 2004c: 13), which is welcomed, but arguably this is still insufficient in the light of the research participants' accounts. Parents and youngsters felt that this younger group were not being catered for and one young person suggested a possible means of beginning to integrate young people into the community:

> We need outreach workers on the street, like they have for the homeless, the kids need people telling them what's available, where they can get things.

Where clubs existed (mostly for the older age group), there were two key issues: self-exclusion from the clubs that exist and cost (*cf.* Measor and Squires 2000; Stephen and Squires 2001).

It's so boring for them here, there's nothing for them. Yes, there's clubs, but the kids that go aren't the ones they want to mix with, they'd get into more trouble with that lot.

They say there are loads of clubs but we need to pay.

The young people felt that they would never be able to derive a sense of investment in their neighbourhood, or indeed society, so long as they felt excluded through leisure. This is not just a leisure issue though. Parents, especially those whose children had ADHD, stressed the need for a safe arena in which their children could expend and channel their energy in productive ways, believing this would have multiple benefits to the youngster, the family and the wider community. Exclusion from leisure is a vital issue given that most of the young people had nothing else to do with their time through exclusion from school.

If you exclude a child from school you're taking away all their life, their friends, because it's all they've got. If they don't go to school they don't go out, they've got nowhere to go. There ought to be more clubs and groups for kids like this, there's nothing here at all for them.

As highlighted in this extract, the young people's exclusion was multi-layered and parents had great problems keeping their children occupied throughout the day. The educational provision for children with special needs (such that it was) seems predicated on there being a parent at home and it is, therefore, difficult for parents to maintain employment and normal family relationships. A common finding where two parents were rearing the family was that they 'took shifts' to monitor the child(ren) and as such had no time or personal space for themselves. The situation for single parents was much worse as they usually had no one to turn to for support. Where the young person was excluded from school, there was no respite whatsoever. Accordingly, parents and the young people were unanimous in identifying what the educational system should offer: full-time or residential specialist schools for children with special educational needs, and local basic literacy skills classes, as a right, not something for which they had to fight.

There's nothing for these children. They say they don't have money or resources. I had to fight for the special school, it's an independent school ... they have not let him down, they know how to handle him, but I'd to fight for that.

Respite care emerged as the single most common factor parents wanted from social services. This, parents maintained, would give them a break from the stresses of looking after a child with behavioural problems, and provide their other children with opportunities to experience 'normal family life', such as days out or holidays. However, and this reveals an important issue of expectations, this did not fall within the remit of social services for, absurdly, none of the young people in this project met the 'High Priority' criteria set by local social services. Locally based support groups for families whose children have mental health problems was a second pressing wish. A couple of parents were keen to set up their own groups, but one said she had been told they needed professional support which had not been forthcoming. Parents were pessimistic for the future of their children, and indeed the local community, if the status quo remains:

Kids like [ABC subject] are vulnerable ... [he] comes under the Mental Health Act, but there's been no one there to protect him. We need real community developments for kids like them, run by people who understand ... Something needs to be done for other excluded kids, they set [him] off and are bad influences ... These kids tend to stick together too, imagine their strength if they all kicked off together on the estate, they need to understand that this could happen if nothing's done ... They're pushing kids like him out of the community, not bringing them in.

The main thing the families wanted was a sense of justice. Most were utterly bewildered that they were threatened with eviction while, they believed, the 'real criminals' were evading any kind of punishment for their more deleterious activities on the estates.

So how come's that family's still on this estate? How come's they haven't been evicted? No, they're all still nicely tucked up in their home causing trouble and selling drugs with no worries over their head ... They're picking on the wrong families for the wrong reasons. They've got to get the drugs off the estate, all the families selling pills, they're all prescription pills ... I saw a new doctor who said to me that she'd never had to give out so many prescriptions for anti-depressants and tranquillisers and that's it, half of them's being sold to the kids.

For the families, the whole emphasis of Community Safety was wrong; the naïve 'broken windows theory' (Wilson and Kelling 1982) clearly bore no resemblance to the actuality of their daily lives:

> It shouldn't be done this way. It's [ABC subject] that needs help, he's needed help for years, but no one listened. If anything, threatening to throw a family on the street's going to make the child worse.

The families felt that no one had bothered to explore their 'side' before formal action was taken and, especially in the case of neighbour disputes, they expressed exasperation that mediation had not been tried before contracts were considered.

> *Mother*: They should talk to both parties, but they don't. The person reporting is taken as the only story. It was easy with [ABC subject], with him being a boy and them being girls, but no one looked into what they'd been doing before …

> *Father*: It's all over nothing, but that's life nowadays. It's been fifty–fifty all the way along, but they made it seem like it was [him] one hundred per cent.

> I felt before they took such a drastic step they should have tried some arbitration or something … If mediation failed, then use the contract, but mediation is more important to start with. There was nothing before the contract.

As indicated earlier, the families also felt strongly about the very nature of the contract itself. For them, a contract meant a partnership of mutual obligations and, in their firm belief, this issue certainly needs to be addressed.

> I feel it's very one-sided … The council don't offer anything in the contract, they ask them to sign that they'll not do all these things, but they're giving nothing in return … What is there on this estate for him to do, he's tried really hard, he likes the outdoors, but it's nothing they're giving him. All they promised is for the older children, they have given ours nothing.

The compounded sense of exclusion and despair arising from their expectations of what a 'contract' might bring in terms of support had been magnified by the imposition of yet another stressor on their already fraught lives, something upon which government ministers need to reflect.

It's so frustrating when you've got kids like this because nobody listens to you. Mostly they are just blaming you for your kids' bad behaviour. They tell you things but they never listen to what you say or what you need.

Fundamental concerns

Parents, and to some extent the young people themselves, knew all too well the impact of the youngsters' anti-social behaviour for they had been living with it, trying to manage it and trying to ameliorate its effects upon themselves and the wider community for years. Alarmingly, in a couple of cases, mothers reported they were on the point of giving up hope for their child completely and, indeed, one mother's sense of compounded isolation, frustration and exhaustion meant she also feared that, without support, she could feasibly end up harming her son herself. Moreover, the finding that over half of the mothers were on anti-depressants and/or tranquillisers indicated the extent to which those mothers, like their children subject to medicinal behavioural coshes, were in need of more concrete interventions and support than these pharmaceutical props. Yet such concrete interventions continue to be minimal despite ongoing government promises:

> I can't change all this from the Home Office. We have a valuable part to play but need to ensure that powers we introduce and the information we build up at the centre are used effectively ... The Government's anti-social behaviour action plan sets out how we will work with the communities blighted by anti-social behaviour to deliver change. The plan will build a new infrastructure, rooted in the experience of frontline practitioners, designated to assist every community and every agency to tackle the problems they face. (David Blunkett, in Home Office 2003d)

The Anti-Social Behaviour Act 2003 expands anti-social behaviour measures and, from a realist perspective, it is difficult to challenge the common-sense assumptions upon which this policy is founded; anti-social behaviour is indeed a harsh lived reality in many marginalised estates throughout the country. Further, no one who upholds humanist values would wish to question the sentiments expressed in the Press Release announcing the White Paper (Home Office 2003a) accompanying the Act

> to give power back to the decent law-abiding majority whose lives are ruined by an out-of-control minority. (Home Office 2003b)

However, taking away the inherent value-judgements, could not such sentiments be applied to the disempowered families who participated in this research too? Sadly no. Within current discourses and practices, any accommodation of understandings more multifarious than the absolutes on offer would be to expose the extent to which it is the failure of the welfare state, not crime, against which a 'war should be waged', a welfare state that requires local social services to impose such high thresholds of 'in priority need' to cope with severe resource constraints (Interview with local social services manager for Stephen and Squires 2003a) that *none* of the families who participated in the research could qualify.

Instead, increasingly punitive and exclusionary measures are directed at marginalised young people and their families, whereupon formal and informal surveillance by local agencies and 'law abiding citizens' (Home Office 2004c) offers perfunctory promises of control and ontological security, with deleterious consequences for those constructed as *Other*. Of great concern is that, within this vista, 'the liberal vision of equality before the law is neutralized by assigning dangerousness to specific social identities' (Lianos with Douglas 2000: 261), notably already marginalised young people and their families. This, as shown throughout this chapter, serves to reinforce rather than redress long-standing processes of marginalisation. This situation, not least in respect of the encouragement of greater community involvement in justice initiatives, for example the 'Together Campaign' and 'Taking a Stand' (Home Office 2004c: 48–9), must be challenged for:

> In a system of low visibility and accountability, where a high degree of discretion is given to administrative and professional bodies ... there is often less room for such niceties as due process and legal rights. (Cohen 1985: 70)

Superficially, the advent of ABCs might have seemed a rather benign development, but, as Cohen shows, the use of informal mechanisms of control, founded in apparently 'humane' sentiments of so-called 'protection' of young people 'at risk' of being 'sucked into crime' is based on narrow behaviourist premises, premises that represent young people's lived experiences through delusive imagery and mask the structured context for their 'anti-social' agency.

Reappraising and updating Cohen's (1985) vista, Pratt (2002) points to important elements of contemporary social control that bear relevance to the accounts offered. Increasingly

> simplistic and binary classifications of populations: divisions based are 'us' ... 'normal', law abiding citizens against demonised

'others'... who are made known to the rest of us ... through representations of them in the popular press (Pratt 2002: 177)

and 'growing public participation in the process of punishment', Pratt suggests, are new elements unforeseen by Cohen which are 'taking us into a new arena of punishment altogether' (Pratt 2002: 178). In this manner, the populist and value-laden ideals of 'Community Safety' dissemble the ways in which this control is mobilised and exercised, not least in harnessing local powers and knowledge (see Garland 2001) in order to 'mould compliance to the dominant values of responsibility and risk management' (Flint 2002: 624–5) among those stigmatised by the shift to decentred, if not also misanthropic, 'actuarial justice' (Feeley and Simon 1994) inherent in community safety enforcement activities.

> Principally it involves a shift in state functions from 'rowing' to 'steering'. Responsibility for crime control has moved from the centre and is increasingly exercised 'at a distance' by a combination of statutory, private and voluntary agencies. This change in formal responsibilities has been accompanied by a blurring of crime and disorder and the collapsing of both into what is now called 'community safety'. (Matthews 2002: 224)

The extracts presented in this chapter indicate that, in practice, this had profound consequences for those young people and their families, not least that fundamental rights could be disregarded (Fox, 2002 Stephen and Squires 2004). There is, therefore, an undoubted need to secure a 'rights-based agenda' (Scraton and Haydon 2002) within youth justice, if not also wider youth welfare systems. Instead of coercion, the young people and their families who participated in this research simply needed respect for their human rights (Home Office 1998), notably their right to 'private and family life' (Article 8) and a 'right to education' (Protocol 1, Article 2). As Cohen implies above, however, of greatest concern is that the 'civilianization' of crime prevention (Hope 1998) can absolve authorities from the rights enshrined in Article 6 ('right to a fair trial'). This disregard for human rights must set alarm bells ringing for this

> new regulatory state is in danger of creating a post-liberal society, in which government becomes ubiquitous and arbitrary. (Hirst, 2000: 283)

Reinforcing such concerns, the accounts from and the casenotes held on those 'dangerous' young people, disturbingly, revealed the quantity of 'grey intelligence' amassed against them and others in their social networks through the net-widening activities (Cohen 1985) inherent in what certainly appears as representative of a shift beyond a 'Foucaultesque strategy for classifying and controlling the problematic behaviour of the young' (Smith, R. 2003: 159) towards a *'nouveau ancien régime'* (Hirst 2000: 283) which neither the young people, nor their families, were in a position to challenge, as these parents explain:

> They also wanted to know if the children were involved in anything going on, they were fishing too … They wanted to extend the contract because of the friends that [he] has.

> The threat of eviction has gone now, but I feel they want to put him on another contract. They said they'd be back next month and the month after, but he's off the contract, they didn't explain why.

> We'd signed the contract seven months earlier, but they'd said he'd broken it just by being out … He never went out at all for the best part of seven months, and they said to us it would be for the best to keep him home, just for his own protection … So that's what we did. But it wasn't part of the contract that we had to keep him like a prisoner in his own home… They even accused him of being out, lighting a fire in someone's garden on a day we knew we'd grounded him. He'd been in all day and he never went out, but they said that someone saw and thought it was him.

> I know for a fact that kids up here, when they're caught in trouble, they give his name if they get challenged by adults. He's got a reputation, people say it's him when it isn't … other kids give his name when they get caught, so everyone picks on him.

Hearsay and apparent professional bias towards perceived 'vulnerable' complainants ensured that 'evidence' inadmissible in the formal criminal justice system could offer sufficient grounds for ABC imposition with ensuing pernicious effects, especially in terms of family well-being. Further, the long-term consequences of sucking progressively minor 'anti-social' behaviours into this system of surveillance and control was found to be exerting injurious determining influences upon the young people's current state of social being which earlier youth justice policies certainly recognised (e.g. Home Office 1988):

> I get pulled over and searched [by the police] for no reason when I'm walking home, everywhere I go I get pulled over now, if I'm out at all, I get pulled over and searched … I ain't been in trouble for a long time, but they still pull me over.

They arrested him and de-arrested him, but there was no apology. If he'd been an adult they would have had to apologise, but because he is a child they just took him home said they'd de-arrested him … He was like a sack of dirt they lifted and then put away again … He was very traumatised by the arrest … The police told him 'we've got your DNA and fingerprints, any trouble and we're going to pick you up'… If anything goes wrong on this estate, it's [him] they blame.

Such accounts were not unique, but when looking at these extracts alone it is possible to appreciate that ABCs had enabled the young people to become objects of further surveillance and harassment. In the first extract above, the young man had just secured a college place and he was desperately trying to establish educational foundations for his later adult life despite a fragmented educational history due to his chronic mental health problems. The second account came from the mother of a 10-year-old with profound mental health and behavioural problems. Notwithstanding the humanitarian concerns these accounts raise, there is the pragmatic issue of the long-term consequences of having this negative reputation upon all of the young people's future life chances, not least their ability to effect the transition to economic independence at adulthood. Davies and Tanner's (2003) large-scale longitudinal study on the effects of labelling on employment shows firm correlation between the way rule-breakers are responded to and the future course of their economic lives. Those authors show that the indirect consequences of early negative judgement encounters with those in a position to label, such as teachers or police officers, have 'a significant and cumulatively damaging' (Davies and Tanner 2003: 399) effect upon youth transitions to adult work roles. The majority of young people in this study were already severely disadvantaged educationally and, as such, their prospects for an effective education to employment transition look bleak. So why can the government not appreciate this when they actually acknowledge this themselves?

Where young people are brought up in a secure and stable environment with role models and constructive activities, they are less likely to get sucked into anti-social behaviour and criminality. If families and children are neglected, we reap problems for generations. (Home Office 2004c: 12)

Instead, in the government's 'Call for Local Heroes' (Home Office 2004b), for a first prize of £5,000 and a hundred secondary prizes of £1,000, communities are called upon to 'celebrate their local heroes' who have taken a stand against anti-social behaviour. Home Office Minister Hazel Blears comments that the government wishes

to reward those people who are saying enough is enough.

The young people and their families who participated in this research were indeed 'saying enough is enough'. All explained that they had participated to have their version of events heard and, as expressed by one father who was on the point of losing his job because of ABC-induced, stress-related illness, 'we just want to make sure that what happened to us won't happen to other families.' Those young people and their families simply sought to be agents for change, but to what extent are we, apparently 'law-abiding citizens' (Home Office 2004c), prepared to listen and actively resist this ever-encroaching *nouveau ancien régime* (Hirst 2000)?

Chapter 6 will fully address the criminological concerns raised in this chapter and lay the foundations for a fuller critique of the 'nipping in the bud' thesis upon which 'anti-social behaviour' measures are founded.

Chapter 6

Nipped in the bud – youthful transitions or criminal careers?

> It seems that offending is part of a larger syndrome of antisocial behaviour that arises in childhood and tends to persist into adulthood ... There is significant continuity over time, since the antisocial child becomes the antisocial teenager and then the antisocial adult, just as the antisocial adult then tends to produce another antisocial child. (Farrington 2002: 658)

The above comment exemplifies that which is of increasing concern not only to 'anti-social behaviour' agendas but to our discipline and its late modern *raison d'être*. Previous chapters have highlighted the rhetorical impetus behind current government 'anti-social behaviour' discourses: to 'nip crime in the bud'. The last chapter also illuminated the extent to which the voices of 'the defined' have been ignored in these same discourses and, especially, the markedly differing understandings produced by the simple act of listening to those usually voiceless *Others*. Drawing heavily as it does from the cultural tradition, the qualitative approach we adopt is certainly not offering any new methodological revelations. Yet, given the dearth of critical empirical work in this area (Smith, D. 2003) in the face of the overwhelming concerns identified in Chapter 5, the potential for offering such critical commentaries is progressively diminishing in the face of the research funding priorities of 'actuarial justice' (Feeley and Simon 1994).

The choice of methodology is an ideological act (Galtung 1977), so what is criminology's 'obsession' (Kane 2004: 304) with positivism saying about the discipline's current status and direction (see also Hayward and Young 2004; Presdee 2004), if not also about the ability to actually 'do something' about youth offending? Positivist hegemony over accounts of criminal careers, as typified by Farrington above and exemplified in the undoubted populist appeal of current 'anti-social behaviour' practices, suggest on the surface that interventions can be made, but these are actually imbued with more than a modicum of pessimism not just about the potential for concrete and durable change, but about the whole human condition itself:

> These 'social facts' stand as 'description' devoid of explanation and theory. They tell us little about crime and criminality as do explanations and theories devoid of description. In short, administrative criminology has produced an overdetermined descriptive criminology, deprived of any social/human dimension. It is an anti-sociological methodology in 'denial'. (Presdee 2004: 275)

Despite confidence in alternative ways of seeing (see Fenwick 2004), any optimism must be tempered for, quite simply, the majority of contemporary mainstream criminological research ignores, if not also denies, the objectified *Other*'s humanity with the grave consequences outlined in the previous chapter. As a discipline, therefore, it seems vital that we, like youth justice itself, take stock of this 'particularly uncomfortable conjuncture' (*cf.* Smith, R. 2003: 187) and, especially, our role in informing Best Value initiatives and wider (tacitly criminalising) policy in respect of young people – to what extent are we leading, or being led by prevailing managerialism? In our complicity with these imperatives, we serve to lend credence to and reinforce the cementing of *Otherness* through pathologised 'prevention' and 'treatment' prescriptions that remain fixed within priorities that mask wider policy insufficiency in respect of 'those underlying structural factors associated with deviant behaviour' (Smith, R. 2003: 187–8).

The hegemonic influence of positivist criminology within contemporary managerialist agendas is subsuming alternative ways of seeing, if not also stifling contemporary criminological imagination in its wake; in many ways, contemporary mainstream criminology is at risk of being reduced to the status of mere handmaid to political paymasters. Nonetheless, as Fenwick (2004) maintains, this is not yet an entirely hopeless situation. The special issue of *Theoretical Criminology* in 2004 was a revitalising reminder that cultural criminology is certainly not a spent force, and we wish to add to the insights advanced therein: that there is still potential 'to counter mainstream criminology's modern (allegedly) "scientific methods"' (Hayward and Young 2004: 271), but even those cultural giants conclude with a caveat:

> Whether we can achieve our goal of derailing contemporary criminology from the abstractions of administrative rationalisation and statistical complexity remains to be seen. (Hayward and Young 2004: 271)

Unquestionably, the core findings of the positivist tradition have laid down a substantial and enduring bedrock of research evidence pointing to the criminogenic circumstances in a young person's life likely to influence involvement in criminal activity. The modernist imperative behind this research is easily apparent, but has tended, as Ulmer and Spencer (1999) note, to throw up ethical questions regarding the contribution of quantitative criminological evidence to criminal risk prediction, a vital issue returned to in Chapter 7. This has, as Feeley and Simon (1992) have argued, somewhat problematic consequences whether one moves from criminological aggregates to potentially deviant individuals or whether one continues to focus upon deprived or excluded communities themselves as the sites for policy intervention.

Thus, on the more individual level, the practice of community safety teams in 'New Deal' areas drawing up league tables of their '50 most prolific' anti-social young people, each with their accompanying dossier of reports on family and social circumstances, correspondence, police reports, criminal records, lists of circumstantial or hearsay evidence, complaints by neighbours or harassment logs and, more often than not, details of anti-social behaviours, curfews or Acceptable Behaviour Contracts (ABCs) employed as management tools, points to the practical influence of this more *actuarial* perspective. The newer policy conclusions drawn from the wealth of criminal career development research focusing upon career onset have tended to distract from the broadly continuous message from the research itself. Consequently the personal, familial, communal, environmental and, especially, structural factors influencing young people's involvement in criminal and/or anti-social activities have been well known for some time, although the ways that this research has been interpreted or used to inform policy-making has changed. Anti-social behaviour is now more definitely perceived as the larger and, typically, prior set of behaviours predicting an offending career path, a path portrayed as inevitable 'truth'.

For example, significant gender differences have been reported with boys participating in anti-social behaviour to a greater extent and at an earlier age than girls (Pakiz *et al.* 1997; Bendixen and Olweus 1999). Males' early disruptive behaviour has been shown to be an important indicator of later adolescent and adult criminality (e.g. Farrington 1994; Haapsalo and Tremblay 1994) and indicators of 'delinquent trajectories' have been demonstrated in boys at very early ages (Pakiz *et al.* 1997; Nagin and

Tremblay 1999) especially aggressive behaviour, bullying and impulsivity (e.g. Pakiz *et al.* 1992; Bendixen and Olweus 1999). This tends to be followed by paths of less to more serious behaviours (Loeber 1991; Bendixen and Olweus 1999). The type of offence has a strong bearing on the peak age of criminality (Farrington 1986). Studies have long shown that male offending peaks at 17 years (e.g. Farrington 1990), teenage criminality is found to peak in the mid-teenage years (e.g. Gottfredson and Hirshi 1990) and serious anti-social behaviour and criminality are indicated to peak in young adulthood or later (respectively Robins and Regier 1991; Smith, 2002). Notwithstanding these insights:

> A sea of numbers with numerical significance decoupled from meaning is of no use. (Kane 2004: 318)

Fundamentally, the clear message is that criminal careers are objectively observable, measurable and, sadly, teleological. In this manner, the young people following such paths are portrayed as 'different', as *Other*, but just how different are they? Acknowledging that very few people subscribe to a neo-classical conception of the criminal career (or even the straight career for that matter) policy remains focused upon the deterministic social positivism of empirical criminology which has devoted considerable time and resources towards demonstrating the factors impelling a mass of young, and largely working-class, 'delinquents' towards a life of crime (see Farrington 2002; Smith, 2002 for overviews). Such analyses often say very little about how these same contexts and circumstances are perceived and experienced by offenders and potential offenders; they also reveal little about the dynamic interaction of structure and agency, or the subjective reality of process. Thus, on the one hand, positivist accounts can offer a sense of optimism that something can be done about youth crime yet, on the other hand, these accounts mirror, and indeed reinforce, the abject sense of hopelessness in deterministic structural accounts of 'youth trajectories'. As demonstrated in Chapter 3, we need to take on board Gadd and Farrall's (2004: 124) reminder to incorporate 'the other processes that have some bearing on involvement in crime' and desistance, not least the subjective accounts that young people themselves provide about their own 'careers':

> … what is important is the analysis of the way in which humankind makes sense of and, at times resists, existing and developing social structures. Such privileging of 'culture' enables cultural theorists to view behaviour as dynamic rather than determined and opens up the possibility of other ways of 'seeing' transgressive and therefore criminal behaviour (Presdee 2004: 275–6)

Youth perspectives and youth transitions

The key objective of this chapter, therefore, is to offer a challenge to positivist-engorged 'risk management' in contemporary youth justice. As in Chapter 5, we try to develop this approach by returning young offenders to centre stage. While we have undoubtedly learned a great deal from modernist accounts of criminal career development, such approaches still remain overly deterministic. Social reaction and 'labelling' approaches, while offering a critical response to mainstream social positivism, contained remarkably similar weaknesses (Ulmer and Spencer 1999) and so we draw upon firmer cultural traditions to achieve a much-needed refocus for, as Henry and Milovanovic have argued:

> The behaviours of human subjects who offend and victimise others cannot be understood in isolation from the society of which they are part. Nor are they understandable as determined products of cultures and structures. (Henry and Milovanovic 1996: x)

The contribution of this thesis for a 'constitutive criminology' is the way in which Henry and Milovanovich highlight the need to understand the 'co-production' that occurs between society's structure and culture, and active human subjects. Within criminology the privileging of such 'co-production' is, arguably, long overdue. But instead of locating our deliberations within a postmodern analysis, as realised by Henry and Milovanovic, this chapter will provide a means of understanding young people's involvement in offending activities through a conceptualisation of their contemporary lived experiences within the risks inherent in late modernity (Beck 1992), especially as they try to effect youth transitions to adulthood (Stephen and Squires 2003b).

Late modernity necessarily underpins our considerations, for the contemporary late modern epoch reflects key continuities with modernity, no less than the impact of the structured limitations upon young people's lived experiences and life chances (see Furlong and Cartmel 1997). Beck argues this effectively in that, despite profound societal changes, individual life chances continue to be highly structured and 'remain relatively unchanged' (1992: 92). Within late modernity, the previously established transition from school to work has been replaced by prolonged, insecure and fragmented periods of training, employment and unemployment (Ainley and Bailey 1997; Evans and Furlong 1998) and those without the necessary 'social capital' (Coleman 1998; Raffo and Reeves 2000) are subject to the greatest insecurities as they try to effect previously predictable school to work transitions; boys without qualifications or skills face the greatest insecurities (e.g. Williamson 1997; Bentley and Gurumurthy 1999). The consequential results for those still at school who hold little hope of subsequent employment are also documented; school is seen as irrelevant and truanting and underachievement prevail (e.g. Booth 1996; France and Wiles 1996; John 1996; Stirling 1996).

Thus nowadays, since young people's transitions to adulthood are neither linear nor predictable, 'alternative careers' develop in response (MacDonald *et al.* 2001) to wider constraints and in the light of cultural experiences. Where such conventional opportunities for employment, income and status are absent, young people are shown to 'invest heavily in peer group relationships' (Green *et al.* 2000: 113). Nonetheless, little remains known about how young people, still 'shaped by customary codes' (Cohen and Ainley 2000: 81) negotiate and make sense of their lifeworld within such wider shifts (Stephen and Squires 2003b).

Many commentators (e.g. Rudd 1997; Jeffs and Smith 1998; MacDonald 1998; Cohen and Ainley 2000; Fergusson *et al.* 2000; Miles 2000; Raffo and Reeves 2000; Stephen 2000; Stephen and Squires 2003b) argue for progress to be made in the development of more sophisticated understanding of young people's contemporary experiences to incorporate cultural meaning and identity. Accordingly, we hope to show that the purposive agency involved in offending behaviour can be seen as a means of resolving the 'epistemological fallacy of late modernity' (Furlong and Cartmel 1997: 109), baldly stated, that young people are encouraged to seek individual solutions for problems that are of a social and structural nature. This, as we shall show, is effected through a process of 'self-culture' creation (Beck and Beck-Gernsheim 2002: 42).

Albeit in the form of 'structured individualisation' (Furlong and Cartmel 1997), through their leisure activities and consumption, young people have been said to be more able to construct their own biographies (Chisholm and Du Bois-Reymond 1993) and identities within individualised transitions to adulthood (Miles 2000). Furlong and Cartmel (1997) argue that the changes associated with late modernity affecting young people, such as in education, employment, family relationships and consumerist pressures, have produced an increased awareness of and willingness to take risks. Thus it is necessary to appreciate that, and how, 'young people can actively shape their social world through the development of identities enhanced by "risk reputations" ' (Green *et al.* 2000: 113). However, in doing so, of late, young people have found themselves running up against the relatively inflexible (but also highly mobile) authority of law enforcement, operating at lower levels of tolerance, increasingly proactive and discriminatory in application, and into the wider nets and tighter surveillance of our new behavioural control agencies as shown in Chapter 5. It is, therefore, exigent to more fully understand the lived experiences and self-conceptions of young people as they make sense of the insecurities inherent in late modernity (e.g. Stephen 2000) and this necessarily requires a more effective means of synthesising structure and agency (e.g. Raffo and Reeves 2000; EGRIS 2001) and the diverse social processes that influence young people's risk-taking behaviour (France 2000).

Consistent with earlier work (e.g. Stephen 2000), therefore, we intend to show how young people denied usual, and accepted, social and material frames of reference (Furlong and Cartmel 1997) construct their own culture and identities within this process of 'self-culture' (Beck and Beck-Gernsheim 2002: 42) creation. Identity is taken here as 'embracing the individual's own perceptions of himself or herself generally and in specific domains' (Banks *et al.* 1992: 12) for, as Banks *et al.* show, this active category plays an important role in goals young people pursue 'consistent with notions of who they are and what they are capable of' (Banks *et al.* 1992: 181). In developing an analysis of this 'self-culture', we acknowledge a further author who argues for an understanding of youth offending activities, not as deviance, but as a 'potential element in a resistance cultural politics' (Stanley 1995: 115). Stanley's thesis offers an important insight into the need for a complete shift away from looking at young people's activities through the prisms of 'causality', and the need to put context and culture at the centre of any analysis. However, Stanley's thesis still presents a substantial reification of the agency inherent in offending behaviour, mirroring earlier essays into 'symbolic rebellion' in wider studies of 'deviance' (e.g. Willis 1977). This conception is questioned through our own empirical findings (e.g. Stephen and Squires 2001; Stephen and Squires 2003a) which, as will be shown, tend to reflect core themes in existing 'normative youth studies' of 'escape' from the mundane aspects of day-to-day life (e.g. Cohen and Taylor 1992) through status and pleasure (e.g. Plant and Plant 1992; Lupton 1999). As we have found, much offending behaviour is rooted in conformity to traditional mores rather than 'resistance' where 'risk' and 'control' are the two main concepts of heuristic import (Stephen and Squires 2003b).

In summary, therefore, there exists a dearth of explanations of the 'lived experience of criminality' in traditional criminological explanations (Hayward 2002: 81) of young people's agency in regard to crime. Accordingly, the 'lived experiences' of young offenders provide a means of highlighting the deficiencies in positivist criminological explanations and current 'anti-social behaviour' assumptions, and the initial direction for this comes from drawing upon Hayward's (2002) analysis of risk be-haviours as a means of obtaining control and self-actualisation in the face of the uncertainties inherent in late modernity. Thus:

Many forms of crime frequently perpetrated in urban areas should be seen for exactly what they are, an attempt to achieve a semblance of control within ontologically insecure social worlds. (Hayward 2002: 86)

Albeit a rather illusory control of strictly limited duration. Nonetheless, the significance of Hayward's work is that he highlights the essential 'normality' of the pursuit of risky activities among young people as a whole which is supported in our own study in regard to non-offending young people's leisure pursuits and aspirations (Stephen and Squires 2001). Moreover, drawing upon Lyng (1990), Hayward indicates the need to develop the notion of 'edgework' and 'escape attempts' as dominant cultural norms which facilitate a process of 'self-actualisation' in a manner akin to the process of identity formation in Banks *et al.'s* (1992) thesis. It is, therefore, from an assumption of the essential 'normality' of this risk-taking (borne out in a wide range of studies, e.g. Lyng 1993; Parker *et al.* 1998; Measor and Squires 2000; Ferrell *et al.*, 2001; Hayward 2002; Stephen and Squires 2001; Beinart *et al.* 2002) rather than the 'deviance' privileged in previous explanations of youth crime that our arguments are premised. In this vein, mainstream youth studies must necessarily provide the starting point for any understanding of the agency inherent in youth offending and the way in which it contributes to the process of self-actualisation as young people negotiate and try to make sense of their social worlds. Further, bearing in mind overarching structural influences, the

reflexive conduct of life, the planning of one's own biography and social relations, gives rise to a new inequality of dealing with insecurity and reflexivity. (Beck 1992: 98)

This reflexivity should be understood as 'self-confrontation' (Beck 1994: 5) and it is, therefore, prerequisite to illuminate the ways through which young people approach and accommodate 'risk' in their biographies since young people's identity development and risk-taking behaviour are strongly linked (Green *et al.* 2000). In the context of the formation of biography and social relations, it is also indispensable to understand more fully why particular forms of offending come to be a preferred leisure activity for significant numbers of young men as a means of 'dealing with' the 'insecurity' Beck postulates, a world where they must negotiate risks largely unbeknown to previous modernist generations (Furlong and Cartmel 1997).

Exploring the lived experiences of criminality and criminalisation

As we have highlighted, the context and culture within which young people's agency is produced must be acknowledged, and firm foundations for the development of more holistic criminological theory exist. Demonstrating our indebtedness to the wider cultural tradition, not least that of the Centre for Contemporary Cultural Studies and their practice of writing 'history from below' (McRobbie 1991: 62), we find much in common between E. P. Thompson's re-evaluation of accounts of 'the mob' (a term he rejects for its implications) and contemporary 'explanatory' depictions of youth offending. In 'The moral economy of the crowd', Thompson (1993a) argues that the eighteenth-century English food 'riots' (another term he rejects for obvious reasons) were not spurred merely by people's reactions to hunger, their actions must be seen as a form of political agency arising from a complex of customary expectations and an essential moral economy. 'Riot' instead becomes 'a sophisticated pattern of collective behaviour, a collective alternative to individualistic and familial strategies of survival' (Thompson 1993a: 266) and he continues to offer a caveat against determinism: 'Hunger rioters were hungry, but hunger does not dictate that they must riot nor does it determine riot's form' (Thompson 1993a: 266).

Interestingly, a similar point was made about anti-social behaviour by one of our Community Safety Team interviewees – but with a rather different purpose in mind:

> Lots of people living up here are poor and have all sorts of family difficulties, but they don't all beat their neighbours up. (Interview with Community Safety Team practitioner for Stephen and Squires 2003a)

Authoritative critiques of traditional structural-determinist conceptions of 'youth trajectories' (e.g. Jeffs and Smith 1998; Cohen and Ainley 2000; Fergusson *et al.* 2000; Miles 2000) provide further impetus for our thinking. While structural accounts of young people's experiences have provided invaluable insights into the ways in which young people's experiences are framed, an overriding focus upon 'trajectories' has served to progressively limit the potential for more holistic understandings of young people's experiences, particularly the active ways in which socially marginalised young people negotiate structure in their everyday lives (Stephen and Squires 2003b) for, indeed, we are all

> part subjects, part objects, the voluntary agents of our own involuntary determinations. (Thompson 1978: 280)

Accordingly, in highlighting that we need to appreciate the dialectical interaction between young people's reflexive agency and the wider structural context, the basic premise for Thompson's thesis and the direction for 'co-production' (Henry and Milovanovic 1996) in under-standings of youth offending in late modernity are firmly established. Thompson captures this point lucidly in his conception of 'lived experience':

> Any theory of culture must include the concept of the dialectical interaction between culture and something that is not culture. We must suppose the raw material of life – experience to be at one pole, and all the infinitely–complex human disciplines and systems, articulate and inarticulate, formalised in institutions or dispersed in the least formal ways, which 'handle', transmit or distort this raw material to be at the other. It is the active process – which is at the same time the process through which men (*sic*) make their history – that I am insisting on. (Thompson 1981: 398)

This extract serves to underline the essence of Thompson's historiography, an approach through which human beings are portrayed as makers of their own history within a wider structured context. Thus this notion as advanced by Thompson provides an efficacious means of connecting human agents and the conditions and consequences of their autonomous action with the structured 'causes' and consequences of the conditions of their existence; empirically, structure, agency and process can be analysed as interdependent variables (Stephen 1998). Key to understanding how Thompson effects this is through the use of the concept of 'experience' which is taken as the way in which human beings convert objective determinations into subjective initiatives:

> What we see – and study – in our work are repeated events within 'social being' – such events being indeed often consequent upon material causes which go on behind the back of consciousness or intention – which inevitably do and must give rise to lived experience, *experience I*, which do not instantly break through as 'reflections' into *experience II*, but whose pressure upon the whole field of consciousness cannot be indefinitely diverted, postponed, falsified or suppressed. (Thompson 1981: 406).

The challenge from history is laid: 'co-production' (Henry and Milovanovic 1996) can be achieved through such an understanding of 'lived experience'. When looking at the contemporary experiences of marginalised young people, therefore, two key theses should be borne in mind: firstly, that 'alternative careers' develop in response (MacDonald *et al.*, 2001) to wider constraints and in the light of cultural experiences; secondly:

> some of the problems faced by young people in [late] modern Britain stem from an attempt to negotiate [structured] difficulties on an individual level. (Furlong and Cartmel 1997: 114).

The need to go beyond 'causal' accounts in the manner we have just described was imperative in our research with young men who were or had been involved in vehicle crime (Stephen and Squires 2001). To further underline why we need a qualitative understanding of young people's 'criminal careers' along the processual lines offered above, and in respect of the three central themes of criminal career onset, maintenance and desistance, one illustrative case study from our vehicle crime project (Stephen and Squires 2001) will be offered. On initial inspection the account from this 21-year-old male, who had been one of the most prolific vehicle offenders we interviewed, certainly seemed to support dominant explanations of young people's involvement in offending behaviour:

> That's another thing about the way they stereotype you: you come from an area, you come from a family, they slag off the estates so the arseholes there try to live up to it ... once your family's known to them, they're on your case the whole time ... you're not given the chance to leave, even now I'm still getting pulled in, they don't give you any chance. Once you're known they won't leave you alone ... We're not bad people, but if you're told all your life you're bad you become what they tell you.

Having a known criminal for a father, being a male of low social class, living in a socially marginalised neighbourhood, offering a history of truanting and expulsion from school at 14 years and becoming immersed in 'deviant' peer group activities and the effects of labelling would all appear to provide various accepted means of 'explaining' the onset and maintenance of this young man's eight-year 'criminal career'; even the ages of onset and desistance conform to the accepted statistical range for young people's involvement in criminal activities. But to focus on such indicators alone would be an erroneous two-dimensional portrayal of the rich biography, and indeed reflexivity, he offered. It soon became clear that, despite such 'objective indicators', we needed to appreciate the interaction between this young man's agency and such apparent 'determinants' as constituents of a process of 'self-actualisation' (Hayward 2002) that were rooted in his conformity to customary mores (*cf.* Cohen and Ainley 2000), and consistent with notions of whom he regarded himself to be and of what he believed he was capable (Banks *et al.* 1992):

> I was kicked out [of school] at fourteen, didn't want to learn Shakespeare or algebra, college is what I wanted to do, get an NVQ, not waste my time learning stuff I'd never use.

His long-standing ambition had been to become a mechanic:

> An apprenticeship would have been ideal, but the opportunity wasn't there. I might not have been good at school, but I'd practical skills. I'd learned myself to strip a car by the age of fifteen.

The academic orientation of school was, for this young man, perceived as a complete irrelevance and, perhaps, before the extension of compulsory formal education to 16 years, he might well have attained his ambition without any criminal record (his first conviction was when he was 15 years old). School, he believed, denied him any formal opportunity to develop the practical skills he privileged which, for him, were integral to his conception of 'being a man', but, as he reflected, he had been unaware of the consequences of his actions at the time:

> That's another stereotype they have. 'Car crime starts other crime'. Car crime does not start more crime … But you're black marked once you get a criminal record and that affects all your other options in life.

Nonetheless, as he became highly proficient and confident in vehicle-taking and police evasion techniques, the 'threat' of harsher penal sanctions came to be regarded as a potential opportunity as he became increasingly aware of his progressive marginalisation from wider opportunities:

> I wasn't scared of prison, my dad's been in and he came through it. Feltham doesn't sound so bad. Instead of having nothing to do at home, I sometimes thought it'd be a good option when I couldn't get an apprenticeship, if I'd've gone to prison I'd've got my NVQ, you can get stuff like that in there, you'd come out qualified for a proper job and have people like probation officers setting things up for you. It's a crazy system when you've gotta break the law to get a better start in life, for the kids it can sometimes be a better option than a life of unemployment and New Deal schemes.

165

We also need to appreciate the psychosocial (Gadd and Farrall 2004) benefits this young man derived from his vehicle-taking activities over and above the mutual 'respect' among peers he, and other research participants, reported this affords: the realisation of control within his 'ontologically insecure' (Hayward 2002: 86) lifeworld. These rewards contrasted markedly with how he felt about his daily life:

> It's a thrill driving, it doesn't really change ... It's all about control, you're in complete control. Control and stability. We're all looking for a bit of stability in our lives, so it's like an achievement we've done, like me with this kid that's coming, it's something we can do for ourselves that's not been handed down to us by anyone.

The important concepts of 'control' and 'escape' (e.g. Cohen and Taylor 1992; Hayward 2002), and 'risk' (e.g. Green *et al.* 2000) in mainstream youth studies contribute greatly to an understanding of this young man's involvement in vehicle-taking; for him, the car became the vehicle, literally and metaphorically, for his process of 'self-confrontation' (Beck 1994) and 'self-actualisation' (Hayward 2002) in the face of weighty 'determining' forces. Significantly, these normative concepts also facilitate understanding of the reasons why this young man withdrew from vehicle offending:

> I've had a good run, but I'm a bit wiser now, older, sick of getting all the hassle. All my mates are getting out of it too, we're all older and it's different, some have jobs, others have responsibilities like kids and I've got the baby on the way. No it's different now, we've all grown up.

Shortly after hearing that his girlfriend was pregnant, this young man secured a labouring job which he reported he did not much want because it was unskilled, but it was 'honest man's work'. Further, he progressively withdrew from vehicle offending, not least since the fatherhood aspect of his conception of 'being a man' was being realised; for the first time in his life, he believed, he was in the process of securing socially acceptable status and identity.

We cannot understand where this young man is coming from without recognising the wider structural context within which his 'criminal career' developed and was sustained. Reliance on 'causal' predictors or 'trajectories' would be to deny his reflexive agency and, certainly, cannot grasp any sense of lived experience and process. This young man was not passive in the face of determining forces, and the ways through which he converted objective circumstances into subjective initiatives or simply the way in which structure was reflexively 'transmuted into process' (Thompson 1978: 362) are clearly evident. Thompson explains clearly how this happens:

> Changes take place within social being, which give rise to changed experience: and this experience is determining, in the sense that it exerts pressure upon existent social consciousness, proposes new questions, and affords much of the raw material which the more elaborate intellectual exercises are about. (Thompson 1981: 406)

As exemplified in this case study, this reflexivity must be understood as 'self-confrontation' (Beck 1994) in a world where young people develop 'alternative careers' (MacDonald *et al*. 2001) as a means of negotiating wider risks largely unbeknown to previous modernist generations (Furlong and Cartmel 1997). To develop these conclusions, these notions of 'alternative careers' and 'self-culture' (Beck and Beck-Gernsheim 2002) will now be developed by drawing further upon our vehicle offending research.

All of the extracts presented derive from 32 semi-structured interviews conducted in 2001, the qualitative component of a study for Sussex Police to engender understanding of local young people's motivations towards vehicle offending (Stephen and Squires 2001). The research participants were aged between 13 and 21 years (mean was just under 17 years). Although official records revealed that many young women were being arrested at the time for 'being carried', despite attempts, we could find none directly involved in 'taking of' activities in this city. Only one young man was of minority ethnic group status.

The young men's reported vehicle-taking histories ranged from a minority who had only fleeting experiences and tended to have been caught by the police early on in their activities to highly proficient takers of hundreds of cars who seemed to have accomplished competence in evading police detection and punishment through their strong 'social capital' (Coleman 1998; Raffo and Reeves 2000) of experience and peer group resources. All lived with at least one parent: around a half lived with both parents, and a quarter each with a lone parent and reconstituted family. Unlike a host of positivist studies (see Farrington 2002 for tidy overview) that focus on pathological family forms and practices, family contexts were not accorded attention in the young men's accounts, significantly until looking at issues of desistance from offending, quite simply because, for the young men, familial influences were minimal as expressed succinctly here:

It's not true that you become who you are because of your parents

They say all car-takers come from broken homes, my parents never argued. I did it 'cause my mates did it. I thought 'he's getting away with it, why can't I?'

excepting, as indicated in the case study above, where external perceptions were felt to have exerted determining forces:

They've stereotyped my whole family, just 'cause of my cousin, but no one else's been in trouble. But no, they think we're all at things.

They could have stopped stereotyping me 'cause of my family 'cause the way I look at it, they call me a criminal so why shouldn't I be it?

The interviews were conducted in the young men's homes or in local community facilities and explored their: biographies, peer and leisure activities; vehicle-taking histories; motivations; experience of, and feelings about the criminal justice system; actual and possible personal deterrents; life aspirations; and their recommendations for reducing young people's involvement in vehicle offending.

Employment aspirations

As argued above, our praxis is premised on appreciating how young people denied usual frames of reference (Furlong and Cartmel 1997) construct their own culture, their 'alternative careers' (MacDonald *et al.* 2001) and identities, and the ways through which these active categories play the central role in the goals young people pursue 'consistent with notions of who they are and what they are capable of' (Banks *et al.* 1992: 181). Accordingly, the accounts presented reveal that, unless we understand those young men's aspirations, it is impossible to recognise why vehicle offending, rather than other forms of offending including substance misuse, was pursued, and thence, importantly, withdrawn from. Moreover, taking on board the earlier caveat about determinism (Thompson 1993a), this approach also offers a rather more normative context for understanding the young men's offending 'careers' in the first place.

Very clear aspirational categories emerged: overwhelmingly, highly gendered 'traditionally male' jobs of skilled trades or building site work, car mechanic and the armed forces (Army and Royal Marines) dominated career aspirations or current employment. Educational issues will be outlined shortly, but those who had been excluded from school or left early because of educational difficulties emphasised the employment quandary they now faced.

> It's not a good situation because I can't get a proper job until I've left officially, but they won't let me leave until June so I'm just working with my Dad now, but I'd like to try to get a proper job ... I was working by the time I was 15, one day a week ... I'm not scared of work, it's what I want to do, get a proper job, but the situation I'm in makes it impossible to get a proper job.

As indicated here, among the majority, problems with and the lack of interest in education did not mean a lack of interest in or motivation towards paid work. All of the research participants very much adhered to hegemonic notions of masculinity and collectivist principles and aspired to highly conventional futures of work and family. The extent to which these ambitions could be realised was to be dependent upon their ability to overcome wider determining forces. The older interviewees recounted a series of jobs that had been lost largely as a result of employers discovering their offending histories and two of the young men who no longer offended were presently setting up their own semi-skilled trades enterprises because they felt they would always have to confront such problems:

> Setting up my own business is the easiest option for me now

Determining forces

The general characteristics of neighbourhoods within which the majority of the young men lived were spoken of in highly negative terms. The lack of facilities and opportunities for young people, and the high levels of crime and drug use were underlined. This was to provide the backdrop to understanding why the theme of 'escape' (*cf.* Cohen and Taylor 1992; Hayward 2002) was to pepper accounts, as typified in the concerns expressed by this active vehicle offender, who was only in his mid-teens himself:

> I worry about what's going to happen to [sister], she's only a kid ... What's this estate got to give them to do anyway, the kids have got nothing to do ... They've got to sort the estate out before they can start to do anything with the kids.

The mother of one young man who was present throughout his interview supported all of the young research participants' accounts:

> If we'd the money we could move away, but that's the problem, people like us just don't have the money to leave, nobody would stay here if they could leave, so we've got to stay here and hope that our kids will be safe. I worry about them, and this one (points to her heavily pregnant abdomen), what future are they going to have?

Recognising this context facilitates understanding another aspect of the research participants' aspirations:

> To get married and have children and live in an area where there are plenty of things for kids to do, not like round here where there's nothing for them.

> I don't think I'd want to get married and stay here. I don't think I'd want my kids to grow up here and end up losers.

For the young men, therefore, escape would, they hoped, be eventually secured through paid employment, but this, they felt and as introduced in the case study above, was being denied them in a world of compulsory schooling to the age of 16 and the privileging of academic rather than practical skills. Accordingly, such feelings of marginalisation arising from growing up in these neighbourhoods were enhanced by the young men's experience of school. Only six of the research participants were either still at school or had left school at the age of 16 without having secured any suspensions or exclusions, most of whom were no longer involved in any vehicle offending activities and whose involvement had been minor and marginal. Two others who were still at school were still truanting and receiving suspensions and a further two had been sent to 'special schools' for 'difficult' youths. Among the majority, however, exclusion for persistent truanting, 'attitude problems' or fighting at the age of 13 or 14 years was the norm:

> I've been excluded from school for about two years ... I'm not doing nothing now. I probably wouldn't be able to handle it in school now, I'm so used to being out of it.

The difficulties with school were not always reported to be of the interviewees' making and in this respect bullying and, especially, educational difficulties emerged as the two overriding factors reported

In Year Ten I started bunking off school because I was getting bullied, couldn't cope with the pressure. They were always giving me detentions and I still kept bunking off. I liked school, I was good at all my subjects, but the bullying was getting worse. I was getting bullied every day and I couldn't take any more and I hit one of the boys over the head with a glass vase and that got me expelled.

They said I was dyslexic because I couldn't do the school work. They gave me learning support for a year, but it failed and I was just left to get on on my own. I started bunking off regularly ... I just couldn't stick the lessons.

Whether education was completed or not, a sense of socially ascribed failure permeated accounts because most of the young men had experienced learning difficulties and many, as indicated above, referred to dyslexia, either diagnosed or a self-ascribed label which produced unresolved feelings of low self-worth and wider exclusion:

My teachers always said I'd never do anything with my life, that I would always be a failure.

I wasn't good at school and, if you've not got any qualifications it's like 'you're not welcome to society'.

For two-thirds of the sample, there was an association between fragmented schooling and involvement in petty crime, and 11 to 12 years was the usual age when this had started:

We were bunking off school and that's when we'd steal from shops, food mainly, and I got nicked. It scared me, upset my mum, so I never did it again.

Most, however, went on to develop their 'careers' citing lack of money as a prime motivator for their early shoplifting activities. Sweets and crisps were the usual commodities taken early on and this usually developed into taking cigarettes, alcohol, CDs, videos and clothes. Among half of those who were involved in such crimes at an early age, breaking into cars was reported almost as a logical extension to their shoplifting activities since there appears to have been early awareness of local distributors and markets.

Like in a shop if I was starving I'd just take something to eat. [Then] we broke into a couple [of cars] first, taking radios and stuff ... you

> just know who you can pass 'em on to, just people round here ... I never did it on my own, always with some mates ... some had done it more than me. It's like just passing the skills on.

Two major clues for developing understanding of the young men's involvement in vehicle-taking as 'self-culture' (Beck and Beck-Gernsheim 2002) have emerged: the importance of peer group capital and skills to the young men's self-conceptions and onset of their process of 'self-actualisation' (Hayward 2002). As shown, consistent with mainstream youth studies outlined earlier, for these marginalised young men school was largely irrelevant and truanting and underachievement prevailed (e.g. Booth 1996; France and Wiles 1996; John 1996; Stirling 1996). Further, in their awareness of the absence of conventional opportunities for the realisation of their life goals, those young men invested 'heavily in peer group relationships' (Green et al. 2000: 113) based upon what were clearly hegemonic masculine mores that are increasingly redundant in late modern Britain. Yet, although heavily subscribing to such anachronistic ideals, the young men, like other young people (e.g. Miles 2000), very much wished to be part of late-modern consumerism.

The process of self-culture

With so much free time on their hands through truanting, expulsion or unemployment, vehicle offending was found to be integral to the young men's leisure and peer group activities. The interrelated themes of 'boredom' and 'lack of money' dominated accounts of those who were involved in both taking of and taking from cars:

> Everyone here does something, they need the money and this is the only way they'll get it. What do they expect, we're young, there's no money here, nowhere to go, so we take what we want.

In everyone's accounts, peer group influences were afforded paramount place; vehicle taking was recounted as an essential part of peer group bonding, and status and identity acquisition:

> Your mates are important to you and you need to see that they respect you.

> The younger ones look up to the older ones and the older ones want people to impress so they let the younger ones hang around with them and it goes on like that.

Overwhelmingly, accounts focused upon the key element of sharing experiences with friends whereupon the notion of 'game' reflected both their young age and their exclusion from formal leisure activities:

> You'd never do it [take vehicles] on your own, what'd be the point? It'd be pointless not showing your mates what you've done ... You play games like how many of the same colour you can get or how many of one make you can get. We change the games all the time, it's just one big game.

> There's no point doing it on your own, what'd be the point, you've got to have people with you for the laugh, it's all for the laugh with your mates. It's always a buzz doing it and talking about it after-wards.

There was also a sense of pragmatism in such accounts, associated with their perceptions of risk, but still the emphasis on a male culture where females at best only played a minor role was ever present, as typified here:

> It's more risky on yer own, and its much more fun when you've got your mates there, flying round corners, going fast ... its really good ... You've bin in a car with your mum but you've never been at the wheel yourself, its not the same, it's totally different, a real rush ... and you're responsible for it, driving it and really buzzin' ... It's really good, you're having a laugh, you feel really good driving around. It's great. First time I had a go I really loved it, I was shitting meself but really loving it as well ... and then I wanted to do it again ... There was two girls in our gang – they could come for a ride in the cars but we wouldn't let 'em drive, but it didn't matter cos they couldn't anyway. Most of the time they didn't want to come with us but sometimes they did ... There are a few girls that drive but ours didn't.

In order to further understanding of how risk was accommodated in the young men's biographies, all asked to recount their first experiences of vehicle offending in general and car-taking in particular. For most this was reported to have occurred between the ages of 9 and 13 years to counteract the tedium they felt characterised their daily lives:

> Boredom that's why I do it, got straight into robbing cars, I can take any car, it's no problem. It doesn't take any time to learn, mates show you and you can do it, there's nothing to it.

More often than not, first experience of vehicle-offending had started opportunistically as part of another earlier game:

> There was a few of us, we were bored so we were walking to [named part of town]. We started checking car doors, that's all we were doing, just checking car doors, they were all parked in rows in the streets. We'd not thought about what we'd do if any of the doors were open, but we were just checking the doors and got one that opened. There was nothing worth taking so we kept trying, it was just a laugh. At the end of the night we'd got some money, little tools and a stereo.

Making the most of opportunities as they arose indicates the young men's resourceful ability to utilise contingent events. Their accounts, therefore, contrast markedly with explanations that focus on 'criminal careers' almost as teleological truths. First, and indeed subsequent, experiences of vehicle-taking seemed quite simply part of a game developed by cultural knowledge and social capital resources dissemination among peer groupings:

> I was out with two friends, we weren't out to get one [a car] but we got bored just walking around one night and we just decided on taking it, there weren't no plans … It was great, we was buzzin' … My mates were older they taught me how to do it … it's easy really an' I learnt to drive in the car park near my mate's house … and off road up on the fields.

The need for greater confidence arising from experiential knowledge was usually mentioned in these reflections, the first occasion appearing to have been a time of uncertainty.

> It was scary at first, not knowing what's going to happen, but when you've done it again it gets easier.

However, any arising fears were always quickly forgotten once the pleasures of learning to drive were felt:

> It was great to drive, thrashing the car with all your mates, that's what got me started, what a buzz.

When reading media reports about so called 'joyriding' (a term the young men rarely referred to and only ever used to describe others in a pejorative sense, *never* to define themselves) it would be reasonable to assume that boasting about their driving prowess would pepper accounts; this was not the case. At no time in the course of the interviews did any of the young men brag about their driving skills. Only a very small number highlighted their expertise, usually when pressed, and this was very much related to peer group respect:

> I'm the driver ... I always drive the car, they all know I'm the top one there so they let me drive it mostly. It feels good, you feel more important, in charge, on the road.

But on the whole, most who acknowledged any skills at all very much underplayed these.

> Normally you're either good at nicking from cars or driving, you don't normally see somebody who's good at everything.

It might also have been assumed that group hierarchy would determine driving opportunities, but instead the usual explanation was that everyone 'took turns':

> I'm a good driver, we took it in turns because we were both good drivers.

However, not everyone wanted to be the driver and here pragmatic reasons usually prevailed:

> You're the one that's in trouble if you're the driver, you're the one the police will go for, the others they can just say they didn't know the car was stolen.

Almost everyone mentioned the need for a clear head and this proves key to understanding why the vast majority did not use drugs or alcohol when taking cars. Despite the fact that several of the young men reported using 'puff' (cannabis) 'to help wind down after a good night's buzzing', the 'hard' drug users the research participants encountered daily on their estates were typically described as 'losers' with 'no hope' or aspirations. 'Strength, guts and to be sober' were the commonest qualities required:

> I've never touched drugs, the thrill is the car.

Thus it becomes possible to understand what the young men derived from taking cars. Most emphasised the lacuna between driving and the mundane nature of their daily lives and this underpins the need to incorporate subjective psychosocial understandings within criminological explanatory frameworks (Gadd and Farrall 2004):

> There's no money up here and you need money to do anything, go anywhere, it's fucking boring ... There's nothing like the buzz you get when you're out, it's a buzz, a laugh with your mates.

> It's an adrenaline rush, you know what it's like on a roller coaster, well it's exactly the same feeling

> It's the air in your face, the thrill, that's why you do it it's the thrill, nothing puts you off when you get the air in your face and you're running.

Such accounts of the enormously positive rewards to be derived were underpinned by a vital theme first seen in the case study presented earlier, the issue of control (*cf.* Hayward 2002) of the car as a metaphor for what those young men yearned for in their ontologically insecure lifeworld:

> You're in control of the car and can do anything. It's a rush and you're the only one in control.

Like their non-offending counterparts, reflexive agency, control, resilience and optimism (e.g. Rudd and Evans 1998; Abbott-Chapman and Robertson 1999; Wyn and Dwyer 1999; Stephen 2000) were discovered as the young men unfolded their narratives. Further, these accounts lend strong support to Lyng's (2004: 362) argument that 'risk-takers describe their experience at the edge as self-actualising'. 'Control' and 'escape' (e.g. Cohen and Taylor 1992; Hayward 2002) and 'risk' (e.g. Green *et al.* 2000) through 'edgework' (Lyng 1990) were essential to their process of 'self-actualisation' (Hayward 2002) for, as we have argued elsewhere (Stephen and Squires 2003b) the acquisition of status through group support and identity, a sense of belonging in a consumer society from which they recognised their own marginalisation, provided a normative context for those young men being proactive in manufacturing their own forms of leisure, if not also employment. Those young men were actively trying to make sense of the protracted limbo within which they found themselves as they awaited that all-important signifier of male adult status for them: paid employment.

It is in the accounts of what was done with the proceeds of goods taken from vehicles that some invaluable insights arose which further affirms the research participants' commitment to the work ethic and collectivist principles:

I'd buy new clothes and things, nothing big, like burgers, it's like well you've not earned the money, so you buy nothing like you would if you'd had to work for it.

Nothing that's useful 'cause it's not hard work. I've bought clothes and food. One night I got twenty pounds for a stereo and took everyone for a twenty pound KFC.

All were asked if they considered the consequences of what they were doing and while many referred to the illegality of their actions, those who merely took vehicles, rather than took from them, were able to rationalise these:

I know I'm breaking the law and I don't like it when my mates' cars get done, but it's not like we're stealing the cars, it's just been borrowed for a laugh, they get it back 'cause it's not torched or anything, just dump it after.

The ability to present themselves as moral actors through such narratives (see Maruna 2001, for invaluable insight) provides a further vital aspect positivism fails to grasp. As implied here, although the young men acknowledged the illegality of their activities, these vehicle-taking activities, for them, proceeded within moral codes that offer insight into why their vehicle offending did not lead to wider 'criminal careers':

Car crime does not start more crime ... I've never burgled in my life, 'cause that would be like rape wouldn't it, it's like rape of someone's home. That's a whole new ball game.

The extent of the moral codes the young men reported to exist within their lifeworld was further underlined by others:

I don't nick cars with baby seats or disabled badges, that'd be depriving a kid or a disabled person, that's plain sick. I wouldn't touch a car with holy beads either 'cause you'd know they were a certain kind of person. There's a lot of us with values, but it's the ones who don't give a damn that's heard of ... I don't see the point in taking work vans either, that'd be depriving a man of his livelihood. I've standards.

While accepting that we need to fully deconstruct such narratives to understand the conscious and unconscious motivations behind them (see Gadd and Farrall 2004), objectification of apparently 'deviant' *Others*, such as these young men, denies that any sense of moral economy (*cf.* Thompson 1993a) can exist within their lifeworld. Instead, positivist modes of explanation and 'risk-management' prescriptions set themselves up to fail quite simply because they cannot accommodate the *Others'* worldview, motivations, reflexivity and moral economy as we have been demonstrating here. As such, extant top-down interventionist measures were regarded by the young men quite simply as:

> The biggest load of bollocks I've ever been to in my life … They teach you 'circles of offending', teambuilding … At the end of the course they make you fill out a questionnaire that shows your risk of re-offending, you just lie your arse off and pass with flying colours. They haven't a clue.

It was not a pathological vista of deviance that we found in the course of this research, rather the contrary: the young men's lifeworld and aspirations were informed by strong codes of practice, over-ascription to somewhat outmoded hegemonic notions of masculinity and collectivist principles, and especially a hoped-for future of 'real work' and nuclear family life. Late modernity does not, however, provide a conducive context for such outdated sentiments. This is a world where opportunities for any sense of ontological security within the young men's self-ascribed parameters of action proceed within risk accommodation:

> You only look at the good side, don't look at the consequences. It's a mad thing, one big rush, not just when you're doing it but after, being able to say you've done it.

> Any long stretch of road we'd race along, didn't care if we'd crash.

The research participants show that 'risk' is a problematic concept (*cf.* Green *et al.* 2000). While the risks associated with vehicle-taking activities are immense, when related to the wider social and material risks associated with their marginalisation, this 'risky' activity became a normative mode of skilful self-expression, leisure and employment generation, peer group bonding and security as they confronted an adult world imbued with the new inequalities and insecurities produced by contemporary 'risk society' (Beck 1992). In these accounts, 'self-concept' (Stephen 2000) and 'risk reputation' (Green *et al.* 2000) were almost indistinguishable facets of their 'alternative careers' (MacDonald *et al.* 2001). Appreciating how those young men had created their own meaningful lifeworlds, status and identity in the manner described here is imperative to understanding that which is usually taken as the final stage of 'criminal careers', desistance, whereupon strong adherence to the 'customary code' (Cohen and Ainley 2000) of anachronistic ideals of male employment is key.

Desistance

Among those research participants who had now stopped all vehicle offending, accounts of the cessation of their illegal activities usually encompassed very clear factors: wanting to secure a driving licence; not wanting a criminal record; and parental influences

> When I realised that I might end up not being able to drive [fear of possible ban before he secured his licence] I thought it's not worth it, I'll wait 'til I pass my test.

> I was worried about getting a criminal record, so it scared me as well … I was scared of getting caught so I stopped.

> I want to do something so my mum and dad will be proud of me.

As suggested in this latter extract, parents were reported to have been instrumental in desistance among the youngest research participants who said they had withdrawn from vehicle-taking directly as a result of parental reaction of 'shame' on their arrest and their parents' direct intervention:

> I got nicked, the police took me home and my mum and dad were ashamed of me. That's why I stopped. They weren't angry, but I knew I'd shamed them, it wasn't fair to see them hurt because of me… I don't go out a lot now, stay in doing my homework. My grades are getting better 'cause I'm doing my homework now and I've no time to get bored.

> Dad came to the police station, he was really annoyed. I could see it in his face. He refused a lawyer for me and sat in for the interview. He took me back next day for the caution too. But yes, he was annoyed … When we got out of the police station he took me to the place up there [near Brighton Racecourse] where the joyriders died, made me get out and look at the flowers and all he said was 'Do you want to end up like that?'

It was evident in our interactions with the parents of many of the young men who participated in this research that they had tried several means of stopping their son's activities, but they felt impotent in the face of the highly positive rewards to be derived for their sons in taking vehicles. Nonetheless, although several of the continuing vehicle offenders expressed regret for what they were putting their parents through:

> My mum gets really upset if I get arrested. I feel bad, I've let 'em down. It's not exactly fair on them. They've been pretty supportive but they've had enough, I've had about ten to fifteen arrests.

Expressed motivations for stopping were not found to be governed by psychosocially-based 'narratives of reform' (Gadd and Farrall 2004: 125), but by rather more pragmatic and materialist concerns. Among those who were approaching the age of 17, this, they believed, was time to consider longer-term consequences. Common street currency held that their treatment by the criminal justice system would change dramatically ('your records get wiped at 17' was the usual information volunteered by research participants) and this was related to the one key factor that, they believed, would stop them offending altogether: legitimate paid employment.

> If I want to get into the Marines I can't have a record.

> I won't do it again, stealing cars, or anything ruins my chances of getting a job and I want to work.

> The only thing that's going to stop me is if I find the job I want and earn the kind of money I want.

> It's only me that'd make me stop. Probably will when I get a job, working doesn't give you much time to hang around with your mates.

Among the older research participants who had extensive and wider criminal careers, the possibility of harsher sanctions was perceived, like the young man in the earlier case study, as a potential opportunity for life change:

> I accept that I'll probably get four years at the trial and I'll take it, use the time to get some qualifications, build myself up and get my head together.

However, the reasons for not regarding stopping as an option at the moment were quite clear for the younger research participants:

I need the money, how am I going to get the money I need if I stop? [and on taking vehicles] It's the best way to get the thrill and there's nothing else to do here.

By locating the young men's accounts in wider youth studies research, especially youth transitions, it became very clear that 'desistance' should not be regarded as an end to an offending path, but instead as a logical, formal and socially recognised extension to their current activities and sense of whom they regard themselves to be (Banks *et al.* 1992) and their own self-appreciated capabilities and aspirations. Vehicle offending was their 'alternative career' (MacDonald *et al.* 2001) in which they secured core attributes highly prized by contemporary employers in the formal economy, not least 'self-starter', 'team-player', 'skilled innovator' so often cited in job advertisements. In late modernity very few adults can offer stable CVs, and individuals often have to prostitute talents, skills and aspirations to engender a source of income, status and sense of ontological security. If portfolio working is increasingly becoming the norm for even the most privileged adults, how then can society expect marginalised young men to act differently? For those young men, therefore, vehicle offending was the means of resolving the inherent disjuncture between the estrangement produced by their current state of social being and their deferred transition to the adult world (Stephen and Squires 2003b). But, vehicle offending became more than a means of coping (e.g. Julkunen 2001) or a 'culture of survival' (MacDonald 1997, 190); it was the means through which those young men could ' "have" and therefore "be" '(Presdee 2004: 280) in their process of late modern self-actualisation (Hayward 2002). Legitimate paid employment, they hoped, would culminate this alternative process of 'becoming a man'.

There is one final important lesson to learn from those young men which our discipline and wider policy-makers cannot ignore, not least in respect of increasingly punitive 'anti-social behaviour' measures. All of the young men who participated in this research offered multifarious, and feasible, suggestions for change ranging from how to improve relations with police, how to alter the court and sentencing system, to a host of wider educational and employment measures and local community initiatives (Stephen and Squires 2001). The young men's suggestions indicated a strong ability and willingness to come up with their own possible preventative and diversional solutions. However, contemporary positivist-biased managerialism fails to grasp that 'young offenders' are the experts who should be consulted if any initiatives are to stand any chance of success. More significantly perhaps, managerialist fixes also mask the wider insecure late-modern context for marginalised young people that really needs to be tackled. Quite simply, 'existing measures do not work' was the resounding conclusion offered by research participants:

> The main problem is that there is a lack of belief that things are going to get better.

'The system', this prolific vehicle offender continued, stands charged with 'lack of relevant imagination' and 'reinforcing criminality' while 'young people with limited options and unable to envisage any alternative future to that handed down by an unequal society' seek 'misplaced status through vehicle offending'. Both sides, he felt:

> continue to conspire in producing a situation of mutual stereotypes and confrontation, instead of collaboration and belief that things can change.

As an inherent part of this system, through the increasing mis-appropriation of our talents and imaginations by administrative doctrines and imperatives, contemporary criminology too stands guilty as charged by this young man. Unless and until we begin to listen much more to such young people, to understand their needs and aspirations, and to work to empower them through providing concrete opportunities, if only to be heard, this situation will remain unchanged. Yet, instead, we augment our beholding to political paymasters and, thus, continue to perpetuate the modernist myth that 'truth' can be found, that 'causes' can be ascertained and that surface, and increasingly punitive, 'expert' prescriptions can be effected to 'cure' such examples of social malaise. In its ongoing efforts to present itself as an objective scientific discipline within modernist modes of acceptance contemporary mainstream criminology increasingly ignores our indebtedness to a richer sagacious humanist history that simply reminds us we should learn to understand the 'lived experience' of those whom we research:

> not as autonomous subjects, 'free individuals', but as persons experiencing their determinate productive situations and relation-ships, as needs and interests and as antagonisms and then 'handling' this experience within their *consciousness* and their *culture* ... in the most complex ... ways, and then ... acting upon their determinate situation in their turn. (Thompson 1978: 356, emphasis in original)

This interaction of structure and reflexive agency is central to understanding the choices young people make and the 'careers' they pursue. In this chapter, we have shown one simple means of drawing upon this firm cultural heritage in pursuit of our own 'constitutive criminology' (Henry and Milovanovic 1996). The young man's concluding analysis above should inspire us all to more rigorously rekindle our criminological imaginations in the further development of a less objectifying and more empathic discipline, 'a more creative, caring criminology' (Presdee 2004: 276), for we cannot lose sight of this fertile interpretative heritage that entreats us to remember:

> Any group of persons ... develop a life of their own that becomes meaningful, reasonable and normal once you get close to it. (Goffman 1961: ix–x)

By drawing upon wider youth studies we can offer a firm challenge to constructions of *Otherness* inherent in mainstream accounts of young people's 'anti-social behaviour' and offending. Positivism continues to deliver mind-boggling causal explanations *ad nauseam*, yet has failed to produce the desired and real 'cost-benefit' results in terms of significant reductions in anti-social behaviour or youth offending. Undoubtedly 'getting close' to the subjects of our research is what is required for 'without concerted attempts to understand the subjective realities ... the *human meaning* of criminal behaviour will always escape us' (Gadd and Farrall 2004: 149) and we shall continue to conspire with the ever-consolidating 'institutionalised mistrust' (Kelly 2003) of marginalised youth, a 'mistrust' that is in danger of criminalising the whole period of youth itself (Stephen and Squires 2004). The inherent caveat in our desire to contribute to revealing the potentialities of cultural criminology (see Hayward and Young 2004) is that we do not stumble where previous modernist structuralist and culturalist accounts fell; late modernity necessitates that we reify neither structure nor agency, that we privilege neither passivity nor resistance, that we prioritise neither objectivity nor subjectivity, but instead seek unified explanatory frameworks. In exploring the 'forgotten spaces' where the 'story of crime ... unfolds' (Hayward and Young 2004: 271), we can ' re-contextualise crime within its human and historical context' (Presdee 2004: 277) and thus become more potent 'Champions of Dissent' (see Thompson 1993b) in the face of our own structured constraints. How will future historians record our response to this vital challenge though?

Chapter 7

Anti-social behaviour, social control and the precautionary principle: new views 'from the boys'

What is it that we do as producers of intellectually grounded knowledge when we take youth as our objects? What might be the consequences of these institutionalised processes of knowledge production for the regulation of the young people who are the objects of these processes? ... What might it mean for the practice of youth studies if we take seriously the proposition that the *governmentalisation* of youthful desires, bodies, thoughts and actions which emerge as a result as a practice of youth studies may have profound, if unintended, consequences for the regulation of youth? No matter that these processes of intellectual knowledge production are framed with the best of intentions. (Kelly 2000: 313, emphasis in original)

Recognising that we are at great risk of being charged with gender-blindness/centrism, the title of this chapter is grounded in pragmatic factors: firstly, and quite simply, the overwhelming bulk of our empirical work has been with marginalised young men. Secondly, we are merely continuing criminology's historical interest in 'lower-class male' youths (Young 1999: 41) for resolutions to these long-standing investigations remain unresolved to any degree of satisfaction. Notwithstanding these more mundane reasons, as implied in the questions posed by Kelly, the third reason is unquestionably concerned with praxis. As we have been arguing, there is a pressing need to re-evaluate our direction as a discipline along the very same lines as Kelly suggests.

Van Swaaningen (1999: 7) succinctly states the underlying problematic: 'why do we actually need criminologists?' There are some strong contemporary dissenting voices for youth (e.g. Pitts 2001; Smith, R. 2003), and alternative creative visions of youth (e.g. Katz 1988; Lyng 1990; Presdee 2000; Hayward 2004). However, if we criminologists continue to nourish, rather than problematise, the ever-consolidating 'institutionalised mistrust' (Kelly 2003) of marginalised youth as effected in and through anti-social behaviour discourses and practices (Stephen and Squires 2004), it suggests we have learned nothing from Schur's (1973) reconsideration of 'delinquency'. Indeed the entire phase of interactionism within our discipline's development may have passed us by. We must, therefore, take time to reflect on the issues Kelly (2000) raises above in respect of the knowledge we are producing and the ensuing intended/ unintended consequences of this knowledge production to young people's governmentalisation through the highly problematic concept of 'anti-social behaviour'.

Returning to our interactionist roots

Perhaps few readers will need to be reminded of Becker's seminal proposition, but it is essential to begin our reconsideration from this point since the fundamental premise bears direct relevance to the notion of 'anti-social behaviour':

> Social groups create deviance by making the rules whose infraction constitutes deviance, and by applying those rules to particular people and labelling them as outsiders. From this point of view, deviance is not a quality of the act a person commits, but rather a consequence of the application by others of rules and sanctions to an 'offender'. The deviant is one to whom the label has been successfully applied; deviant behaviour is behaviour that people so label. (Becker 1963: 9)

In returning to these basics, considerations focus upon three factors: that which is labelled 'anti-social'; the processes inherent in the labelling of 'anti-social behaviour'; and the active impact of the application of the label 'anti-social' upon the young people thus labelled. Further, the concept of deviance may not hold much currency nowadays, but in failing to incorporate this notion into our explanatory frameworks for the contemporary governance of youth we throw the baby out with the bath water because 'anti-social behaviour' is such a highly problematic, value-laden, subjective and politically-loaded construct. Nowhere is this made more clear than in the perceptions of anti-social behaviour results of the 2003/4 British Crime Survey which include a range of reported behaviours from speeding traffic to people sleeping rough (see Wood 2004).

In adhering to more individualistic concerns of labelling theory, previous chapters have shown that we need to appreciate the processual impact of the label upon young people to their progressive marginalisation. However, as also argued, this focus on the individual is not enough: this process does not proceed in a vacuum. It is the political intentionality, not least in advancing the myth that ('deviant') 'anti-social behaviour' can be distinguished from ('normal') youthful agency (cf. Schur 1973) which lies behind this process that needs to be examined, as Schur demonstrates lucidly:

> Human behaviour is deviant *to the extent* that it comes to be viewed as involving a *personally discreditable* departure from a group's normative expectations, *and it elicits* interpersonal or collective reactions that serve to 'isolate', 'treat', 'correct' or punish *individuals* engaged in such behaviour. (Schur 1971: 24, emphasis in original)

The significance of Schur's thesis is that, like other interactionists, he shows the need to appreciate the relative nature of that which is labelled anti-social, that

> the 'deviantness' of an act or an individual is always relative, changeable, a matter of degree, and that the degree depends mainly upon the extent to which the behaviour is viewed and responded to in certain ways. (Schur 1971: 25)

But, as shown in the preceding extract, Schur's argument draws our attention to rather more profound questions. These concern the wider social and political processes at work in the current discursive frenzy surrounding 'anti-social behaviour' and the part this plays in consolidating a 'lack of respect for freedom and dignity of all, and lack of regard for established rights and systems of legality' (Hudson 2003: 73). 'Anti-social behaviour', therefore, becomes a 'sensitising concept' (Schur 1971: 26), the prism through which we must necessarily engage critically with the structures and processes at work in and through the contemporary governance of, especially marginalised, youth by anti-social behaviour discourses and practices. This 'reordering of emphasis' (Schur 1971: 173) is imperative if we are to address the vital questions posed by Kelly at the start of this chapter and so, to achieve this, we necessarily return to another seminal interactionist:

The State, dismayed at the failure of its conditioning agencies such as the school, the church, the social services and community development projects, resorts to coercion through 'terreur'. (Parker 1974: 186)

As argued in our earlier chapters, the flexible boundaries of anti-social behaviour labelling runs counter to those principles long held sacrosanct within the British criminal justice system, not least 'innocent until proven guilty', 'beyond reasonable doubt' and 'right to a fair trial'. In bypassing criminal law through the civil injunctions of ASBOs and ABCs, hearsay is admissible, guilt presumed and 'swift justice' encouraged (Home Office 2004c). Yet, failure to comply with these seemingly benign interventions can lead to a magnification of criminal penalties and, as such, the very foundations of our criminal justice system become adulterated, if not also, at times, abandoned. This legally confusing (and morally dubious) situation is further confused by the ambiguous position of young people within the law. A long-standing ambiguity (see, for example, Goldson 2000) here construes young people both in need of protection (e.g. Children Act 1989) *and* in need of control (e.g. Crime and Disorder Act 1998: section 37). However, as indicated by Parker (and as discussed in Chapter 4), nowadays where local authorities fail in their duties, for example to provide services to children in need under the Children Act 1989, the new apparatus of civil control can be brought in to paper over the cracks (Walsh 1999; Jones 2001b).

In this manner, through the rhetoric of 'responsibilisation' (e.g. Flint 2002), society becomes absolved and individuals, already essentialised as 'thugs' and 'yobs' (e.g. Home Office 2004b, 2004c, 2004d) are held solely culpable, and the 'epistemological fallacy' (Furlong and Cartmel 1997) is cemented. Instead of fostering any sense of inclusion for already marginalised young people, this essentialism 'facilitates the process of social exclusion' (Young 1999: 116). Indeed, as a 'paramount strategy of exclusionism' (Young 1999: 104), Young shows there are distinct advantages of this essentialism for the so-called 'decent law-abiding majority whose lives are supposedly threatened by an out-of-control minority' (Home Office 2003b: 1). It 'provides ontological security; legitimises both privilege and deference; allows us to blame the Other; is the basis for projection' (Young 1999: 104–5). These aspects are vital to understanding the place and purpose of contemporary constructs of marginalised young people and anti-social behaviour policy responses against them, as we will demonstrate shortly.

Accordingly, we 'isolate' (Schur 1971: 24), through crude exclusionary restrictions and controls that circumscribe young people's 'anti-social' agency and the geography within which that agency may proceed, reducing the horizons (cf. Parker 1974: 194) of their youthful agency, and thus *a priori* deviancy. In our study (Stephen and Squires 2003a) we found young people coerced into signing Acceptable Behaviour Contracts containing such terms as 'I will not swear', 'I will not throw stones' or 'I will not hang around' in given areas, with the threatened eviction of the entire family ensuring compliance. Drawing upon Schur's (1973) vital insights, therefore, it is truly impossible to identify the point at which, for example, 'hanging around' with friends (when there are no relevant youth facilities in the neighbourhood) becomes 'anti-social' when there is so much subjectivity embraced by the discourse of Anti-Social Behaviour. However, as we shall explore later, it is both the symbolism and the fear (*cf.* Lianos with Douglas 2000) that this visible youthful signifier of perceived danger engenders that is of paramount value within the contemporary political economy of power (Foucault 1977). Consequently, instead of tackling the roots of the supposed 'anti-social behaviour', the managerial measures of 'success' (outputs such as contracts signed, arrests made, interventions completed) served to reassure the Community Safety Team, the New Deal sponsors and the 'decent law-abiding majority' within those estates that the system is working. As we have argued, there is rather more to it.

This much we have learned from our interactionist predecessors, but there is another important lesson we would do well to recall. It concerns the impact of the label itself and its role in magnifying the *self*-processes of marginalisation and exclusion of individuals who are without yet a secure foothold in society. Chapter 6 offered a critique of voluntarist and teleological understandings of 'criminal career', yet the justification for anticipatory interventions at increasingly younger ages (see Bandalli 2000) through anti-social behaviour measures is grounded in these very same assumptions. The result is not the supposed management of risk envisaged by 'actuarial justice' (Feeley and Simon 1994) but, rather, young men, fully cognisant of their marginalised position, finding ontological security and status in offending practices. This was their process of 'becoming a man' in the absence of socially acceptable signifiers in a late-modern world where they 'grow up with less than they need' (Parker 1974: 186). Those young men had developed their own ways of having and being (*cf.* Presdee 2000) which mirrored the values of a society always just out of legitimate reach by virtue of their young age, and the aggregate marginalising processes inherent in their social, economic and neighbourhood heritage. Thus, while their lifeworld may appear 'deviant' to supposedly 'law-abiding citizens', the young men's values and aspirations are almost hyper-'normal'. In other, legitimate, circumstances such enterprise would be applauded since their vehicle offending agency was found to be a creative and pragmatic response to the social and material *'rareté'* (Parker 1974: 186) within which they had been reared. And, even when the uncompromising realities of late-modern life became compounded by the effects of progressive criminal sanction, those young men came to regard the ultimate sanction available within our criminal justice system, prison, as opportunity rather than deterrent. For them, prison had the potential of being their 'New Deal'. The question hardly needs asking, but what is this telling us about the opportunities for marginalised young people in contemporary Britain? In the next section, therefore, we wish to expand upon a point we made earlier in that the risk *of* the 'Other' in contemporary Community Safety discourses obscures the real risks *to* the 'Other' resulting from their social exclusion (Stephen and Squires 2004). There is an important difference, sometimes obscured by contemporary discourses of community safety and ASB, between *being a risk* and being *at risk*.

The twin fallacies

> The problem of crime control in late modernity has vividly demonstrated the limits of the sovereign state. (Garland 2002: 205)

Garland's assertion needs to be borne in mind in the remainder of this chapter. Undoubtedly, the contemporary governance of marginalised youth is rooted in and symptomatic of the realpolitik of late modern Britain (Pitts 2000), although the government have often sought to obscure this with discourses of inclusion, community and consensus. While a core theme of this book has been Furlong and Cartmel's (1997) 'epistemological fallacy' thesis, within criminology, however, there is another fallacy to which we have been alluding throughout, but which we have yet to fully explicate. This 'cosmetic fallacy' (Young 1999) bears direct relevance to our problematisation of 'anti-social behaviour' discourses and regarding young people. The 'cosmetic fallacy'

> conceives of crime as a superficial problem of society, skin deep, which can be dealt with using the appropriate ointment, rather than any chronic ailment of society as a whole. (Young 1999: 130)

Young people, and especially marginalised young men, have historically been society's *bêtes noires*, objects of the gaze of criminal justice surveillance and interventions, and, of course, of our discipline. This is not as a matter of actuality, but merely through their 'perceived probability of being dangerous' (Lianos with Douglas 2000: 263). It could, therefore, quite easily be questioned why we bother to raise this issue at all. Yet it is important for the contemporary regulatory processes, effected in and through anti-social behaviour discourses and practices, appear to be consolidating the 'institutionalised mistrust' (Kelly 2003) of the period of youth itself.

This is a mistrust which, through superficial policy and highly visible practice, not least in local newspapers, is creating a climate of *Otherness* that hyper-inflates the 'moral panic' parameters of Cohen's (1973) seminal work. A report in the *Mid-Sussex Times* (30 September 2004) followed a headline 'You're barred – Court slaps no-go areas on yob 16'. Naturally this newspaper report was accompanied by a supporting photograph of a suitably furtive looking young man. While 'the yob' story received the majority of front-page space, in stark contrast a report of a missing 14-year-old was relegated to a third of the space at the bottom of the page. This fairly typical illustration of the increasing imbalance between societal concern *for* young people's well-being and concern *about* young people indicates that the long-standing uncomfortable equilibrium between protection and control has been destabilised. Young people are now firmly constructed symbolically as dangerous Other (Stephen and Squires 2004). This, as we have been arguing throughout this text, is an imbalance with highly deleterious consequences:

> [T]hose whose lives and opportunities have not yet been improved will be held responsible and enmeshed at an ever younger age in the current expansion of the criminal justice system with little concern either for their rights or for the principles of criminal law. (Bandalli 2000: 94)

Ironically, the front-page headline story in the same mid-Sussex newspaper the following week indicated that anti-social behaviour measures were not, however, working to plan, 'Yobs "migrating" after crackdown' (*Mid-Sussex Times* 7 October 2004). The story begins 'A tough police clamp-down in Burgess Hill is pushing troublemakers into Haywards Heath [town nearby], it is claimed.' Something is clearly going awry. 'Teen found safe' received two sentences on page 10 despite the youngster having been missing for four days.

These local illustrations therefore draw our attention to the 'cosmetic' (Young 1999) nature of contemporary policy and practices. Populist headline-grabbing clamp-downs and exclusionary measures may simply displace the 'problem of anti-social behaviour'. The very fact that such measures have limited impact will undoubtedly provide justification for wider and increasingly more punitive 'solutions', for example, as witnessed in the announcement of new powers for parish councils on 28 October 2004 (Home Office 2004e). More significantly, as we demonstrated earlier, even where young people do comply with the terms of these measures, it often comes at unacceptable increased cost to already fragile family units and the young persons' psycho-social well-being and current and future life chances.

Yet, increasingly, a new more condemnatory political consensus suggests that competition for the title of party of law and order will only intensify the 'cosmetic fallacy', creating a sense that society can absolve itself through individualised responsibilisation strategies. The theme of 'respect and responsibility' sees both of the main party leaders trying to outdo each other in what proves to be an impossible game of 'spot the difference':

It was John Stuart Mill who articulated the modern concept that with freedom comes responsibility. But in the 1960s revolution, that didn't always happen. Law and order policy still focussed on the offender's rights, protecting the innocent, understanding the social causes of their criminality. All through the 1970s and 1980s, under Labour and Conservative Governments, a key theme of legislation was around the prevention of miscarriages of justice. Meanwhile some took freedom without the responsibility. The worst criminals became better organised and more violent. The petty criminals were no longer the bungling but wrong-headed villains of old but drug pushers and drug abusers, desperate and without any residual moral sense. And a society of different lifestyles spawned a group of young people who were brought up without parental discipline, without proper role models and without any sense of responsibility to or for others. (Tony Blair 19 July 2004)

As a society we are in danger of being overrun by values which eat away at people's respect for themselves, each other, their homes and their neighbourhood. Most damaging of all has been the dramatic decline in personal responsibility. Many people now believe that they are no longer wholly responsible for their actions. It's someone else's, or something else's fault – the environment, society, the government. Remember the lines from *West Side Story*, when the gangs of hoods try to excuse their actions: 'I'm depraved on account of I'm deprived' says one. 'Juvenile delinquency is purely a social disease' says another. *West Side Story* may have been written by an American at the end of the 1950s, but these attitudes are all too prevalent in British society today. These excuses shift the balance away from the yob, the shoplifter, the joy-rider, the mugger, any criminal, on to someone or something else. What more harmful message could we send than to say 'It's not your fault, it is society's fault.' (Michael Howard 10 August 2004)

Yet in stark contrast, the launch of the Positive Images campaign in Westminster on 13 October 2004, appeared to represent a challenge towards such typical representations of young people. These are representations that, as we have shown, tend to portray them as 'Yobs, thugs, louts, monsters, scum, brutes, crooks' (Goddard 2004). The campaign is supported by a range of organisations and both Tessa Jowell, Secretary of State for Culture, Media and Sport, and Margaret Hodge, Minster for Young People. Highlighting MORI research findings that 71 per cent of media stories about young people are negative and a third focus on crime, the campaign is to be commended. However, this much-needed reappraisal will be undermined as long as other senior government ministers perpetuate young people's demonisation.

> 'Youth crime', and the fear of it, has emerged in Anglo-American politics as a kind of electoral glue. On the one hand 'fear of youth crime', can bind together an otherwise disparate band of electors into a new 'post-industrial' political constituency which transcends traditional class affiliations. On the other, it may be used to repair rifts within political parties, generating an impression of unity and common purpose. (Pitts 2003: 1–2)

The promises of order, security and 'prevention' by party leaders, through earlier and earlier interventions in young people's lives (e.g. Bandalli 2000), find a receptive adult audience. This discourse of control internalises the values and fears of contemporary 'Risk Society' (Beck 1992), and combines them with neoclassicist notions of 'zero tolerance' of youthful transgressions for the supposed greater good of community cohesion and safety. This is a 'community', however, founded in adultist agendas and increasing intolerance that fails to appreciate the realities of growing up, especially on the margins, in late-modern Britain. Already essentialised, these young people are offered for sacrifice on the altar of utilitarianism without a murmur of protest from the supposedly 'law-abiding majority' who lap up the superficial and misleading, analyses on offer as typified in the following illustration.

> Police in Mid-Sussex are right to be wary of troublesome youths migrating to another area in the face of a crackdown in their usual haunts. It's a known pattern of behaviour ... So no-one should be surprised that the troublemakers in Burgess Hill town centre are finding somewhere else to ply their evil behaviour. However, the police have promised 'relentless' action and that's to be welcomed. They are using anti-social behaviour orders to bring these hooligans to book. When they break the ASBO – as most of them surely will –

the courts must back the police and the public and hand down appropriate sentences. There should be no shilly-shallying from magistrates – the louts have had their chance with the issue of the ASBO. (Tubthumper, *Mid-Sussex Times* 14 October 2004: 9)

Burgess Hill is certainly not deluged by crime and anti-social behaviour, but, like any English town, it has its element of young 'troublemakers'. Nonetheless, current anti-social behaviour discourses guarantee that the fears and antagonisms engendered are echoed, as much from Middle England as from those who have to endure disproportionate levels of genuine 'anti-social' behaviour, by virtue of their residency in the marginalised and deprived estates throughout the country (see Wood 2004). Even in saying this, however, we need to maintain a healthy scepticism, for the very fact that more anti-social behaviour can be 'found in social housing estates' could simply be an artefact of 'the physical presence of "investigatory" people and technology [who] ensure that it will be found' (Brown 2004: 210), reported and responded to within the new political economy of power (Foucault 1977). The opacity of definitions of anti-social behaviour, in turn, provide fertile grounds for ever-increasing numbers of reports, and, in due course, form the basis for the further development of the growing 'anti-social behaviour' industry. Mindful of Kelly's opening challenge to this chapter, as a discipline we are also directly complicit in spawning this culture of intolerance through our own long-standing veneration of hybridised positivist utilitarianism:

One method of preventing the spread of diseases is through quarantine. This clearly involves some costs to the individual who is isolated. However, it is felt that the benefits to the community of preventing diseases outweigh the costs to the individual being quarantined. (Farrington 1987: 89).

However, through the punitive quarantining of 'anti-social' individuals, we do not, in fact, provide 'the greatest good for the greatest number'. Instead, as our interactionist predecessors have clearly shown, it engenders an environment whereby exclusion becomes consolidated because

the treatment of deviants denies them the ordinary means of carrying on the routines of everyday life open to most people (Becker 1963: 35)

offering progressively fewer opportunities for their social reintegration and inclusion resulting in 'a cycle of increasing deviance' (Becker 1963: 37). Refining this understanding by focusing upon the psychosocial notion of commitment some years later, Ullmer (1994) develops the picture:

1. Restricted availability of conventional alternatives increases the attractiveness of deviant alternatives. Actors may thus adjust by continuing deviant activities and further exploring deviant opportunities and networks.
2. This adjustment, in turn, can lead to further reduction in the availability and attractiveness of conventional alternatives through unfitting processes.
3. Adjustment to deviant identity placement conditions irretrievable investment in deviant activities and network relationships. These investments, in turn, further reduce the attractiveness of conventional alternatives. (Ullmer 1994: 149)

Yet we are unwilling to face up to the fact that social censure, either through the formal criminal justice system or through the civil 'anti-social behaviour' measures, can be counterproductive (cf. Schur 1973; Hudson 1993). One good example of this was unearthed during our ABC research. We were informed by both professionals and young people that the list of the 50 young people 'at risk of offending' drafted for selection to the Youth Inclusion Project had come to be regarded almost as a competitive league table by many young people who wanted to know the precise position they held. Further, this Youth Inclusion Project, despite its laudable aims and achievements, was marred by its exclusivity in offering exciting opportunities, such as quad biking, only for a select minority. Younger, lesser and non-'offenders', denied such episodes of escape from the boredom of their estates, could only look on with envy. 'Early intervention' through such intensive measures may, therefore, simply serve to intensify and extensify 'deviant' agency among a wider population of young people to secure opportunities denied them. The dangers of 'over-prediction' (and thereby net-widening) have been long established (see Schur 1973). Yet in under-predicting the potential consequences of current 'anti-social' discourses and selective practices, we are at great risk of magnifying problems for the future, not just for young people themselves, but for society as a whole. The remainder of this chapter will, therefore, be devoted to contemplating the view that, perhaps, the government too may have come to realise this.

The governmentalisation of becoming and belonging

In modernity positivism provided us with the notion of a small number of distinct criminals with their own individualistic aetiology – maverick characters, the product of dire and atypical situations – whilst neo-classicism delineated the clear-cut legal parameters of crime. Late modernity loses the precision of both offender and the offence; offenders are everywhere, offences blur together with a host of anti-social behaviours. (Young 1999: 133)

If, as our own research and that of our interactionist predecessors has shown, early interventions do not produce favourable or lasting outcomes for either the individuals targeted or the wider society, what, therefore, is being achieved? One clear answer to this question is the politicisation of all kinds of risk (see Douglas 1992). In the extract above, Young clearly captures the substance of the present situation. Despite government and media assurances that 'yobs' and 'thugs' can be readily identified and 'controlled' through anti-social behaviour measures, the lack of clarity in definitions of 'anti-social behaviour' and the promotion of an increasingly intolerant climate ensure a masking of the increasing state penetration into our own lives. Thus, in mobilising against 'anti-social behaviour' we merely acquiesce to subtle, target-driven processes of risk control (see Clear and Cadora 2001). Accordingly, there are two interrelated concerns which must be acknowledged:

Dangers are being produced by industry, externalised by economics, individualised by the legal system, legitimised by the sciences and made to appear harmless by politics. (Beck 1998: 16)

The *needs of the organisation* often affect and even determine the nature of delinquency-processing. This factor frequently has a greater bearing on the outcomes in delinquency cases than either the supposed needs of the processed individuals or the specific details of their law-violating behaviour. Organisational needs partly centre around the sheer necessity of getting a job done, of managing an overwhelming number of cases. (Schur 1973: 131, emphasis in original)

The 'industry' we wish to oppugn is the ever-expanding 'anti-social behaviour' industry, an industry that, on the one hand, through appro-priation of public fear and the structuring of intolerance, encourages ever more reports of 'anti-social behaviour'. On the other hand, legitimised by administrative criminology's doctrines and imperatives, ASB managers offer perfunctory promises that control and order can be realised. In this manner, instead of trying to understand, practitioners work to identify; instead of offering empathy we are urged to condemn; instead of recognising the need for systematic reform, we are encouraged to isolate and responsibilise deviant individuals; and instead of hope we in-creasingly find cynicism and despair. Writing this as the British Labour government has recently set out its 'security'-centred programme in a Queen's Speech designed to take us through to the next election, the ability of governments to manipulate, manage and benefit from late modern fears and insecurities is very apparent. Perhaps just as apparent is their ability to mobilise people around specious notions of morality. Bauman, in particular (2002: 69), has neatly summarised why politicians find the 'law and order' issue so attractive.

> 'Being tough on crime' is the expedient to which politicians resort with particular zeal, and for a twofold reason. First, when fighting crime, politicians of all levels can be seen as doing something tangible, 'real' and easily understandable while, secondly, none of them can do anything remotely as tangible and real about any other source of their voters' insecurity.

Young's (1999) work also addresses how governments demonstrate to a sceptical public that they are 'getting the job done'. Governments might be trying to maintain cohesion, order and stability in the face of late-modern insecurity and dislocation – while simultaneously ensuring a ready supply of scapegoats upon which all our fears can be projected, for example 'asylum-seekers', 'Muslim extremists' and, of course, that long-standing target of public chagrin, marginalised young people. Then, through appeals to morality, tougher rhetoric and policy, and myriad upbeat evaluations of crime and anti-social behaviour initiatives, a sense of ontological security may be fostered. It seeks to reassure us that we are different, upstanding beings whose government is acting in our best interests through these moralised measures (see Blair 2004). Whereas the sense of optimism and progress inherent in modernity allowed us to indulge in such delusions, late-modernity only offers a profound, and certainly insatiable, desire that risk should be managed and contained. However, in lapping up such 'cosmetic' assurances, we fail to see that *we* are also part of that risk, a factor camouflaged by our late-modern structured understanding of ourselves as a fellowship of potential victims (see Hudson 2003). Such an understanding is troubling, for the surveillance of our everyday lives has become so commonplace that we readily cede rights in the name of 'risk prevention'. As students of the potentialities inherent in the inheritance of Lombroso's project are only too aware, there are feasibly no limits to what can be done in the name of 'security' (Zedner 2000), especially in a world of increasing scarcity, not least in terms of material and creative opportunities for young people on the margins. Thus, although this short extract is not presented in the context Miles intended, it captures a point that needs to be developed:

Not only can young people be described as an index of social ills and a barometer of social change, but also as beacons of economic stresses and strains. (Miles 2002: 61)

We, therefore, need to deviate slightly to be in a stronger position to contend why marginalised young people are so symbolically essential to the exercise of contemporary governance. To develop Simon's (1997) point, just as young people are increasingly governed *through* crime and disorder, so risky, out-of-control and marginalised young people are offered up as the justification for much of our current criminal justice policies and infrastructure. It is necessary to return to a vital issue, first raised in Chapter 6 and identified by Schur in his critique of naive social reformism:

Direct and meaningful measures to eliminate or reduce poverty, inequality of opportunity, and associated living conditions appear to have a particularly strong potential for ultimately reducing crime and delinquency. To the professional sociologist, this line of argument presents several difficulties ... As a formal causal explanation that is both theoretically grounded and empirically testable, the assertion that poverty causes crime or delinquency is not really acceptable. It clearly does not explain why some of the poor become delinquent and others do not. Then too ... sociologists increasingly question the assumption that usually underlines this thesis – namely, that delinquency is heavily concentrated in the working or lower-class segments of the population. But even if these limitations could be disregarded, simply to attribute delinquency to poverty would in no way indicate the specific processes that produce it. (Schur 1973: 106)

As argued earlier, the young men we interviewed underlined the need for an appreciation of their activities as a process of 'becoming', and this notion appears prerequisite in analysis of contemporary youth experiences. It is already an established aspect of youth transition literature (Skelton 2002). The term 'transition', an essential defining feature of the period of 'youth', is helpful for it reveals further potentialities inherent in more interactionist understandings of young people's agency, agency that is always enabled or constrained by wider structural forces. Wider youth studies conceive of youth as an intermediate phase in the life course between childhood and adulthood (e.g. Jones and Wallace 1992; Furlong and Cartmel 1997). While the fundamental problems in attempting to define both of these latter concepts must be acknowledged, as is the need to avoid the pitfalls of reifying developmental approaches and adulthood (see Wyn and Dwyer 1999; Skelton 2002), the constituents of this 'intermediate phase' afford invaluable means of not just understanding the active process of 'becoming', but more fundamentally, that of *belonging*.

As a social construct, the period of youth has no clear beginning nor end but is understood as a time wherein individuals are accorded staged rights and responsibilities. They acquire a status of 'semi-dependency and semi-independence', childhood being accepted as a state of dependence on parents or 'surrogate' parents (Coles 1995). Analysis, therefore, of the transitionary markers and processes through which individuals move from perceived 'dependency' to the rights and obligations implicit in conceptions of 'adulthood' affords a means of offering a critical account of contemporary criminological constructs of youth. Key material constituents of this intermediate phase have been described. These include the education to employment transition, the domestic transition and the housing transition (Coles 1995; Furlong and Cartmel 1997) with mediating factors, such as class, gender and 'race' (e.g. Coles 1995) and wider socio-economic change (e.g. MacDonald 1998) exerting strong influences upon young people's ability to acquire these markers of 'status passage' (Du Bois-Reymond 1998). Grasping this structural context for offending practices is a necessary component, but a focus on this alone, as Schur (1973) implies, is naïve and misplaced. It is, therefore, necessary to move from traditional structural conceptions of youth transitions (see critiques in Jeffs and Smith 1998; Cohen and Ainley 2000; Fergusson *et al.* 2000; Miles 2000) to an analysis that encompasses young people as active agents in this process of becoming and belonging, a process in which outcomes are also reliant upon the ways in which society responds to this agency as our interactionist predecessors have shown. Further, we need to bear in mind that, nowadays, these transitions proceed within a fundamental shift in orientation away from collective state welfare to competitive individualised market provision. Accordingly, at present, the prognosis for society playing a positive enabling role in marginalised young people's processes of becoming and belonging looks bleak:

> Without the willingness of government to exercise a degree of direct regulation and control over key resources for the young (*sic*), the prospects for any significant improvement in the fortunes of most school leavers will continue to remain in doubt. At best, the importance placed on investing in young people's education and training will most likely make little substantive difference to the lives of the majority, whether judged in terms of their individual life chances, ability to participate in society or in relation to the fortunes and status that accrue from the possession of certain forms of

qualification. At worst, New Labour's 'progressive competitiveness' in policy for young workers will most likely further deepen the problems that large numbers are increasingly experiencing as responsibility for poor educational outcomes, unemployment, low quality work, meagre earnings, marginality to the social security system, and so on is further shifted on to the young themselves. (Mizen 2003: 472)

Mizen's paper is a welcome contribution to appreciating the Janus-face of current youth policies, an approach depicted as 'rooted in a melange of Fabian optimism and neo-liberal nihilism' (Pitts 2003: 135). The 'epistemological fallacy' (Furlong and Cartmel 1997), is clearly visible in Mizen's concluding sentence above: young people are increasingly being required to find their own ways of becoming and belonging. And, with the advent of 'anti-social behaviour' measures, where young people fail in this onerous task the new civil controls will assuredly be ready to prompt them. Acknowledging that the meaning of transition has changed since the initial conceptions were formulated (Wyn and Dwyer 1999), late modernity has eroded the previously more predictable transitions young people were able to effect. This is a world in which marginalised young people, subject to the vagaries and risk of late-modern markets, must become increasingly reliant on their own agency (MacDonald 1998; Kelly 1999). And this exposes the fundamental contradiction in policy thinking. In late modernity we expect young people to be more reliant on their reflexive agency (Kelly 1999) than ever before, yet, like no time in the past, we are subjecting marginalised young people to ever-limiting constraints on that agency. In an earlier chapter, the two motors driving this reflexive agency were described by the young: aspiration and, relatedly, an awareness of their marginalised status. These, we contend, are vital issues that conventional searches for 'causes' of offending or 'anti-social behaviour', material or otherwise, have ignored. In advancing this proposition, we are developing earlier work:

> What is important here at the policy and research levels is that if this increasing emphasis on individualisation implies an understanding of youth as an active process, rather than a stage of development, it also implies that for young people their own sense of agency carries a degree of personal investment that looks forward to – even insists on – positive outcomes. (Wyn and Dwyer 1999: 14)

Policies for marginalised young people, therefore, instead of becoming progressively enabling for the reflexive agency and anticipatory investment of young people in their futures, are increasingly constraining,

199

placing inflated emphasis on academic achievement, and punitive, as current trends in anti-social behaviour enforcement demonstrate. As we have argued elsewhere (Stephen and Squires 2003b), although the young men who participated in our vehicle offending research recognised their own marginalisation from mainstream opportunities, excepting the focus on academic achievement, they did not express any sense of alienation. However, they very much adhered to hegemonic notions of masculinity and to collectivist principles and they aspired to conventional futures of work and family. The prolonged period of youth structured by now extended periods of formal education created a lacuna their similarly practical skill-orientated forefathers did not have to confront by virtue of early entry into apprenticeships or manual employment within a more secure economy. It is, therefore, these values and the part they played in the young men's ambitions that proved essential to understanding their agency. Through these we can grasp the ways they sought to resolve the gulf between an acute awareness of a social status of marginalisation and their own more normative, and anticipatory, self-conceptions and aspirations.

Further, a central characteristic arising in Chapters 5 and 6 is school exclusion. The young people on ABCs with behavioural and mental health problems were found to be in dire educational need, while the young vehicle offenders, despite alienation from school, were found to have a strong commitment to the work ethic. Their energy and creativity found outlets in the skills and knowledge required for their offending activities. The key feature which unites both groups' lived experiences, therefore, was the lack of formal educational and recreational opportunities on their estates in which they might have expended mental and physical energies, this being particularly acute for young people with ADHD. Without formal opportunities for release of these energies their 'anti-social' and offending activities can be seen quite simply as responses to the boredom (Ferrell 2004) that characterised the long and repetitive days of their young lives.

Accordingly, the key to addressing Schur's (1973) conundrum of why not all marginalised young people offend seems, for us, quite clearly rooted in young people's aspirations and self-conceptions in the face of acute under-occupation. If young people can successfully marry their self-conceptions and aspirations to social mores and opportunities, and be offered concrete means to do so, their process of becoming and consequently belonging should not produce problematic outcomes for them or society. This is not to imply 'cause', but instead it serves to underline the need to recognise the interactionist and processual nature of outcomes for young people. Thus self-identity and aspirations play important roles in the goals young people pursue (Banks *et al.* 1992), however apparently different from the norm (Stephen 2000), and in their reflexive agency. But society must play a key enabling role for this reflexive agency. So, when young people respond creatively to '*rareté*' (Parker 1974) to facilitate their process of becoming and belonging, while rejecting monotonous and repetitive daily lives, we should not be at all surprised when they turn to alternative means of doing so (see MacDonald *et al.* 2001). It is that simple, but in searches for quantifiable 'causes' we have ignored the voices of the young people themselves and, therefore, such insights they afford to their fundamental needs and strong aspirations. To the same degree we also deny their hopes for a different, better future.

Instead, somewhat reminiscent of a Foucauldian signification of spectacle (1977), we are supposed to celebrate 'effective enforcement':

> A year ago I said to communities that I wanted them to use the powers we have given them to tackle anti-social behaviour. Since then, a tremendous amount has been done to reclaim our communities for the law-abiding majority. We have brought in tough new laws and, with local partners, driven forward an ambitious national action plan. The TOGETHER campaign has produced real results, with around 100,000 cases of thuggery and nuisance dealt with over the past year. And this is against a background of record numbers of police officers – nearly 140,000 – backed up by more than 4,000 community support officers and cuts in crime on both statistical measures ... But there is no room for complacency. We know that too many communities are still blighted by anti-social behaviour, with the yobbish behaviour of a few thugs ruining the quality of life within communities. In the summer I set out the Government's plans to tackle crime over the next five years, and dealing with anti-social behaviour is a key part of that. There will be no let up in our campaign against crime, disorder and thuggery ...
> (David Blunkett in Home Office 2004e)

The glad tidings continue: we are informed that, in the past year, 5,383 ABCs were made 2,633 ASBOs issued, 418 Dispersal Orders applied to 'tackle intimidating groups' and 66,000 (undefined) cases of anti-social behaviour 'tackled' (Home Office 2004e). We are further reassured that 'causes' remain of concern to the government:

> Treating the causes, as well as the effects of anti-social behaviour, is vital, which is why I am announcing today plans to get drug-misusing people who behave anti-socially into treatment, closing a gap for those who have not already entered the criminal justice system. (David Blunkett in Home Office 2004e)

But in revealing starkly the now superficial, and unquestionably hopeless, interpretation of 'causes', Mr Blunkett failed to consider why people take drugs in the first place and why detox programmes, without more profound change, are not the solution. The political spin on Wood's (2004) findings bears further witness to the government's blinkered approach to anti-social behaviour. While respondents mentioned as a 'very big' or 'fairly big' problem, 'speeding traffic' (43 per cent), 'cars parked illegally or inconveniently' (31 per cent), 'rubbish or litter' (29 per cent), and 'fireworks' (29 per cent), *Findings 252* (Home Office 2004f), devotes disproportionate attention to the *sixth* most common category reported 'teenagers hanging around' (28 per cent). Justification for this appears to arise in figures for those with 'actual experience of anti-social behaviour'. Among those *'perceiving* problems in their local area' (emphasis in original), 'incidents with young people hanging around' were reported as the highest category of experience mentioned (94 per cent). At no point are we informed that measures will be strengthened against inconsiderate drivers or a war waged on the third category, rubbish and litter, for which laws already exist.

Instead we are presented with a breakdown of the 'incidents relating to young people hanging around' (Home Office 2004f: 3). In the interests of social justice this is simply not acceptable for the young people, or the communities who report a much wider range of problems. It does, however, suggest a more profound ideological shift about which we should be concerned: the advent of a new *precautionary injustice* in crime and disorder policy.

The era of precautionary injustice?

Many notable commentators have focused upon the punitive shift that has occurred in recent years and the impact this is having on justice itself (e.g. Castel 1991; Feeley and Simon 1992; Young 1999; Clear and Cadora 2001; Garland 2002; Hudson 2003). In small part, we wish to add to this literature, by developing our ideas in relation to 'precautionary injustice', a concept already employed in environmentalist circles:

> In order to protect the environment, the precautionary approach shall be widely applied by States according to their capabilities. Where there are threats of serious or irreversible damage, lack of full scientific certainty shall not be used as a reason for postponing cost-effective measures to prevent environmental degradation. (United Nations Conference on Environment and Development 1992: Principle 15)

A somewhat unsettling remark captures the essence of this paradigm shift into what Hudson (2003: 45) describes as 'gloves-off crime control' : 'It's an ideal way of doing politics because you don't have to prove anything' (Jaap Hanekamp, Dutch scientist, cited in Lowry Miller 2003). 'The precautionary principle' has been widely used in the realm of environment protection for many years (see helpful critical accounts in Morris 2000). It offers a means of understanding the fundamental shift in policy beyond risk management and towards zero tolerance of 'anti-social' agency – which appears to be inspired by a 'precautionary principle' whereupon 'the remoteness of harm is not an excuse of inaction' (Morris 2000: 7). Our concern here is not to engage in debate about whether any given precautions need to be adopted in relation to particular en-vironmental (or social) risks, but rather to reflect upon the implications of a form of precautionary governance (in other words, the precautionary principle as a governmental rationality). Applied to crime policy, this new approach extends well beyond all hitherto preventative methods adopted in liberal democracies towards reliance upon half-truths, hearsay, prejudice and exclusion. In doing so, as we have been arguing:

> The precautionary principle undermines legal certainty by providing bureaucrats with an excuse to change the rules of the game in an essentially arbitrary manner ... the regulator in these matters is typically influenced less by the quality of the scientific research than by what the most vocal and influential interest groups demand. (Morris 2000: 19)

The management of risk, effected in and through 'actuarial justice' (Feeley and Simon 1994), has served its managerialist purpose. However, in a late-modern world where the management of public perceptions and fears must also be administered by governments (Young 1996), risk management cannot alone assuage these concerns. According to Walters (2004: 162) the risk management perspective identified 'how "risks" can be defined and manipulated by government and corporate entities'. Furthermore, his own analysis directs our attention towards the ways in which perceptions of risks (like our fears and insecurities) might them-selves be created and monopolised (or dispelled) for political or economic gain.

The Prime Minister himself seems to have grasped this point well as is evidenced by his speech to the Royal Society in 2002:

> Responsible science and responsible policymaking operate on the same precautionary principle. (Blair, 2002)

203

To take one sentence out of context is rather unfair, especially when the Prime Minister continued on a more cautious note: 'But that principle should make us proceed with care on the basis of fact, not fail to proceed at all on the basis of prejudice.' However, an earlier comment in the same speech belies more significant sentiments already touched upon in this chapter:

> Science doesn't replace moral judgement. It just extends the context of knowledge within which moral judgements are made. It allows us to do more, but it doesn't tell us whether doing more is right or wrong. (Blair 2002)

Anti-social behaviour, as we have been arguing, is not a matter of modernist objectivity, evidence and certainty. Its signification is a more instinctive response. In a late-modern world the need of the state to engender a sense of security in the face of contemporary fears and uncertainties and mistrust of metanarratives finds expression in more emotive appeals to subjective judgements and questions of morality. These appeals, however, are quite contradictory for such questions of morality, in their reification of crude dichotomous understandings of the world, notably 'right' and 'wrong', 'good' and 'evil', 'us' and 'them', are firmly pre-modern. At the same time, the essentialisation of marginalised young people as the dangerous Other is a decidedly modern phenomenon. The existence of such contradictory and ambiguous ideas perhaps marks a tacit acknowledgement that, despite positivism's best efforts, we still cannot clearly ascertain 'cause' for crime nor guarantee its control. Modernist explanatory frameworks are, therefore, exposed as deficient and this coincides with a seeming recognition that 'risk-management' techniques are not producing the desired results either. But how could they, when subjective perceptions and fears are potentially infinite, constrained only by the limits of our own darkest imaginings?

Thus, to develop our arguments, we find it helpful to draw upon the critique of environmental 'risk-assessment' by Tickner *et al.* proponents of 'the precautionary principle', for the core insights to anti-social behaviour enforcement it affords. Tickner *et al.* (n.d.: 14–15) argue that, among others, 'risk-assessment' alone is flawed because it:

- assumes 'assimilative capacity';
- focuses on quantifying and analysing problems rather than solving them;
- is susceptible to model uncertainty;
- allows dangerous activities to continue under the guise of 'acceptable risk';

- is costly and time-consuming;
- is fundamentally undemocratic;
- puts responsibility in the wrong place.

Considering these points in the light of current approaches to anti-social behaviour, Tickner et al.'s arguments help us recognise the advent of the contemporary precautionary governmentalisation of marginalised youth. In particular, they expose a shift beyond the limitations of risk-management. Despite a plethora of studies over the years which have attempted to ascertain 'cause', while it is possible to identify predisposing factors with some degree of accuracy, we still have no certainties, no absolutes upon which we can 'solve' the problem. This position has now become particularly acute in the context of late modernity. As we have been arguing, empirical, conceptual and policy failure lies in the reality that neither the macroscopic structural sphere nor the microscopic realm of reflexive agency have been subject to equivalent investigative rigour. Consistent holistic approaches have been thwarted by short-term political imperatives, if not also our own discipline's pursuit of modernist modes of acceptance. As such, too much attention and resources have focused on reinventing the particularly rickety wheels of causality and polishing up our surface 'treatments' without beginning to address more profound issues needing to be tackled, but which would simply be regarded too costly, economically and politically.

Consequently, in encouraging a climate of intolerance, the idealism inherent in believing that small amounts of 'anti-social behaviour' can be 'assimilated' by communities is no longer plausible. Under current policy anti-social perpetrators must be removed from communities to prevent further 'contamination' and future examples prevented through the enlistment of the structures of civil society onto the crime prevention front of this relentless war. Under the guises of apparently benign empowering and just themes of 'community safety' and 'community involvement', an illusionary appearance of democracy-in-action is presented, for we are now all obliged to recognise our part, as active 'stakeholders', in eradicating risk to ourselves and from our communities. We are expanding relations of responsibilisation to a wider range of agents (neighbourhood wardens and shopping mall security staff (Fox 2002), theme park employees (Shearing and Stenning 1996), even 'bouncers' (Hobbs et al. 2003) and, not least, as recent debates about citizen arrests, vigilantism and self-defence might testify, to private citizens (Johnston 1996). We are also delegating – in the British case – the enforcement tools of ABCs and ASBOs which, as we have been arguing, readily absolve society from its part in producing deviant outcomes by means of placing responsibility for change squarely upon the targeted individuals themselves.

To return to the terms in which we first encountered the problem of anti-social behaviour in Chapter 1, we appear to be attempting to fill the 'justice gap' with enforcement action, seemingly unaware that these precaution-ary interventions engender further processes of exclusion generating still greater injustices. Having essentialised the problems of our social order, we argue that we no longer subscribe to naïve notions of 'acceptable risk'. Nonetheless, we still have an insatiable appetite for knowledge of these risks, as the environmentalists reflect:

> Criticisms aside, risk assessment can play a role in implementing the precautionary principle. Instead of using risk assessment to establish 'safe' levels of exposure, levels that are fundamentally unknowable, it can be used to better understand the hazards of an activity and to compare options for prevention. It can also be used in conjunction with democratic decision-making methods to prioritise activities … But the underlying basis of policy and decision-making must be pre-caution and prevention, rather than risk. (Tickner *et al.* (n.d.: 15)

In focusing upon future risk minimisation within the parameters of 'the precautionary principle', we are at risk of losing all sense of justice and, not insignificantly, long-term security for ourselves and for society. As we have argued, this 'politics of risk and safety is a politics of inequality' (Hudson 2003: 73). It is a politics that shamelessly employs erroneous portrayals of marginalised young people symbolically to ensure com-pliance within a looming *'nouveau ancien régime'* (Hirst 2000: 283). In finding comfort within our own (and our government's) construction of 'decent law-abiding citizens', we are encouraged to welcome this shift with open arms and tolerate increasing penetration into our own lives as a necessary side-effect of preventative treatment. The advent of precaution-ary injustice, effected in and through anti-social behaviour measures, must, therefore, serve as a timely call to arms reminiscent of the sentiments contained within Martin Niemoller's classic poem. Perhaps this might be dismissed as paranoia? For although we write as a substantial section of the British legal establishment voice their collective concerns about the government's new Security Bill, rather few commentators have felt equally moved to criticise the growing ASB enforcement machine now taking shape. No doubt the symbolic significance of the threat of terrorism and the measures deemed necessary to resist it far exceed the risks posed by the more mundane question of ASB, even though countless more people are likely to be affected by the latter compared to the former. Then again, perhaps great legal minds are not fully exercised by minor nuisances. This would be unfortunate and, we would argue, probably a mistake. For, to incorporate a remark of Foucault's, 'from such trifles … a political awareness of small things' (1977: 141), the modes of behaviour management characteristic of late modernity have emerged.

Furthermore, the failure to challenge ASB discourses and management practices also represents a serious cause for concern because the parameters of the 'anti-social' seem to have very few bounds. Without recourse to a safety net of long-held principles and procedures of justice within the formal criminal justice system, who will be 'left to speak up' unless we, as critical social scientists, exert our own check on this now.

Thus, by means of concluding the arguments and reflections prompted by Kelly's opening questions it is necessary to draw upon Mizen's important paper once more:

> New Labour's 'youth policy' may thus ostensibly lay claim to safe-guarding tomorrow's future, but the reality is that it is much more likely to continue to misspend our youth. (Mizen 2003: 473)

This 'misspending' provides the impetus for our praxis as criminologists. In stressing the primacy of adopting a new 'view from the boys' (Parker 1974), we have demonstrated the importance of appreciating the benefits of a more interactionist approach, not least one that incorporates an understanding of the aspirations of the young men deemed 'anti-social' and 'offenders'. A notable majority of the young men with whom we have worked over the years aspired to join the Armed Forces. So, there is some irony when we see the different constructions placed upon these young men. Out of uniform they are perceived by politicians and media alike as a risk and a threat to 'decent law-abiding citizens', yet when 'disciplined' and in uniform and risking their lives, they are hailed by these commentators as heroes in the struggle for 'freedom and democracy'. But they are still the very same young men who, like countless generations before them, have sought escape and a sense of becoming and belonging as foot soldiers in other people's wars in the absence of more concrete opportunities.

In some senses the Iraq War can serve as a stark reminder of our indebtedness to often socially and economically marginalised young people. In this light we can begin to reappraise another long and entrenched 'war', in this case against crime, which also cynically employs a demonology of young people to rally a disparate population to a seemingly moral cause. But we also need to reconsider this notion of risk so 'often conceptualised as a purely bad thing' (Morris 2000: vi). Instead, as Morris shows in citing Wildavsky's (1988) insightful remark, 'there can be no safety without risk' (Morris 2000: vi).

'Community safety' can only begin to be realised if we as a society take a risk with young people, a risk that, without criminalising interventions (e.g. Schur 1973), they will probably grow out of crime and anti-social behaviour; that, without pejorative labelling (e.g. Becker 1963), they will assuredly not be subjected to fortified processes of social and self-exclusion; and that, without our discipline's supine buttressing of the twin fallacies (as exposed by Furlong and Cartmel 1997; Young 1999), young people's anticipatory agency could be channelled into concrete life chances afforded by a resuscitated welfare state and a more humane economy. In other words, strategies of exclusion and criminalisation (the 'abandonment' we discussed at the end of Chapter 4) need replacing by positive and supportive social polices. Schur's critique did not make a case for no social intervention at all. On the contrary, it was an argument for social justice and that young people's primary experiences of public policy ought not to be defined by enforcement, punishment and criminalisation. To develop these alternatives, we must begin to engage more effectively with the real hopes and needs of marginalised young people, and channel our energies into challenging the new precautionary injustice.

Perhaps we were offered a faint glimmer of hope on Valentine's Day 2005, in the Home Office announcement that intensive support will be offered to 'anti-social' families in fifty *TOGETHER Anti-Social Behaviour Action Areas* (Home Office Press Release 14 February 2005). However, only two weeks later, taking up where his predecessor left off, Charles Clarke signalled a further erosion of young people's (still essentialised as 'yobs') rights with a forceful endorsement of the 'name and shame' approach adopted in many areas (Home Office Press Release 1 March 2005). Stigmatising local publicity, now directly orchestrated by local government, will attach to ASBO recipients (justified as necessary for effective enforcement) in a way never even comtemplated for perpetrators of more serious crimes. Arguably, in terms of the need for anonymity to protect children from long-term stigma, the policy breaches the 1985 UN Standard Minimum Rules for the Administration of Youth Justice (see Muncie 2005). We are, therefore, left to contemplate how such increasing politicised misconceptions of 'justice' will impact upon the lives of successive generations of young people and then what impact this will have on the integrity of our notions of 'community safety'.

Above all, returning to Morris, we need to ask what this all says about us, for the 'piecemeal erosion of the rule of law ultimately makes of us less civilized men and women' (Morris 2000: 19). As a society we have acknowledged a putative 'justice gap' but sought to fill it with enforcement practices based upon a dubious precautionary principle in which 'due process' and the 'rule of law' (hitherto regarded as constituent elements of Justice) become sidelined by political and administrative priorities. And the most likely outcome is not justice at all, but the reinforcement of social exclusion and greater social injustice.

References

Abbott-Chapman, J. and Robertson, M. (1999) 'Home as private space: some adolescent constructs', *Journal of Youth Studies*, 2 (1): 23–43.

Ainley, P. and Bailey, W. (1997) *The Business of Learning*. London: Cassell.

Allen, J. (2004) 'Worry about crime', in S. Nicholas and A. Walker (eds), *Crime in England and Wales 2002/2003 Supplementary Volume 2: Crime, Disorder and the Criminal Justice System – Public Attitudes and Perceptions*. London: Home Office Research and Statistics Directorate.

Allsopp, J. F. and Feldman, M. P. (1976) 'Personality and anti-social behaviour', *British Journal of Criminology*, 16 (4): 337–51.

Ancel, M. (1965) *Social Defence: A Modern Approach to Criminal Problems*, London: Routledge & Kegan Paul.

Anderson, B. (1999) 'Youth crime and the politics of prevention', in B. Goldson (ed.), *Youth Justice: Contemporary Policy and Practice*. Aldershot: Gower.

Anderson, S., Kinsey, R., Loader, I. and Smith, C. (1994) *Cautionary Tales: Young People, Crime and Policing in Edinburgh*. Avebury: Ashgate.

Andrews, K. and Jacobs, J. (1990) *Punishing the Poor: Poverty under Thatcher*. London: Macmillan.

Aries, P. (1962) *Centuries of Childhood*. London: Cape.

Armitage, R. (2002) *Tackling Anti-Social Behaviour – What Really Works?* London: NACRO.

Armstrong, D. (2004) 'A risky business? Research, policy, governmentality and youth offending', *Youth Justice*, 4 (2): 100–16.

Ashford, M. (1998) 'Making criminals out of children: abolishing the presumption of *doli incapax*', *Criminal Justice*, 16: 16–17.

Ashworth, A., Gardner, J., Morgan, R., Smith, A., Von Hirsch, A. and Wasik, M. (1998) 'Neighbouring on the oppressive: the government's "Anti-Social Behaviour Order" proposals', *Criminal Justice*, 16 (1): 7–14.

Association of London Government (ALG) (2004) *The London Anti-Social Behaviour Strategy: Proposals for Consultation with Stakeholders*. Greater London Authority.

Asthana, A. and Bright, M. (2004) 'I would rather be dead than live next door to them', *The Observer*, 4 July.

Audit Commission (1996) *Misspent Youth*. London: Audit Commission.

Audit Commission (2004) *Youth Justice 2004: A Review of the Reformed Youth Justice System*. London: Stationery Office.

Austin, B. and Krisberg, J. (1981) 'Wider, stronger and different nets', *Journal of Research in Crime and Delinquency*, 18 (1): 165–96.

Australian Institute of Family Studies (2003) *Patterns and Precursors of Adolescent Antisocial Behaviour: Types, Resiliency and Environmental Influences*, Executive Summary, 2nd Report. Victoria: Department of Justice and AIFS.

Autoglass (2004) *Cracking Car Crime Report 2004*. London: Autoglass. www.autoglass.co.uk/press/

Bailey, V. (1987) *Delinquency and Citizenship: Reclaiming the Young Offender: 1914–1948*. Oxford: Clarendon Press.

Bandalli, S. (1998) 'Abolition of the presumption of *Doli Incapax* and the criminalisation of children', *Howard Journal*, 37 (2): 114–23.

Bandalli, S. (2000) 'Children, responsibility and the new youth justice', in B. Goldson (ed.), *The New Youth Justice*. Lyme Regis: Russell House.

Banks, M., Bates, I., Breakwell, G., Bynner, J., Emler, N., Jamieson, L. and Roberts, K. (1992) *Careers and Identities*. Buckingham: Open University Press.

Barlow, A. and Duncan, S. (2000a) 'Supporting families? New Labour's communitarianism and the "rationality mistake": Part I', *Journal of Social Welfare and Family Law*, 22 (1): 23–42.

Barlow, A. and Duncan, S. (2000b) 'Supporting families? New Labour's communitarianism and the "rationality mistake": Part II', *Journal of Social Welfare and Family Law*, 22 (2): 129–43.

Barton, A. and Gilling, D. (1997) 'Crime prevention and community safety: a new home for social policy?', *Critical Social Policy*, Number 52, 17 (3), August.

Bateman, T. (2003) 'Living with Final Warnings: Making the best of a bad job?', *Youth Justice*, 2 (3): 131–40.

Bauman, Z. (1982) *Memories of Class: The Pre-History and After Life of Class*. London: Routledge & Kegan Paul.

Bauman, Z. (1998) *Globalisation: The Human Consequences*. Cambridge: Polity Press.

Bauman, Z. (2002) 'Violence in the age of uncertainty', in A. Crawford (ed.), *Crime and Insecurity: The Governance of Safety in Europe*. Cullompton: Willan.

Bauman, Z. (2004) *Wasted Lives: Modernity and Its Outcasts*. Cambridge: Polity Press.

Bayley, E. (ed.) (1999) *Transforming Children's Lives: The Importance of Early Intervention*, Occasional Paper 25. London: Family Policy Studies Centre. Proceedings of a conference on the importance of early intervention, held in London, 12 March 1998.

Beck, U. (1992) *Risk Society: Towards a New Modernity*. London: Sage.

Beck, U. (1998) 'Politics of risk society', in J. Franklin (ed.), *The Politics of Risk Society*. Cambridge: Polity Press.

Beck, U. and Beck-Gernsheim, E. (2002) *Individualization*. London: Sage.

Becker, H. (1963) *The Outsiders*. New York: Free Press.

Beckett, K. and Western, B. (2001) 'Crime control, American style: from social welfare to social control', in P. Green and A. Rutherford (eds), *Criminal Policy in Transition*. Oxford: Hart Publishing.

Beinart, S., Anderson, B., Lee, S. and Utting, D. (2002) *Youth at Risk? A National Survey of Risk Factors, Protective Factors and Problem Behaviour among Young People in England, Scotland and Wales*. London: Communities that Care.

Bell, C. (1999) 'Appealing for justice for children and young people: a critical analysis of the Crime and Disorder Bill 1998', in B. Goldson (ed.), *Youth Justice: Contemporary Policy and Practice*. Aldershot: Ashgate.

Bendixen, M. and Olweus, D. (1999) 'Measurement of antisocial behaviour in early adolescence and adolescence: psychometric properties and substantive findings', *Criminal Behaviour and Mental Health*, 9: 323–54.

Bentley, T. and Gurumurthy, R. (1999) *Destination Unknown: Engaging with the Problems of Marginalised Youth*. London: Demos.

Berlins, M. and Wansell, G. (1972) *Caught in the Act*. London: Penguin.

Blair, T. (1997) Speech at the Aylesbury Estate, Southwark, 2 June.

Blair, T. (2002) *Science Matters*. Speech by the Prime Minister to the Royal Society, 10 April (available at: http://www.number10.gov.uk/output/page1715.asp – checked 1 November 2004).

Blair, T. (2004) *A New Consensus on Law and Order*. Speech by the Prime Minister at the launch of the Home Office and Criminal Justice System strategic plans, 19 July (available at: http://www.labour.org.uk/news/tbcrimespeech – checked 8 October 2004).

Bland, N. (1997) *Measuring Public Expectations of Policing: An Evaluation of Gap Analysis*, Police Research Series Paper 24. London: Home Office.

Bland, N. and Read, T. (2000) *Policing Anti-Social Behaviour*, Police Research Series No. 123. London: Home Office Police Research Group.

Booth, T. (1996) 'Stories of exclusion: natural and unnatural selection', in E. Blyth and J. Milner (eds), *Exclusion from School*. London: Routledge.

Bottomley, A. K. (1973) *Decisions in the Penal Process*. Oxford: Martin Roberstson.

Bottoms, A. E. (1974) 'On the decriminalisation of the English juvenile court', in R. Hood (ed.), *Crime, Criminology and Public Policy*. London: Heinemann.

Bottoms, A. E. and Wiles, P. (1997) 'Environmental criminology', in M. Maguire, R. Morgan and R. Reiner (eds), *Oxford Handbook of Criminology*, 3rd edn. Oxford: Oxford University Press.

Bowlby, J. (1946) *Forty-Four Juvenile Thieves: Their Characters and Home Lives*. London: Baillière, Tyndall & Cox.

Boys, L. and Warburton, F. (2000) *Preventing Anti-Social Behaviour*, Crime and Social Policy Briefing. London: NACRO.

Bradford, S. (1997) 'The management of growing up: youth work in community settings', in J. Roche and S. Tucker (eds), *Youth in Society*. London: Sage.

Braye, S. and Preston-Shoot, M. (1995) *Empowering Practice in Health and Social Care*. Buckingham: Open University Press.

Bright, J. (1997) *Turning the Tide: Crime, Community and Prevention*. London, Demos.

Bright, M. (2004) 'Most problem kids go on to thrive', *The Observer*, 13 June.

Brown, A. P. (2004) 'Anti-social behaviour, crime control and social control', *Howard Journal*, 43 (2): 203–11.

Brown, S. (1998) *Understanding Youth and Crime*. Buckingham: Open University Press.

Brownlee, I. (1998) 'New Labour, New Penology? Punitive rhetoric and the limits of managerialism in criminal justice policy', *Journal of Law and Society*, 25 (3): 313–35.

Bryson, A. and Jacobs, J. (1992) *Policing the Workshy: Benefit Controls, the Labour Market and the Unemployed*. Aldershot: Ashgate.

Burchell, G. (1981) 'Putting the child in its place', *Ideology and Consciousness*, 8: 73–95.

Burlingham, D. and Freud, A. (1942) *Young People in Wartime*. London: Allen & Unwin.

Burlingham, D. and Freud, A. (1944) *Infants without Families*. London: Allen & Unwin.

Burnett, R. and Appleton, C. (2004) 'Joined up services to tackle youth crime: a case study in England', *British Journal of Criminology*, 44 (1): 34–54.

Burney, E. (1999) *Crime and Banishment: Nuisance and Exclusion in Social Housing*. Winchester: Waterside Press.

Burney, E. (2002) 'Talking tough, acting coy: what happened to the Anti-Social Behaviour Order?', *Howard Journal*, 41 (5): 469–84.

Butler, I. and Drakeford, M. (1997) 'Tough guise: the politics of youth justice', *Probation Journal*, 44: 216–19.

Butler, S. (1998) *Access Denied: The Exclusion of People in Need from Social Housing*. London: Shelter.

Byrne, D. (1999) *Social Exclusion*. Buckingham: Open University Press.

Campbell, B. (1993) *Goliath: Britain's Dangerous Places*. London: Methuen.

Campbell, S. (2002a) *A Review of Anti-Social Behaviour Orders*, Home Office Research Study 236. London: Home Office Research and Statistics Directorate.

Campbell, S. (2002b) *Implementing Anti-Social Behaviour Orders: Messages for Practitioners*, Findings 160. London: Home Office.

Carlen, P. (1996) *Jigsaw: A Political Criminology of Youth Homelessness*. Buckingham: Open University Press.

Carr-Saunders, A. M., Mannheim, H. and Rhodes, E. C. (1942) *Young Offenders*. Cambridge: Cambridge University Press.

Castel, R. (1991) 'From dangerousness to risk', in G. Burchell, C. Gordon and P. Miller (eds), *The Foucault Effect: Studies in Governmentality*. Chicago, IL: University of Chicago Press.

Cavadino, M. and Dignan, J. (1997) *The Penal System: An Introduction*. London: Sage.

Chawla, L. (2001) *Growing Up in an Urbanised World*. London: Earthscan/UNESCO.

Chisholm, L. and Du Bois-Reymond, M. (1993) 'Youth transitions, gender and social change', *Sociology*, 27: 259–79.

Christie, N. (2004) *A Suitable Amount of Crime*. London: Routledge.

Clarke, Charles (2005) Press Release 042/2005. London: Home Office.

Clarke, J. (1980) 'Social democratic delinquents and Fabian familes: a background to the 1969 Children and Young Persons Act', in National Deviancy Conference (ed.), *Permissiveness and Control*. London: Macmillan.

Clear, T. and Cadora, E. (2001) 'Risk and community practice', in K. Stenson and R. R. Sullivan (eds), *Crime, Risk and Justice: The Politics of Crime Control in Liberal Democracies*. Cullompton: Willan.

Cohen, P. and Ainley, P. (2000) 'Youth studies and cultural studies in Britain', *Journal of Youth Studies*, 3 (1): 79–95.

Cohen, S. (1973) *Folk Devils and Moral Panics: The Creation of the Mods and Rockers*. St Albans: Paladin.

Cohen, S. (1979) 'Community control: a new utopia', *New Society*, 15 March.

Cohen, S. (1985) *Visions of Social Control*. Cambridge: Polity Press.

Cohen, S. and Taylor, L. (1992) *Escape Attempts: The Theory and Practice of Resistance to Everyday Life*, 2nd edn. London: Routledge.

Coid, J. W. (2003) 'Formulating strategies for the primary prevention of adult antisocial behaviour: "high risk" or "population" strategies?', in D. P. Farrington and J. W. Coid, *Early Prevention of Adult Antisocial Behaviour*. Cambridge: Cambridge University Press.

Coleman, J. (1998) 'Social capital in the creation of human capital', *American Journal of Sociology*, 94: 95–120.

Coles, B. (1995) *Youth and Social Policy: Youth Citizenship and Young Careers*. London: University College Press.

Commission on Social Justice (CSJ) (1993) *The Justice Gap*. London: IPPR.

Corrigan, P. (1979) *Schooling the Smash Street Kids*. Basingstoke: Macmillan.

Crawford, A. (1997) *The Local Governance of Crime*. Oxford: Oxford University Press.

Crawford, A. (1998) *Crime Prevention and Community Safety*. Harlow: Longman.

Crawford, A. (2002) 'The governance of crime and insecurity in an anxious age: the trans-European and the local', in A. Crawford (ed.), *Crime and Insecurity: The Governance of Safety in Europe*. Cullompton: Willan.

Crofts, T. (2002) *The Criminal Responsibility of Children and Young Persons: A Comparison of English and German Law*. Aldershot: Ashgate.

Currie, E. (1996) *Is America Really Winning the War on Crime and Should Britain Follow Its Example?* London: NACRO.

Davies, B. (1986) *Threatening Youth*. Buckingham: Open University Press.

Davies, S. and Tanner, J. (2003) 'The long arm of the law: effects of labelling on employment', *Sociological Quarterly*, 44 (3): 385–404.

Davis, G., Boucherat, J. and Watson, D. (1989) 'Pre-court decision-making in juvenile justice', *British Journal of Criminology*, 29: 219–35.

De Berker, P. (1960) 'State of mind reports: the inadequate personality', *British Journal of Criminology*, 1 (1): 6–20.

Dean, M. (1999) *Governmentality*. London: Sage.

Delaney, L. T. (1954) 'Establishing relationships with anti-social groups and an analysis of their structure', *British Journal of Delinquency*, 5: 24–42.

Department for Education and Science (DfES) (2003) *Every Child Matters*, Green Paper, Cm 5860. London: Stationery Office

Department of the Environment (DoE) (1993) *Crime Prevention on Housing Estates*. London: HMSO.

Dodd, T., Nicholas, S., Povey, D. and Walker, A. (2004) *Crime in England and Wales 2003/2004*. London: Home Office Research and Statistics Directorate.

Donnison, D. (1997) 'Creating a safer society', *Social Policy and Administration*, 31 (5): 3–21.

Donzelot, J. (1979) *The Policing of Families*. London: Hutchinson University Press.

Douglas, M. (1992) *Risk and Blame: Essays in Cultural Theory*. London: Routledge.

Downes, D. (1966) *The Delinquent Solution: A Study in Subcultural Theory*. London: Routledge.

Downes, D. and Rock, P. (2002) *Understanding Deviance*, 4th edn. Oxford: Oxford University Press.

Doyal, L. and Gough, I. (1991) *A Theory of Human Need*. Basingstoke: Macmillan.

Du Bois-Reymond, M. (1998) '"I don't want to commit myself yet": young people's life concepts', *Journal of Youth Studies*, 1 (1): 63–79.

Eadie, T. and Canton, R. (2002) 'Practising in a context of ambivalence: the challenge for youth justice workers', *Youth Justice*, 2 (1): 14–26.

Earle, R., Newburn, T. and Crawford, A. (2003) 'Referral Orders: some reflections on policy transfer and "What Works"', *Youth Justice*, 2 (3): 141–50.

Edwards, A. and Hughes, G. (2002) 'The community governance of crime control', Introduction to A. Edwards and G. Hughes (eds), *Crime Control and Community: The New Politics of Public Safety*. Cullompton: Willan.

Edwards, L. and Hatch, B. (2003) *Passing Time: A Report about Young People and Communities*. London: Institute for Public Policy Research

Ellis, H. (1895) *The Criminal*, 2nd edn. London: Walter Scott Publishers.

European Group for Integrated Social Change (EGRIS) (2001) 'Misleading trajectories: transition dilemmas of young adults in Europe', *Journal of Youth Studies*, 4 (1): 101–18.

Evans, K. and Furlong, A. (1998) 'Metaphors of youth transitions: niches, pathways, trajectories or navigations', in J. Bynner, L. Chisholm and A. Furlong (eds), *Youth, Citizenship and Social Change*. Aldershot: Ashgate.

Evans, R. and Ellis, R. (1997) *Police Cautioning in the 1990s*, Research Findings No. 52. London: Home Office Research and Statistics Directorate.

Eysenck, H. J. (1964) *Crime and Personality*. London: Routledge & Kegan Paul.

Family Policy Studies Centre (1998) *The Crime and Disorder Bill and the Family*. London: FPSC.

Farrington, D. P. (1986) 'Age and crime', in M. Tonry and N. Morris (eds), *Crime and Justice: An Annual Review of Research*, Vol. 7. Chicago, IL: University of Chicago Press.

Farrington, D. P. (1987) 'Predicting individual crime rates', in D. Gottfredson and M. Tonry (eds), *Prediction and Classification: Criminal Justice Decision-Making*. Chicago, IL: University of Chicago Press.

Farrington, D. P. (1994) 'Childhood, adolescent and adult features of violent males', in L. R. Huesmann (ed.), *Aggressive Behaviour: Current Perspectives*. New York: Plenum Press.

Farrington, D. P. (1996) *Understanding and Preventing Youth Crime*, Social Policy Research Findings No. 93. York: Joseph Rowntree Foundation.

Farrington, D. P. (2002) 'Developmental criminology and risk-focussed prevention', in Maguire et al. (eds), *Oxford Handbook of Criminology*, 3rd edn. Oxford: Oxford University Press.

Farrington, D. P. (2003) 'Advancing knowledge about the early prevention of adult antisocial behaviour', in D. P. Farrington and J. W. Coid, *Early Prevention of Adult Antisocial Behaviour*. Cambridge: Cambridge University Press.

Farrington, D. and Bennett, T. (1981) 'Police cautioning of juveniles in London', *British Journal of Criminology*, 21 (2): 123–35.

Farrington, D. P. and Coid, J. W. (2003) *Early Prevention of Adult Antisocial Behaviour*. Cambridge: Cambridge University Press.

Faulkner, D. (2001) *Crime, State and Citizen*. Winchester: Waterside Press.

Feeley, M. M. and Simon, J. (1992) 'The new penology: notes on the emerging strategy of corrections and its implications', *Criminology*, 30 (4): 452–74.

Feeley, M. M. and Simon, J. (1994) 'Actuarial justice: the emerging new criminal law', in D. Nelkin (ed.), *The Future of Criminology*. Thousand Oaks, CA: Sage.

Feilzer, M., Appleton, C., Roberts, C. and Hoyle, C. (2004) *The National Evaluation of the Youth Justice Board's Cognitive Behaviour Projects*. London: Youth Justice Board.

Felson, M. (1994) *Crime and Everyday Life*. Thousand Oaks, CA: Sage.

Fenwick, M. (2004) 'New directions in cultural criminology', *Theoretical Criminology*, 8 (3): 377–86.

Fergusson, R., Pave, D., Esland, G., McLaughlin, E. and Muncie, J. (2000) 'Normalized dislocation and new subjectivities in post-16 markets for education and work', *Critical Social Policy*, 20 (3): 283–305.

Ferrell, J. (2004) 'Boredom, crime and criminology', *Theoretical Criminology*, 8 (3): 287–302.

Ferrell, J., Milovanovic and Lyng, S. (2001) 'Edgework, media practices, and the elongation of meaning', *Theoretical Criminology*, 5 (2): 177–202.

Finney, A. (2004) 'Perceptions of changing crime levels', in S. Nicholas and A. Walker (eds), *Crime in England and Wales 2002/2003 Supplementary Volume 2: Crime, Disorder and the Criminal Justice System – Public Attitudes and Perceptions*. London: Home Office Research and Statistics Directorate.

Finney, A., Thorpe, K. and Toofail, J. (2004) *Crime in England and Wales: Quarterly Update to June 2004*. London: Home Office Research and Statistics Directorate.

Fionda, J. (1999) 'New Labour, old hat: youth justice and the Crime and Disorder Act', *Criminal Law Review*, XXX: 36–47.

Flint, J. (2002) 'Social housing agencies and the governance of anti-social behaviour', *Housing Studies*, 17 (4): 619–37.

Flint, J., Atkinson, R. and Scott, S. (2003) *A Report on the Consultation Responses to 'Putting our Communities Together: A Strategy for Tackling Anti-Social Behaviour'*. University of Glasgow, Department of Urban Studies.

Foucault, M. (1967) *Madness and Civilisation*. London: Tavistock.

Foucault, M. (1977) *Discipline and Punish: The Birth of the Prison*. London: Allen Lane.

Foucault, M. (1990) 'Governmentality', in G. Burchell (ed.), *The Foucault Effect: Studies in Governmentality*. Hemel Hempstead: Harvester-Wheatsheaf.

Fox, C. (2002) 'The real life pre-crime officers: widening the net of criminal justice', *Safer Society*, Winter: 9–10.

France, A. (2000) 'Towards a sociological understanding of youth and their risk-taking', *Journal of Youth Studies*, 3 (3): 317–31.

France, A. and Wiles, P. (1996) *The National Evaluation of Youth Action*. London: Department for Education and Employment.

Fry, M., Mannheim, H., Radzinowicz, L. and Grunhut, M. (1947) *Lawless Youth: A Challenge to the New Europe*. London: George Allen & Unwin.

Furedi, F. (2001) *Paranoid Parenting*. London: Allen Lane.

Furlong, A. and Cartmel, F. (1997) *Young People and Social Change: Individualisation and Risk in Late Modernity*. Buckingham: Open University Press.

Fyvel, T. R. (1961) *The Insecure Offenders: Rebellious Youth in the Welfare State*. London: Penguin.

Gadd, D. and Farrall, S. (2004) 'Criminal careers, desistance and subjectivity: interpreting men's narratives of change', *Theoretical Criminology*, 8 (2): 123–56.

Galtung, J. (1977) *Methodology and Ideology: Essays in Methodology*, Vol. 1. Copenhagen: Christian Ejlers.

Garland, D. (1985) *Punishment and Welfare: A History of Penal Strategies*. Aldershot: Gower.

Garland, D. (1996) 'The limits of the sovereign state: strategies of crime control in contemporary society', *British Journal of Criminology*, 36 (4): 445–71.

Garland, D. (2000) 'The culture of high crime societies: some preconditions of recent law and order policies', *British Journal of Criminology*, 40 (3): 347–75.

Garland, D. (2001) *The Culture of Control*. Oxford: Oxford University Press.

Gelsthorpe, L. (1999) 'Youth crime and parental responsibility', in A. Bainham, S. D. Sclater and M. Richards (eds), *What Is a Parent: A Socio-Legal Analysis*. Oxford: Hart.

Gelsthorpe, L. and Morris, A. (1999) 'Much ado about nothing: a critical comment on key provisions relating to children in the Crime and Disorder Act 1998', *Child and Family Law Quarterly*, 11 (3): 209–21.

Gilbert, J. (1986) *Cycle of Outrage: America's Reaction to the Juvenile Delinquent in the 1950s*. New York: Oxford University Press.

Gilling, D. (1997) *Crime Prevention: Theory Policy and Politics*. London: UCL Press.

Gillis, J. R. (1981) *Youth and History: Tradition and Change in European Age Relations, 1770–Present*. London: Academic Press.

Girling, E., Loader, I. and Sparks, R. (2000) *Crime in Middle England*. London: Routledge.

Glueck, E. T. (1952) 'Predicting juvenile delinquency', *British Journal of Delinquency*, 2: 275–86.

Glueck, S. and Glueck, E. T. (1950) *Unraveling Juvenile Delinquency*. New York: Commonwealth Fund.

Goddard, C. (2004) "Positive Images: Young People Now" campaign wins backing from ministers', *Young People Now* (available at: http://www.ypnmagazine.com/campaign/index.cfm – checked 14 October 2004).

Goffman, E. (1961) *Asylums*. New York: Doubleday.

Goldson, B. (1999) 'Youth (in)justice: contemporary developments in policy and practice', in B. Goldson (ed.), *Youth Justice: Contemporary Policy and Practice*. Aldershot: Ashgate.

Goldson, B. (ed.) (2000a) *The New Youth Justice*. Lyme Regis: Russell House.

Goldson, B. (2000b) 'Children in need or young offenders? Hardening ideology, organisational change and new challenges for social work with children in trouble', *Child and Family Social Work*, 5 (3): 255–65.

Goldson, B. and Chigwada-Bailey, R. (1999) '(What) justice for Black children and young people?', in B. Goldson (ed.), *Youth Justice: Contemporary Policy and Practice*. Aldershot: Ashgate.

Goldson, B. and Jamieson, J. (2002) 'Youth crime, the "parenting deficit" and state intervention: a contextual critique', *Youth Justice*, 2 (2): 82–99.

Goodey, J. (2005) *Victims and Victimology: Research, Policy and Practice*. Harlow: Longman.

Gottfredson, M. and Hirshi, T. (1990) *A General Theory of Crime*. Stanford, CA: Stanford University Press.

Graham, G. and Bowling, B. (1995) *Young People and Crime*, Home Office Research Study No. 145. London: HMSO.

Graham, J. (1998) 'What works in preventing criminality?', in P. Goldblatt and C. Lewis (eds), *Reducing Offending*, Home Office Research Study No. 187. London: HMSO.

Grayling, T., Hallam, K., Graham, D., Anderson, R. and Glaister, R. (2002) *Streets Ahead: Safe and Liveable Streets for Children*. London: IPPR.

Green, E., Mitchell, W. and Bunton, R. (2000) 'Contextualizing risk and danger: an analysis of young people's perceptions of risk', *Journal of Youth Studies*, 3 (2): 109–26.

Grier, A. and Thomas, T. (2003) '"A war for civilisation as we know it": some observations on tackling anti-social behaviour', *Youth and Policy*, 82, Winter.

Gutfreund, R. (1993) 'Towards 2000: which direction for the Youth Service?', *Youth and Policy*, 41: 13–19.

Haapsalo, J. and Tremblay, R. E. (1994) 'Physical aggressive boys from ages 6 to 12: family background, parenting behaviour and prediction of delinquency', *Journal of Consulting and Clinical Psychology*, 62: 1044–52.

Hagan, J. (1993) 'The social embeddedness of crime and unemployment', *Criminology*, 31: 455–91.

Hagell, A. and Newburn, T. (1994) *Persistent Young Offenders*. London: Policy Studies Institute.

Haines, K. (2000) 'Referral Orders and Youth Offender Panels', in B. Goldson (ed.), *The New Youth Justice*, Lyme Regis: Russell House.

Haines, K. and Drakeford, M. (1999) *Young People and Youth Justice*, Basingstoke: Macmillan.

Hall, S. (1979) 'The great moving right show', *Marxism Today*, 23 (1): January.

Hall, S., Critcher, T., Jefferson, T., Clarke, J. and Roberts, B. (1978) *Policing the Crisis: Mugging, the State and Law and Order*. Baskingstoke: Macmillan.

Halleck, S. L. (1971) *Psychiatry and the Dilemmas of Crime*. Berkeley, CA: University of California Press.

Hallsworth, S. (2002) 'Representations and realities in local crime prevention: some lessons from London and lessons for criminology', in G. Hughes and A. Edwards (eds), *Crime Control and Community: The New Politics of Public Safety*. Cullompton: Willan.

Hancock, L. (2001) *Communities, Crime and Disorder: Safety and Regeneration in Urban Neighbourhoods*. Basingstoke: Palgrave.

Hansen, R., Bill, L. and Pease, K. (2003) 'Nuisance offenders: scoping the public policy problems', in M. Tonry (ed.), *Confronting Crime: Crime Control Policy under New Labour*. Cullompton: Willan.

Harcourt, B. E. (2001) *Illusions of Order: The False Promises of Broken Windows Policing*. Cambridge, MA: Harvard University Press.

Hartjen, C. (1977) *Possible Trouble: An Analysis of Social Problems*. New York: Praeger.

Harvey, A. (1960) *Casualties of the Welfare State*, Fabian Tract Number 321. London: Fabian Society.

Hathaway, S. R. and Monaschesi, E. D. (1953) *Analysing and Predicting Juvenile Delinquency with the MMPI*. Minneapolis, MN: University of Minnesota Press.

Haworth, A. and Manzi, T. (1999) 'Managing the underclass: interpreting the moral discourse of housing management', *Urban Studies*, 36 (1): 153–65.

Hayes, M. and Williams, C. (1999) 'Offending behaviour and children under 10', *Family Law*, May: 317–20.

Hayward, K. (2002) 'The vilification and pleasures of youthful transgression', in J. Muncie, G. Hughes and E. McLaughlin (eds), *Youth Justice. Critical Readings*. London: Sage.

Hayward, K. (2004) *City Limits: Crime, Consumer Culture and the Urban Experience*. London: Glass House/Cavendish.

Hayward, K. and Young, J. (2004) 'Cultural criminology: some notes on the script', *Theoretical Criminology*, 8 (3): 259–73.

Henry, S. and Milovanovic, D. (1996) *Constitutive Criminology: Beyond Postmodernism*. London: Sage.

Her Majesty's Inspectorate of Prisons (HMIP) (1997) *Young Prisoners: A Thematic Review*. London. HMIP.

Hine, J. and Celnick, A. (2001) *A One-Year Reconviction Study of Final Warnings*. University of Sheffield.

Hirst, P. (1981) 'The genesis of "the social"', *Politics and Power*, No. 3. London: Routledge.

Hirst, P. (2000) 'Statism, pluralism and social control', *British Journal of Criminology*, 40 (2): 279–95.

Hobbs, D., Hadfield, P., Lister, S. and Winlow, S. (2003) *Bouncers: Violence and Governance in the Night-time Economy*. Oxford: Oxford University Press.

Holdaway, S. and Desborough, S. (2004) *The National Evaluation of the Youth Justice Board's Final Warning Projects*. London: Youth Justice Board.

Hollway, W. and Jefferson, T. (2000) 'The role of anxiety in fear of crime', in T. Hope and R. Sparks (eds), *Crime, Risk and Insecurity*. London: Routledge.

Home Office (1964) *The Child, The Family and the Young Offender*, Cmnd. 2742. London: HMSO.

Home Office (1988) *Punishment, Custody and the Community*, Cm. 424. London: HMSO.

Home Office (1991) *Safer Communities* ('The Morgan Report'), Home Office Standing Conference on Crime Prevention. London: HMSO.

Home Office (1997a) *No More Excuses*, Cm 3809. London: HMSO.

Home Office (1997b) *Tackling Youth Crime: A Consultation Paper*. London: Home Office.

Home Office (1998a) *The Human Rights Act*. London: Stationary Office.

Home Office (1998b) 'Draft Guidance Document: Anti-Social Behaviour Orders'. London: Home Office.

Home Office (2000) *Crime and Disorder Act 1998: Anti-Social Behaviour Orders – Guidance on Drawing Up Local Protocols*. London: Home Office Communication Directorate.

Home Office (2002a) *Narrowing the Justice Gap*. London: Home Office Justice Gap Taskforce.

Home Office (2002b) *A Guide to Anti-Social Behaviour Orders and Acceptable Behaviour Contracts*. London: Home Office.

Home Office (2003a) *Respect and Responsibility – Taking a Stand Against Anti-Social Behaviour*. London: Home Office.

Home Office (2003b) *Respect and Responsibility – David Blunkett Publishes Anti-Social Behaviour White Paper*, Press Release 069, 12 March. London: Home Office.

Home Office (2003c) *Use Powers to Take a Stand Against Yobs*, Press Release 174/2003, 24 June. London: Home Office.

Home Office (2003d) *Communities Must Not Take No for an Answer on Antisocial Behaviour*, Press Release 278/2003, 14 October. London: Home Office.

Home Office (2004a) Press Release 155/2004, 23 April. London: Home Office.

Home Office (2004b) *Call for Local Heroes*, Press Release 216/2004, 29 June. London: Home Office.

Home Office (2004c) *Confident Communities in a Secure Britain: The Home Office Strategic Plan 2004–08*. London: Home Office.

Home Office (2004d) *Confident Communities in a Secure Britain: Home Office Publishes Strategic Plan*, Press Release 237/2004, 19 July. London: Home Office.

Home Office (2004e) *One Year On: Significant Progress on tackling Anti-Social Behaviour*, Press Release 336/2004, 28 October. London: Home Office.

Home Office (2004f) *Perceptions and Experiences of Anti-Social Behaviour*, Research Findings 252. London: Home Office.

Home Office (2004g) *Together: Tackling Anti-Social Behaviour, One Year On*. London: Home Office.

Home Office (2005a) *Rehabilitation for Neighbours from Hell*, Press Release 030/2005, 14 February. London: Home Office.

Home Office (2005b) *Yobs Will Face the Consequences of Their Actions* – Home Office, Research and Statistics Directorate (2004) *Defining and Measuring Anti-Social Behaviour*, Briefing Note (available at: www.homeoffice.gov.uk/antisocialbehaviour/daycount/index.html).

Hope, T. (1994) *Communities, Crime and Inequality in England and Wales*, Cropwood Conference Proceedings, 'Preventing Crime and Disorder', Cambridge.

Hope, T. (1998a) 'Community crime prevention', in P. Goldblatt and C. Lewis (eds), *Reducing Offending*, Home Office Research Study No. 187. London: HMSO.

Hope, T. (1998b) 'Letting social policy off the hook', *Criminal Justice Matters*, 37: 5–6.

Hope, T. (2000) 'Inequality and the clubbing of private security', in T. Hope and R. Sparks, *Crime, Risk and Insecurity*. London: Routledge.

Hope, T. (2001) 'Crime victimisation and inequality in risk society', in R. Matthews and J. Pitts (eds), *Crime, Disorder and Community Safety*. London: Routledge.

Hope, T. and Foster, J. (1992) 'Conflicting forces: changing the dynamics of crime and community on a "problem" housing estate', *British Journal of Criminology*, 32: 488–504.

Hope, T. and Shaw, M. (1988) 'Community approaches to reducing crime', in T. Hope and M. Shaw (eds), *Communities and Crime Reduction*. London: HMSO.

Hough, M. and Mayhew, P. (eds) (1982) *Crime and Public Housing*, Research and Planning Unit Paper 6. London: Home Office.

Howard, M. (2004) Speech on crime from the Conservative leader delivered in Middlesbrough, 10 August (available at: http://politics.guardian.co.uk/conservatives/story/0,9061,1280083,00.html. – checked 8 October 2004).

Howard League (1999a) Factsheet Number 3. London: Howard League for Penal Reform.

Howard League (1999b) Factsheet Number 19. London: Howard League for Penal Reform.

Howarth, C. et al. (1999) *Monitoring Poverty and Social Exclusion*. London: Joseph Rowntree Foundation.

Howarth, C. et al. (2002) *Responsibility for All: A National Strategy for Social Inclusion*. London: New Policy Institute and Fabian Society. http://www.socresonline.org.uk/5/4/macdonald.html – checked 6 September 2004).

Hudson, B. (1993) *Penal Policy and Social Justice*. Basingstoke: Macmillan.

Hudson, B. (2003) *Justice in the Risk Society*. London: Sage.

Hughes, G. (1998) *Understanding Crime Prevention*. Buckingham: Open University Press.

Humphries, S. (1981) *Hooligans or Rebels? An Oral History of Working Class Childhood and Youth, 1889–1939*. Oxford: Blackwell.

Hunter, C. (2000) 'Dealing with anti-social behaviour: tenancy terms and conditions', *Journal of Housing Law*, 1: 3–7.

Hunter, C. and Nixon, J. (2001) 'Taking the blame and losing the home: women and anti-social behaviour', *Journal of Social Welfare and Family Law*, 23 (4): 395–410.

Hunter, C., Nixon, J. and Shayer, S. (2000) *Neighbour Nuisance, Social Landlords and the Law*. Coventry: Chartered Institute of Housing for the Joseph Rowntree Foundation.

Hurry, J. and Moriarty, J. (2004) *The National Evaluation of the Youth Justice Board's Education, Training and Employment Projects*. London: Youth Justice Board.

Innes, M. (2003) *Understanding Social Control: Deviance, Crime and Social Order*. Maidenhead: Open University Press.

James, M. (2001) *Understanding and Responding to Crime and Older People*. Paper to the 4th National Outlook Symposium on Crime in Australia, convened by the Australian Institute of Criminology, Canberra, 21–22 June.

Jeffrey, C. R. (1960) 'The historical development of criminology', in H. Mannheim (ed.), *Pioneers in Criminology*. London: Stevens & Son.

Jeffs, T. and Smith, M. (1996) 'Getting the dirtbags off the street – curfews and other solutions to juvenile crime', *Youth and Policy*, 53: 1–14.

Jeffs, T. and Smith, M. (1998) 'The problem of "youth" for youth work', *Youth and Policy*, 62: 45–66.

Jenks, C. (1996) *Childhood*. London: Routledge.

Jennings, D. (2003) *One-Year Juvenile Reconviction Rates: First Quarter of 2001 Cohort*, Home Office Online Report 18/03. London: Home Office.

John, P. (1996) 'Damaged goods? An interpretation of excluded pupils' perception of schooling', in E. Blyth and J. Milner (eds), *Exclusion from School*. London: Routledge.

Johnston, L. (1996) 'What is vigilantism?', *British Journal of Criminology*, 36 (2): 220–36.

Jones, C. and Novak, T. (1999) *Poverty, Welfare and the Disciplinary State*. London: Routledge.

Jones, D. (2001a) 'Misjudged youth: a critique of the Audit Commission's reports on youth justice', *British Journal of Criminology*, 41 (3): 362–80.

Jones, D. (2001b) 'Questionning New Labour's youth justice strategy: a review article', *Youth Justice*, 1 (3): 14–26.

Jones, G. and Wallace, C. (1992) *Youth, Family and Citizenship*. Buckingham: Open University Press.

Jones, H. (1956) *Crime and the Penal System*, 2nd edn. London: University Tutorial Press.

Julkunen, I. (2001) 'Coping and mental well-being amongst unemployed youth – a Northern European perspective', *Journal of Youth Studies*, 4 (3): 261–78.

Kane, S. C. (2004) 'The unconventional methods of cultural criminology', *Theoretical Criminology*, 8 (3): 303–21.

Katz, C. (1998) Disintegrating developments: global economic restructuring and the eroding of ecologies of youth', in T. Skelton and G. Valentine (eds), *Cool Places: Geographies of Youth Cultures*. London: Routledge.

Katz, J. (1988) *Seductions of Crime*. New York: Basic Books.

Kelly, P. (1999) 'Wild and tame zones: regulating the transition of youth at risk', *Journal of Youth Studies*, 2 (2): 193–211.

Kelly, P. (2000) 'Youth as an artefact of expertise: problematizing the practice of youth studies in an age of uncertainty', *Journal of Youth Studies*, 3 (3): 301–15.

Kelly, P. (2003) 'Growing up as risky business? Risks, surveillance and the institutionalized mistrust of youth', *Journal of Youth Studies*, 6 (2): 165–80.

Kemp, P., Sorsby, A., Liddle, M. and Merrington, S. (2002) *Assessing Responses to Youth Offending in Northamptonshire*, Research Briefing 2. London: NACRO.

Kempf-Leonard, K. and Peterson, E. (2002) 'Expanding realms of the new penology: the advent of actuarial justice for juveniles', in J. Muncie, G. Hughes and E. McLaughlin (eds), *Youth Justice: Critical Readings*. London: Sage in association with The Open University.

Knight, B. J. and West, D. J. (1978) 'Criminality and welfare dependency in two generations', *Medicine, Science and Law*, 17: 64–7.

Labour Party (1995) *A Quiet Life: Tough Action on Criminal Neighbours*. London: Labour Party.

Labour Party Study Group (1964) *Crime: A Challenge to Us All* (The Longford Report). London: Labour Party.

Lacey, N. and Zedner, L. (1995) 'Discourses of community in criminal justice', *Journal of Law and Society*, 32: 301–25.

Lea, J. and Young, J. (1984) *What Is to Be Done About Law and Order*. London: Penguin.

Levitas, R. (1996) 'The concept of social exclusion and the new Durkheimian hegemony', *Critical Social Policy*, Number 46, 16 (1).

Lianos, M. with Douglas, M. (2000) 'Dangerization and the end of deviance: the institutional environment', *British Journal of Criminology*, 40 (2): 261–78.

Little, A. (1963) 'Professor Eysenck's theory of crime and empirical test', *British Journal of Criminology*, 4 (2): 152–63.

Little, M., Kogan, J., Bullock, R. and Van Der Laan, P. (2004) 'ISSP: an experiment in multi-systemic responses to persistent young offenders known to Children's Services', *British Journal of Criminology*, 44 (2): 225–40.

Loader, I. (1996) *Youth, Policing and Democracy*. Basingstoke: Macmillan.

Loeber, R. (1991) 'Antisocial behaviour: more enduring than changeable?', *Journal of the American Academy of Child and Adolescent Psychiatry*, 30: 393–7.

Loeber, R. and Dishion, T. (1983) 'Early predictors of male delinquency', *Psychological Bulletin*, 94: 68–99.

Lowry Miller, K. (2003) 'The battle over caution', *Newsweek*, 15 December.

Lupton, D. (1999) *Risk*. London: Routledge.

Lyng, S. (1990) 'Edgework: a social psychological analysis of voluntary risk taking', *American Journal of Sociology*, 95 (4): 887–921.

Lyng, S. (2004) 'Crime, edgework and corporeal transaction', *Theoretical Criminology*, 8 (3): 359–75.

Lyon, D. (1994) *The Electronic Eye*. Cambridge: Polity Press.

Lyon, D. (2001) *Surveillance Society*. Buckingham: Open University Press.

MacDonald, R. (1997) 'Dangerous youth and the dangerous class', in R. MacDonald (ed.), *Youth, the Underclass and Social Exclusion*. London: Routledge.

MacDonald, R. (1998) 'Youth, transitions and social exclusion: some issues for youth research in the UK', *Journal of Youth Studies*, 1 (2): 163–76.

MacDonald, R., Mason, P., Shildreck, T., Webster, C., Johnston, L. and Ridley, L. (2001) 'Snakes and ladders: in defence of studies of youth transition', *Sociological Research Online*, 5 (4) (available at: http://www.socresonline.org.uk/5/4/macdonald.html – checked 6 September 2004).

Mannheim, H. (1946) *Criminal Justice and Reconstruction*. London: Routledge & Kegan Paul.

Mannheim, H. (1955) *Group Problems in Crime and Punishment*. London: Routledge.

Maruna, S. (2001) *Making Good: How Ex-Convicts Reform and Rebuild Their Lives*. Washington, DC: American Psychological Association Press.

Matthews, R. (2002) 'Crime and control in late modernity', *Theoretical Criminology*, 6 (2): 224.

Mawby, R. (1988) 'Age vulnerability and the impact of crime', in M. Maguire, and J. Pointing (eds), *Victims of Crime: A New Deal?* Buckingham: Open University Press.

Mawby, R. and Walklate, S. (1994) *Critical Victimology*. London: Sage.

Mays, J. B. (1959) *Growing Up in the City*. Liverpool: University Press.

McDonagh, S. (2004) 'Taking the fight to the yobs', *The Guardian*, 28 October.

McDonald, S. (2003) 'The nature of the Anti-Social Behaviour Order – R. (McCann and others) v Crown Court at Manchester', *Modern Law Review*, July: 630–9.

McLaughlin, E. (2002) 'The crisis of the social and the political materialization of community safety', in G. Hughes, E. McLaughlin and J. Muncie (eds), *Crime Prevention and Community Safety*. London: Sage.

McLaughlin, E., Muncie, J. and Hughes, G. (2001) 'The permanent revolution: New Labour, new public management and the modernization of criminal justice', *Criminal Justice*, 1 (2): 301–18.

McRobbie, A. (1991) *Feminism and Youth Culture*. Basingstoke: Macmillan.

Measor, L. and Squires, P. (2000) *Young People and Community Safety: Inclusion, Risk, Tolerance and Disorder*. Aldershot: Ashgate.

Miles, S. (2000) *Youth Lifestyles in a Changing World*. Buckingham: Open University Press.

Miles, S. (2002) 'Victims of risk? Young people and the construction of lifestyle', in M. Cieslik and G. Pollock (eds), *Young People in Risk Society: The Restructuring of Youth Identities and Transitions in Late Modernity*. Aldershot: Ashgate.

Miller, W. B. (1966) 'Violent crime in city gangs', *Annals of the American Academy of Political and Social Science*, 343: 97–112.

Mizen, P. (2003) 'The best days of your life? Youth, policy and Blair's New Labour', *Critical Social Policy*, 23 (4): 453–76.

Moir, A. and Jessel, D. (1995) *A Mind To Crime: The Controversial Link between the Mind and Criminal Behaviour*. London: Michael Joseph.

Moore, R. et al. (2004) *The National Evaluation of the Youth Justice Board's Intensive Supervision and Surveillance Projects*. London: Youth Justice Board.

Moore, S. (2000) 'Child incarceration and the new youth justice', in B. Goldson (ed.), *The New Youth Justice*. Lyme Regis: Russell House.

Moore, T. and Lawrence, B. (2000) *The Concept of Anti-Social Behaviour*. Middlesex University (available at: www.middx.ac.uk/www/concl/dc2.htm).

MORI (2002) *Quality of Life Indicators. A Survey on Behalf of the Audit Commission*. London: MORI.

Morris, J. (ed.) (2000) *Rethinking Risk and the Precautionary Principle*. Oxford: Butterworth-Heinemann.

Morris, L. (1994) *Dangerous Classes: The Underclass and Social Citizenship*. London: Routledge.

Morris, T. (1989) *Crime and Criminal Justice since 1945*. Oxford: Blackwell.

Morrison, W. (1995) *Theoretical Criminology: From Modernity to Post-Modernism*. London: Cavendish.

Moss, P. and Petrie, P. (2002) *From Children's Services to Children's Spaces*. London: Routledge.

Muncie, J. (1999a) *Youth and Crime: A Critical Introduction*. London: Sage.

Muncie, J. (1999b) 'Institutionalised intolerance: youth crime and the 1998 Crime and Disorder Act', *Critical Social Policy*, 19 (2): 147-75.

Muncie, J. (2000a) 'Pragmatic realism: searching for criminology in the new youth justice', in B. Goldson (ed.), *The New Youth Justice*. Lyme Regis: Russell House.

Muncie, J. (2000b) 'Decriminalising criminology', in G. Lewis, S. Gewitz and J. Clarke (eds), *Rethinking Social Policy*. London: Sage and The Open University.

Muncie, J. (2002) A New Deal for youth? Early intervention and correctionalism', in G. Hughes, E. McLaughlin and J. Muncie (eds), *Crime Prevention and Community Safety*. London: Sage.

Muncie, J. (2005) 'The globalization of crime control – the case of youth and juvenile justice', *Theoretical Criminology*, 9 (1): 35–64.

Muncie, J. and McLaughlin, E. (2001) *The Sage Dictionary of Criminology*. London: Sage.

Murray, C. (1990) *The Emerging British Underclass*. London: Institute of Economic Affairs.

NACRO (1988) *Nuisance Problems in Brixton: Describing Local Experiences, Designing Effective Solutions*. London: NACRO.

NACRO (2003) *A Balanced Approach to Preventing Anti-Social Behaviour*. London: NACRO.

Nagin, D. and Tremblay, R. E. (1999) 'Trajectories of boys' physical aggression, opposition, and hyperactivity on the path to physically violent and non-violent juvenile delinquency', *Child Development*, 70: 1181–96.

National Audit Office (2004) *Youth Offending: The Delivery of Community and Custodial Services. A Report by the Comptroller and Auditor General*. HC 190 Session 2003–2004, 21 January.

Newburn, T. (1998) 'Tackling youth crime and reforming youth justice: the origins of "New Labour" policy', *Policy Studies*, 19 (3): 199–213.

Newburn, T. (2002) 'Young people, crime and youth justice', in M. Maguire, R. Morgan and R. Reiner (eds), *The Oxford Handbook of Criminology*, 3rd edn. Oxford: Oxford University Press.

Newburn, T. et al. (2002) *The Introduction of Referral Orders into the Youth Justice System, Final Report*, Home Office Research Study 202. London: Home Office.

Nozick, R. (1974) *Anarchy State and Utopia*. Oxford: Blackwell.

ODPM (Office of the Deputy Prime Minister) (2003) *Survey of English Housing 2002–03, August. National Centre for Social Research*. London: Stationery Office.

O'Malley, P. (1992) 'Risk, power and crime prevention', *Economy and Society*, 21 (3): 252–75.

Osborn, S. and Bright, J. (1989) *Policing Housing Estates*. London: NACRO.

Osborn, S. and Shaftoe, H. (1996) *Safer Neighbourhoods: Successes and Failures in Crime Prevention*. London: Safe Neighbourhoods Unit. Oxford: Butterworth-Heinemann.

Page, D. (1993) *Building for Communities: A Study of New Housing Association Estates*. York: Joseph Rowntree Foundation.

Page, D. (2000) *Communities in the Balance: The Reality of Social Exclusion on Housing Estates*. York: York Publishing Services for Joseph Rowntree Foundation.

Pakiz, B., Reinherz, H. Z. and Frost, A. K. (1992) 'Antisocial behaviour in adolescence. A community study', *Journal of Early Adolescence*, 12: 300–13.

Pakiz, B., Reinherz, H. Z. and Giaconia, R. M. (1997) 'Early risk factors for serious antisocial behavior at age 21: a longitudinal community study', *American Journal of Orthopsychiatry*, 67 (1): 92–101.

Papps, P. (1998) 'Anti-social behaviour strategies – individualistic or holistic?', *Housing Studies*, 13 (5): 639–56.

Parker, H. (1974) *View from the Boys*. London: David & Charles.

Parker, H., Aldridge, J. and Measham, F. (1998) *Illegal Leisure: The Normalisation of Adolescent Recreational Drug Use*. London: Routledge.

Pearson, G. (1983) *Hooligan: A History of Respectable Fears*. Basingstoke: Macmillan.

Pitts, J. (1988) *The Politics of Juvenile Crime*. London: Sage.

Pitts, J. (1990) *Working with Young Offenders*. Basingstoke: Macmillan.

Pitts, J. (2000) 'The new youth justice and the politics of electoral anxiety', in B. Goldson (ed.), *The New Youth Justice*. Lyme Regis: Russell House.

Pitts, J. (2001) 'Korrectional karaoke: New Labour and the zombification of youth justice', *Youth Justice*, 1 (2): 3–16.

Pitts, J. (2003) *The New Politics of Youth Crime*. Lyme Regis: Russell House.

Pitts, J. (2004) 'What do we want? The "SHAPE" campaign and the reform of youth justice', *Youth Justice*, 3 (3): 134–51.

Piven, F. F. and Cloward, R. A. (1972) *Regulating the Poor*. London and New York: Tavistock.

Plant, M. and Plant, M. (1992) *Risk Takers: Alcohol, Drugs, Sex and Youth*. London: Routledge.

Platt, A. (1969) *The Child Savers: The Invention of Delinquency*. Chicago, IL: Chicago University Press.

Pollock, C. B. R. (1960) 'A case of neurotic exhibitionism', *British Journal of Criminology*, 1 (1): 37–49.

Power, M. (1997) *The Audit Explosion*. Oxford: Oxford University Press.

Pratt, J. (1989) 'Corporatism: the third model of juvenile justice', *British Journal of Criminology*, 29 (3): 236–54.

Pratt, J. (2002) 'Critical criminology and the punitive society: some new "visions of social control"', in K. Carrington and R. Hogg (eds), *Critical Criminology*. Cullompton: Willan.

Presdee, M. (2000) *Cultural Criminology and the Carnival of Crime*. London: Routledge.

Presdee, M. (2004) 'Cultural criminology: the long and winding road', *Theoretical Criminology*, 8 (3): 275–85.

Prince's Trust (2004) *No Ball Games*. London: Prince's Trust.

Radzinowicz, L. (1999) *Pioneers in Criminology*. London: Routledge.

Radzinowicz, L. and Hood, R. (1990) *The Emergence of Penal Policy in Victorian and Edwardian England*. Oxford: Clarendon Press.

Raffo, C. and Reeves, M. (2000) 'Youth transitions and social exclusion: developments in social capital theory', *Journal of Youth Studies*, 3 (2): 147–66.

Raynor, P. and Vanstone, M. (2002) *Understanding Community Penalties: Probation, Policy and Social Change*. Buckingham: Open University Press.

Reeves, R. (2003) 'The battle for childhood', *New Statesman*, October.

Reid, K. (1997) 'The abolition of cautioning? Juveniles in the "Last Chance" saloon', *Criminal Lawyer*, December: 4–8.

Reiner, R. (2000) *The Politics of the Police*. Oxford: Oxford University Press.

Ringham, L. (2004) 'Policing and the public', in S. Nicholas and A. Walker (eds), *Crime in England and Wales 2002/2003 Supplementary Volume 2: Crime, Disorder and the Criminal Justice System – Public Attitudes and Perceptions*. London: Home Office Research and Statistics Directorate.

Ringham, L. and Wood, M. (2004) 'Property crime', in T. Dodd, S. Nicholas, D. Povey and A. Walker (eds), *Crime in England and Wales 2003/04*, Home Office Statistical Bulletin 10/04 July. London: Stationery Office.

Robins, L. N. (1966) *Deviant Children Grown Up: A Sociological and Psychiatric Study of Sociopathic Personality*. Baltimore, MD: Williams & Wilkins.

Robins, L. N. and Ratcliff, K. S. (1979) 'Risk factors in the continuation of childhood antisocial behaviours into adulthood', *International Journal of Mental Health*, 1: 96–116.

Robins, L. N. and Regier, D. A. (eds) (1991) *Psychiatric Disorders in America: The Epidemiologic Catchment Area Study*. New York: Free Press.

Rodgers, J. (1995) 'Family policy or moral regulation?', *Critical Social Policy*, 15: 5–25.

Rose, N. (1985) *The Psychological Complex: Psychology, Politics and Society in England, 1869–1939*. London: Routledge.

Rose, N. (1989) *Governing the Soul: The Shaping of the Private Self*. London: Routledge.

Rose, N. (1996) 'The death of the social: refiguring the territory of government', *Economy and Society*, 25 (3): 327–56.

Rose, N. (1999) *Powers of Freedom: Reframing Political Thought*. Cambridge: Cambridge University Press.

Rose, N. (2000) 'Government and control', *British Journal of Criminology*, 40 (2): 321–39.

Roshier, R. (1989) *Controlling Crime*. Buckingham: Open University Press.

Ruck, S. K. (ed.) (1951) *Paterson on Prisons*. London: F. Muller.

Rudd, P. (1997) 'From socialisation to postmodernity: a review of theoretical perspectives on the school-to-work transition', *Journal of Education and Work*, 10 (3): 257–79.

Rudd, P. and Evans, K. (1998) 'Structure and agency in youth transitions: student experiences of vocational further education', *Journal of Youth Studies*, 1 (1): 30–62.

Ruggiero, V. (1997) 'Punishing children: the manufacture of criminal careers in Hellion Town', *Theoretical Criminology*, 1 (3): 341–61.

Rutherford, A. (1992) *Growing out of Crime: The New Era*. Winchester: Waterside Press.

Rutherford, A. (2002) 'Youth justice and social inclusion', *Youth Justice*, 2 (2): 100–7.

Rutter, M. and Giller, H. (1983) *Juvenile Delinquency: Trends and Perspectives*. London: Penguin.

Rutter, M. and Madge, N. (1982) *Cycles of Disadvantage*. London: Heinemann.

Rutter, M., Giller, H. and Hagell, A. (1998) *ASB by Young People*. Cambridge: Cambridge University Press.

Safe Neighbourhoods Unit (1993) *Crime Prevention on Housing Estates*. London: Department of the Environment/HMSO.

Schur, E. M. (1971) *Labelling Deviant Behaviour: Its Sociological Implications*. London: Harper & Row.

Schur, E. M. (1973) *Radical Non-Intervention. Rethinking the Delinquency Problem*. Englewood Cliffs, NJ: Prentice-Hall.

Scott, P. (1956) 'Gangs and delinquent groups in London', *British Journal of Delinquency*, 7 (1): 425.

Scraton, P. and Haydon, D. (2002) 'Challenging the criminalization of children and young people', in J. Muncie, G. Hughes and E. McLaughlin (eds), *Youth Justice: Critical Readings*. London: Sage in association with The Open University.

Scull, A. (1977) *Decarceration, Community Treatment and the Deviant: A Radical View*. Englewood Cliffs, NJ: Prentice-Hall.

Shearing, C. D. and Stenning, P.C. (1996) 'From the Panopticon to Disney World: the development of discipline', in J. Muncie, E. McLaughlin and M. Langan (eds), *Criminological Perspectives: A Reader*. London: Sage.

Simon, J. (1997) 'Governing through crime', in L. Friedman and G. Fisher (eds), *The Crime Conundrum*. Boulder: CO: Westview Press.

Singer, S. I. (1996) *Recriminalising Delinquency: Violent Juvenile Crime and Juvenile Justice Reform*. Cambridge: Cambridge University Press.

Skelton, T. (2002) 'Research on youth transitions: some critical interventions', in M. Cieslik and G. Pollock (eds), *Young People in Risk Society: The Restructuring of Youth Identities and Transitions in late Modernity*. Aldershot: Ashgate.

Skelton, T. and Valentine, G. (eds) (1998) *Cool Places: Geographies of Youth Cultures*. London: Routledge.

Skogan, W. (1990) *Disorder and Decline: Crime and the Spiral of Decline in American Neighborhoods*. New York: Free Press.

Smith, C. (2000) 'Healthy prisons: a contradiction in terms?', *Howard Journal*, 29 (4): 339–53.

Smith, D. J. (2002) 'Crime and the life course', in M. Maguire, R. Morgan and R. Reiner (eds), *The Oxford Handbook of Criminology*, 3rd edn. Oxford: Oxford University Press.

Smith, D. (2003) 'New Labour and youth justice', *Children and Society*, 17 (3): 226–35.

Smith, R. (2003) *Youth Justice. Ideas, Policies, Practice*. Cullompton: Willan.

Social Exclusion Unit (1998) *Bringing Britain Together: A National Strategy for Neighbourhood Renewal*, Cm. 4045. London: Stationery Office.

Social Exclusion Unit (2000) *Policy Action Team Report 8: Anti-Social Behaviour*. London: Office of the Deputy Prime Minister.

Social Exclusion Unit (2001) *National Strategy for Neighbourhood Renewal: Policy Action Team Audit*. London: Cabinet Office.

Spencer, J. C. (1950) 'The unclubbable adolescent: a study in the prevention of juvenile delinquency', *British Journal of Delinquency*, 1: 113–24.

Spencer, J. C. (1954) 'Comment on Delaney', *British Journal of Delinquency*, 5: 43–7.

Squires, P. (1990) *Anti-Social Policy: Welfare, Ideology and the Disciplinary State*. Hemel Hempstead: Harvester-Wheatsheaf.

Squires, P. (2003) *An Independent Evaluation of the Installation of CCTV Crime Prevention Cameras on the Whitehawk Estate, Brighton*. Brighton: University of Brighton/HSPRC.

Squires, P. (forthcoming) 'Anti-social behaviour and New Labour', *Critical Social Policy*.

Squires, P. and Measor, L. (1996) *CCTV Surveillance and Crime Prevention in Brighton*. Brighton: Health and Social Policy Research Centre, University of Brighton.

Squires, P. and Measor, L. (2001) 'Breaking in: partnership working, prison walls and health promotion', in D. Taylor (ed.), *Breaking Down Barriers: Reviewing Partnership Practice*. Brighton: Health and Social Policy Research Centre, University of Brighton.

Squires, P. and Measor, L. (2005) 'Below decks on the flagship: evaluating youth justice', in D. Taylor and S. Balloch (eds), *The Politics of Evaluation*. Bristol: Policy Press.

Squires, P. and Stephen, D. (2002) 'Criminal Careers or Risky Transitions: Rethinking Criminal Careers'. Unpublished paper to British Criminological Social Conference, University of Keele.

Squires, P., Cunningham, L. and Fyvie-Gauld, M. (2004) *Perceptions of Anti-Social Behaviour in the London Borough of Sutton*. Brighton: Health and Social Policy Research Centre, University of Brighton.

Stanley, C. (1995) 'Teenage kicks: urban narratives of dissent not deviance', *Crime, Law and Social Change*, 23: 91–119.

Stedman-Jones, G. (1971) *Outcast London*. Oxford: Oxford University Press

Stenson, K. (2000) 'Crime control, social policy and liberalism', in G. Lewis et al. (eds), *Rethinking Social Policy*. London: Sage.

Stenson, K. and Edwards, A. (2003) 'Crime control and local governance: the struggle for sovereignty in advanced Liberal politics', *Contemporary Politics*, 9 (2): 203–17.

Stephen, D. E. (1998) *Understanding Context, Agency and Process in the Health of Homeless Young Women in Glasgow: A Qualitative Study*, PhD thesis. Glasgow: University of Glasgow.

Stephen, D. E. (2000) 'Young women construct themselves: social identity, self-concept and psychosocial well-being in homeless facilities', *Journal of Youth Studies*, 3 (4): 445–60.

Stephen, D. E. and Squires, P. (2001) *Vehicle Crime and Young People in Brighton and Hove*. Brighton: Health and Social Policy Research Centre, University of Brighton.

Stephen, D. E. and Squires, P. (2003a) *Community Safety, Enforcement and Acceptable Behaviour Contracts*. Brighton: Health and Social Policy Research Centre, University of Brighton.

Stephen, D. E. and Squires, P. (2003b) '"Adults don't realize how sheltered they are". A contribution to the debate on youth transitions from some voices on the margins', *Journal of Youth Studies*, 6 (2): 145–64.

Stephen, D. E. and Squires, P. (2004) '"They're still children and entitled to be children". Problematising the institutionalised mistrust of marginalised youth in Britain', *Journal of Youth Studies*, 7 (3): 351–69.

Stephen, D. E. (forthcoming) 'Young people and community safety', in P. Squires (ed.), *Community Safety: Critical Perspectives in Policy and Practice*. Bristol: Policy Press.

Stirling, M. (1996) 'Government policy and disadvantaged children', in E. Blyth and J. Milner (eds), *Exclusion from School*. London: Routledge.

Stone, N. (2003) 'Legal commentary: anti-social behaviour orders: naming juveniles', *Youth Justice*, 2 (3): 163–9.

Stone, N. (2004) 'Orders in respect of anti-social behaviour: recent judicial developments', *Youth Justice*, 4 (1): 46–54.

Stott, D. H. (1960) 'The prediction of delinquency from non-delinquent behaviour', *British Journal of Delinquency*, 10 (3): 195–210.

Stott, D. H. (1963) *The Social Adjustment of Children*. London: University Press.

Stott, D. H. (1964) 'Sociological and psychological explanations of delinquency', *International Journal of Social Psychiatry* (Congress edn no. 4): 35–43.

Tarling, R. (1993) *Analysing Offending: Data, Models and Interpretations*. London: HMSO.

Tarling, R., Davison, T. and Clarke, A. (2004) *The National Evaluation of the Youth Justice Board's Mentoring Projects*. London: Youth Justice Board.

Taylor, I. (1981) *Law and Order: Arguments for Socialism*. Basingstoke: Macmillan.

Taylor, I. (1999) *Crime in Context: A Critical Criminology of Market Societies*. Cambridge: Polity Press.

Taylor, R. S. (1960) 'The habitual criminal', *British Journal of Criminology*, 1 (1): 21–36.

Thompson, E. P. (1978) *The Poverty of Theory*. London: Merlin Press.

Thompson, E. P. (1981) 'The politics of theory', in R. Samuel (ed.), *People's History and Socialist Theory*. London: Routledge & Kegan Paul.

Thompson, E. P. (1993a) *Customs in Common*. New York: New Press.

Thompson, E. P. (1993b) *Witness Against the Beast: William Blake and the Moral Law*. Cambridge: Cambridge University Press.

Thorpe, K. and Wood, M. (2004) 'Attitudes to anti-social behaviour', in S. Nicholas and A. Walker (eds), *Crime in England and Wales 2002/2003 Supplementary Volume 2: Crime, Disorder and the Criminal Justice System – Public Attitudes and Perceptions*. London: Home Office Research and Statistics Directorate.

Tickner, J., Raffensperger, C. and Myers, N. (n.d.) *The Precautionary Principle in Action: A Handbook*. Science and Environmental Health Network (available at: http://www.biotech-infonet/precautionary.html – checked 1 November 2004).

Tilley, N. (2000) 'Doing realistic evaluation of criminal justice', in V. Jupp, P. M. Davies and P. J. Francis (eds), *Doing Criminological Research*. London: Sage.

Tonry, M. (1995) *Malign Neglect: Race, Crime and Punishment in America*. Oxford: Oxford University Press.

Tonry, M. (2004) *Punishment and Politics: Evidence and Emulation in the Making of English Crime Control Policy*. Cullompton: Willan.

Ulmer, J. (1994) 'Revisiting Stebbins: labelling and commitment to deviance', *Sociological Quarterly*, 35 (1): 137–57.

Ulmer, J. and Spencer, J. W. (1999) 'The contributions of an interactionist approach to research and theory on criminal careers', *Theoretical Criminology*, 3 (1): 95–124.

United Nations Environmental Programme (UNEP) (1992) *Rio Declaration on Environment and Development* (available at: http://www.unep.org/Documents Default.asp?DocumentID=78&ArticleID=1163 – checked 1 November 2004).

Utting, D. (1996) *Reducing Criminality Among Young People: A Sample of Relevant Programmes in the UK*, Home Office Research Study No. 161. London: HMSO.

Utting, D., Bright, J. and Henricson, C. (1993) *Crime and the Family: Improving Child-rearing and Preventing Delinquency*. London: Family Policy Studies Centre.

Van Swaaningen, R. (1999) 'Reclaiming critical criminology: social justice and the European tradition', *Theoretical Criminology*, 3 (1): 5–28.

Vold, G. B., Bernard, T. J. and Snipes, J. B. (2002) *Theoretical Criminology*, 10th edn. Oxford: Oxford University Press

Wacqant, L. (2001) 'Deadly symbiosis: when ghetto and prison meet and merge', *Punishment and Society*, 3 (1): 95–133.

Waddington, P. (1999) *Policing Citizens*. London: UCL Press.

Walker, N. (1965) *Crime and Punishment in Great Britain*. Edinburgh: Edinburgh University Press.

Walker, N. (1999) 'The end of an old song?', *New Law Journal*, 15 January.

Walsh, C. (1999) 'Imposing order: child safety orders and local child curfew schemes', *Journal of Social Welfare and Family Law*, 21 (2): 135–49.

Walsh, C. (2002) 'Curfews: no more hanging around', *Youth Justice*, 2 (2): 70–81.

Walsh, C. (2003) 'Dispersal of rights: a critical comment on specified provisions of the Anti-Social Behaviour Bill', *Youth Justice*, 3 (2): 104–11.

Walters, R. (2004) 'Criminology and genetically modified food', *British Journal of Criminology*, 44 (2): 151–67.

Warren, W. (1951) 'Conduct disorders in children aged five to fifteen', *British Journal of Delinquency*, 1: 164–8.

Wedd, S. (2000) 'The criminal lawyer's reaction to youth court referral orders', *Criminal Practitioners Newsletter*, Law Society, 1–2 October.

West, D. J. (1967) *The Young Offender*. London: Duckworth.

West, D. J. (1969) *Present Conduct and Future Delinquency*. London: Heinemann.

West, D. J. (1982) *Delinquency: Its Roots, Careers and Prospects*. London: Heinemann.

West, D. J. (1988) 'Psychological contributions to criminology', in P. Rock (ed.), *A History of British Criminology*. Oxford: Oxford University Press.

West, D. J. and Farrington, D. P. (1973) *Who Becomes Delinquent?* London: Heinemann.

West, D. J. and Farrington, D. P. (1977) *The Delinquent Way of Life*. London: Heinemann.

White, P. (1999) *The Prison Population in 1998: A Statistical Review*, Research Findings No. 94. London: Home Office.

Wikstrom, T. and Loeber, R. (1997) 'Individual risk factors, neighbourhood SES and juvenile offending', in M. Tonry (ed.), *The Handbook of Crime and Punishment*. New York: Oxford University Press.

Wilcox, A. (2003) 'Evidence based youth justice? Some valuable lessons from an evaluation for the Youth Justice Board', *Youth Justice*, 3 (1): 19–32.

Wilcox, A. and Hoyle, C. (2004) *The National Evaluation of the Youth Justice Board's Restorative Justice Projects*. London: Youth Justice Board.

Wildavsky, A. (1988) *Searching for Safety*. New Brunswick, NJ: Transaction.

Wilkins, L. T. (1960) *Delinquent Generations*, Studies in the Causes of Delinquency and the Treatment of Offenders No. 3. London: HMSO.

Williamson, H. (1997) 'Status zero youth and the underclass', in R. MacDonald (ed.), *Youth, the Underclass and Social Exclusion*. London: Routledge.

Willis, P. (1977) *Learning to Labour*. Westmead: Saxon House.

Wilson, D. and Ashton, D. (2001) *What Everyone in Britain Should Know about Crime and Punishment*. Oxford: Oxford University Press.

Wilson, J. Q. and Kelling, G. L. (1982) 'Broken windows', *Atlantic Monthly*, March: 29–38.

Wohl, A. S. (1977) *The Eternal Slum: Housing and Social Policy in Victorian London*. London: Edward Arnold.

Wonnacott, C. (1999) 'The counterfeit contract: reform, pretence and muddled principles in the new Referral Order', *Child and Family Law Quarterly*, 11 (3): 271–87.

Wood, M. (2004) *Perceptions and Experience of Anti-Social Behaviour: Findings from the British Crime Survey 2003/04*. London: Home Office.

Wootton, B. (1959) *Social Science and Social Pathology*. London: George Allen & Unwin.

Worpole, K. (2002) *No Particular Place to Go? Children, Young People and Public Space*. Birmingham: Groundwork UK (available at: www.groundwork.org.uk).

Wyn, J. and Dwyer, P (1999) 'New directions in research on youth in transition', *Journal of Youth Studies*, 2 (1): 5–21.

Young, A. (1996) *Imagining Crime*. London: Sage.

Young, J. (1999) *The Exclusive Society*. London: Sage.

Young, J. (2002) 'Incessant chatter', in M. Maguire, R. Morgan and R. Reiner (eds), *The Oxford Handbook of Criminology*, 3rd edn. Oxford: Oxford University Press.

Youth Justice Board (1998) *The Juvenile Secure Estate: Preliminary Advice from the Youth Justice Board for England and Wales to the Home Secretary, 17th December*. London: YJB.

Youth Justice Board (2003) *Annual Report 2002–03*. London: Youth Justice Board.

Youth Justice Board (2004) *Annual Report 2003–04*. London: Youth Justice Board.

Zedner, L. (2000) 'The pursuit of security', in T. Hope and R. Sparks (eds), *Crime, Risk and Insecurity*. London: Routledge.

Zimring, F. (1998) *American Youth Violence*. Oxford: Oxford University Press.

Zimring, F. E. and Hawkins, G. (1997) *Crime Is Not the Problem: Lethal Violence in America*. Oxford: Oxford University Press.

Zuckerman, M. (1991) *Psychobiology of Personality*. Cambridge: Cambridge University Press.

Index